1,000,000 Books

are available to read at

Forgotten Books

www.ForgottenBooks.com

Read online
Download PDF
Purchase in print

ISBN 978-0-259-46850-9
PIBN 10818543

This book is a reproduction of an important historical work. Forgotten Books uses
state-of-the-art technology to digitally reconstruct the work, preserving the original format
whilst repairing imperfections present in the aged copy. In rare cases, an imperfection in
the original, such as a blemish or missing page, may be replicated in our edition. We do,
however, repair the vast majority of imperfections successfully; any imperfections that
remain are intentionally left to preserve the state of such historical works.

Forgotten Books is a registered trademark of FB &c Ltd.
Copyright © 2018 FB &c Ltd.
FB &c Ltd, Dalton House, 60 Windsor Avenue, London, SW19 2RR.
Company number 08720141. Registered in England and Wales.

For support please visit www.forgottenbooks.com

1 MONTH OF FREE READING

at

www.ForgottenBooks.com

By purchasing this book you are eligible for one month membership to ForgottenBooks.com, giving you unlimited access to our entire collection of over 1,000,000 titles via our web site and mobile apps.

To claim your free month visit:
www.forgottenbooks.com/free818543

* Offer is valid for 45 days from date of purchase. Terms and conditions apply.

English
Français
Deutsche
Italiano
Español
Português

www.forgottenbooks.com

Mythology Photography **Fiction** Fishing Christianity **Art** Cooking Essays Buddhism Freemasonry Medicine **Biology** Music **Ancient Egypt** Evolution Carpentry Physics Dance Geology **Mathematics** Fitness Shakespeare **Folklore** Yoga Marketing **Confidence** Immortality Biographies Poetry **Psychology** Witchcraft Electronics Chemistry History **Law** Accounting **Philosophy** Anthropology Alchemy Drama Quantum Mechanics Atheism Sexual Health **Ancient History** **Entrepreneurship** Languages Sport Paleontology Needlework Islam **Metaphysics** Investment Archaeology Parenting Statistics Criminology **Motivational**

REVELATION INTERPRETED

BY

REV. G. A. KRATZER

*Lecturer, Teacher and Practitioner of Christian Science,
Author of "Dominion Within", "Spiritual
Man", and Various Pamphlets*

First Edition

Copyrighted 1915
By The Author

PUBLISHED AND FOR SALE BY
THE CENTRAL CHRISTIAN SCIENCE INSTITUTE
5521 CORNELL AVE.
CHICAGO; ILLINOIS

DECLARATION OF INDEPENDENCE

"Christian Science has its Declaration of Independence. God has endowed man with inalienable rights, among which are self-government, reason and conscience. Man is properly self-governed only when he is guided rightly and governed by his Maker, divine Truth and Love. Man's rights are invaded when the divine order is interfered with."—*"Science and Health,"* 106:6-12.

"For this Principle [of Science] there is no ecclesiastical monopoly."—*"Science and Health,"* 141:17.

"I once thought that in unity was human strength; but have grown to know that human strength is weakness—that unity is Divine might giving to human power, peace."—Mrs. Eddy, in *"Miscellaneous Writings,"* page 138.

"Aspirations pure and Godward, steadfast purpose, honesty, understanding and *independent action* alone fit us for the science of Life."—Mrs. Eddy, in First Edition of *"Science and Health."*

To

My Uncle, Charles Kratzer—a life of helpfulness to others, of noble sacrifices and faithfulness to duty—this book is affectionately dedicated.

THE AUTHOR.

TABLE OF CONTENTS

	PAGE
INTRODUCTION	1
PROLOGUE	29

SECTIONS
I.	Messages to the Seven Churches	45
II.	The Vision of the Seven Sealed Letters	105
III.	The Sounding of the Seven Trumpets	167
IV.	The Woman, The Dragon, and The Beasts	249
V.	Vision of Christ Judging the World	315
VI.	The Vision of the Last Days	333
VII.	The Vision of the Holy City	367

EPILOGUE	377
PERSONAL APPLICATION	383
GLOSSARY	387
ST. JOHN, THE EVANGELIST	391
ANNOUNCEMENTS	397

PREFACE

As Jacob wrestled with the angel through a long night of darkened understanding, but would not let him go until he had gained the victory and won his way into the morning light of spiritual illumination, so the author has wrestled, not with one angel, but with many—the Angels of the Apocalypse—through a night much longer than that of an arctic winter, during which he was unable to clearly understand their heavenly message. Wrestling until he prevailed, he has been blessed in seeing the ladder of mediatorial consciousness* which links the human to the divine, and by which the angels or divine ideas descend, only that they may ascend to lead humanity upward. He hopes that the perusal of the following interpretation of the Apocalypse may aid every reader in gaining a more clear and helpful understanding of the word of God as presented in St. John's vision.

G. A. K.

*"*That life-link forming the connection through which the real reaches the unreal.*"—Science and Health, 350:18.

INTRODUCTION

In the last chapter of the Gospel of St. John, it is related that Peter, looking upon John, "saith to Jesus, Lord, and what shall this man do? Jesus saith unto him, If I will that he tarry till I come, what is that to thee? Follow thou me. Then went this saying abroad among the brethren, that that disciple should not die; yet Jesus said not unto him, He shall not die; but, If I will that he tarry till I come, what is that to thee?" Long after all of the other original twelve disciples had passed away, and even after the apostle Paul had suffered martyrdom, St. John was still living; and, in the last few verses of chapter 1 of the Apocalypse, its author tells us that Christ Jesus appeared to him, when "he was in the isle that is called Patmos", and he further adds: "He laid his right hand upon me, saying unto me, Fear not; I am the first and the last: I am he that liveth and was dead; and, behold, I am alive forevermore, Amen; and have the keys [the solution of the problem] of hell and of death. Write the things which thou hast seen [observed], and the things which are, and the things which shall be hereafter." It is not to be presumed that Christ Jesus appeared in the flesh to the author of the Apocalypse at this time, but, rather, in some such sense as he appeared to Paul on his famous journey to Damascus, though with a much fuller message than that given to Paul,—the message of the Apocalypse itself. So it would seem that St. John did "tarry" till the Christ came to him again after the ascension and gave him the message which is to be the subject of our study.

Arguments for Authorship by Evangelist John

The perfect fulfilment of the prophecy at the end of the Gospel of John through the giving of the Apocalypse by Christ to a man named John, as related above, would seem to the author, when taken in connection with the other considerations which are to follow, to establish beyond question that the Apocalypse was written by the same person who wrote the fourth Gospel, and not by some other man named John, as a few scholars still contend. ❧In the second verse of chapter 1, the author of the Apocalypse declares that he was the servant of Jesus Christ "who bare record [in the Greek, *emarturêse*, the historical past tense] of the word of God, and the testimony of Jesus Christ, and of all things that he saw". This is but a declaration that the author of the Apocalypse was the John who, in the fourth Gospel, written many years before, was already well known to have borne record "of the word of God, and of the testimony of Jesus Christ, and of all things that he saw." This declaration also sounds characteristically similar to the opening words of the First Epistle General of John: "That which was from the beginning, which we have heard, which we have seen with our eyes, which we have looked upon, and our hands have handled of the word of life. . . . That which we have seen and heard, declare we unto you." Any seeming discrepancies in the literary style of the fourth Gospel and of the Apocalypse can be explained by the fact that they were doubtless written many years apart and under widely varying circumstances; in other words, in very different periods of John's experience and literary and spiritual development. It is regarded as practically certain that John wrote his Gospel in Hebrew during his residence in Jerusalem and then later translated it into Greek—or possibly employed a scribe to translate it under his supervision. On the other hand, it seems clear that John wrote or dictated the Apocalypse directly in Greek,—in extreme age, and during his residence at Ephesus; and there seem to be internal evidences that he wrote under great stress, if not under excitement,—haste to put into writing the great message that was crowding in upon him faster than he could inscribe it,—a very common experience with those who write by inspiration. To more than counterbalance apparent differences between the literary style of the Gospel, the Epistle of John, and the Apocalypse, there are striking resemblances,— notably the occurrence in all of these works of a characteristic technical use of many Greek words and phrases, such as would be developed in the diction of a writer who was expressing himself on some definite line of thought with scientific accuracy and discrimination in order that he might bring out fine shades of meaning. This fact was first observed perhaps by Bishop Westcott and is now freely commented on among scholarly critics and interpreters of the New Testament. The summation of the entire question may be found in the fact pointed out by a careful student of the whole situation, that, from all the records of the different Christians of the period, which have come down to us, it is impossible to decide upon any one, save John the son of Zebedee, who could have had anything like the spiritual experience and the other special qualifications which were necessary in order to have written this work.

Evidences of Greek Influence

John was a Jew, thoroughly familiar with Jewish customs and habits of thought, and with the Hebrew Scriptures, although he wrote in Greek. It is also doubtless true, though not as evident to the average reader of the present day, that John was familiar with Greek literature, and especially with the writings of Plato, and that the form of the Book and some of its contents are due to Greek influence. The line of thought symbolized in the letters to the seven churches of Asia is strongly suggestive of the philosophy of Plato. When we remember that, from the time of Alexander the Great onward, the Greek language was the language of literature and of culture over a large part of Western Asia and Northwestern Africa, we can at once understand that the Greek dramas and Greek philosophy, and even the Greek mythology, would naturally have been read by any person of even moderate learning, living in that part of the world; and that St. John, in his later years, came strongly under Greek influence, need not, therefore, seem surprising. We remember that, as related in the seventeenth chapter of Acts, St. Paul quoted from one of the Greek poets in a way which indicates his familiarity with the Greek literature.

References to Astronomy

In that time, there was not, of course, much well-defined knowledge in the realm covered by what we call natural science. There was some knowledge of the anatomy of the human body, and there was an elaborately developed system of astronomy, far more correct on its descriptive side than on its physical and mathematical sides, as measured by present standards. This system of astronomy, including its signs of the zodiac and subdivisions thereof, was currently used in reckoning time; and we have to take this fact into account in order to understand some phrases in the Apocalypse.

Problem of Interpretation Not Unsolvable

At the beginning of the Apocalypse, John represents himself as being commanded to write a book embodying a message given to him; and he has done so, expressing the thought in a series of images and symbols which have proven so intricate and confusing to all readers, that, until very recent years, hardly a beginning of a successful interpretation of the greater portion of the Book had been made, notwithstanding that scores of commentators, from the third century down to the present time, have tried to unravel the mystery, among whom there is the widest imaginable divergence of opinion as to the interpretation of many chapters.* As explained in the chapter on the Prologue, following, this figurative expression was probably the way in which the ideas came to John's aspiring thought, and the figures which he used were clear to him, but it would seem that only those can unravel their meaning who have attained a consciousness in some degree approximating John's spiritual level, and thus have sufficient understanding of the ways of God with men to know what must be approximately the right idea in a given situation, and hence approximately what St. John might be expected to teach. Having in this way a clear indication as to what *general* meaning to look for in connection with a given symbol, the investigator is, after more or less thought, able to see exactly what the meaning must certainly be. The meaning having thus been once seen, it will be found to fit upon the image or symbol perfectly, and usually the interpretation of the symbol brings out and enforces a lesson of great value.

The Author's Experience

Like all students of human development, personal and racial, the author has long been perplexed as to what attitude he should hold toward certain human problems. In studying the Apocalypse, he came, after a time, to see that in certain chapters St. John is dealing with just these problems, and

---

* Mr. F. L. Rawson, M.I.E.E., A.M.I.C.E., of London, author of "Life Understood," a book which students of metaphysics would do well to read, suggests that perhaps the principal reason why the message of the Apocalypse was not given in plain language is, that it was better that what was to transpire in the future should not be made known to mankind except as the Science of spiritual understanding was more fully attained, so that men would know how to mentally handle and destroy evil as its fuller workings became revealed. It might have had a disastrous effect if all the evil uncovered in the Apocalypse should have been made known to mankind when there were none who would understand how to scientifically utilize the power of God to meet this evil.

with this cue, after further meditation upon the symbolism used, he reached the conviction that St. John takes a definite attitude with regard to these problems. His teaching, thus interpreted, was found to be extremely helpful and convincing. It has clarified the mind of the author with regard to several vexed questions in relation to which he had not previously felt the conviction of certitude. He is therefore led to think that many other students of the Book may reach the same satisfying conclusions, and that, when St. John's teaching is clearly understood by them, it will bear witness for itself as being authoritative and final,—as being indeed the very *dictum* of the Christ, to be implicitly followed and obeyed.

Christian Science the Key

In verse 7 of chapter 10, John represents the Christ as declaring solemnly that "In the days of the voice of the seventh angel, when he shall begin to sound, the mystery of God should be finished." As is well known, in Scripture the symbolical sense of "seven" is *completeness* or *completion*. Hence, the proclamation of the seventh angel must be considered as representing the *completion* of the revelation of Truth; and this is what those who understand Christian Science believe that Science to be. Accordingly, this verse of Scripture declares that after Christian Science begins to be proclaimed in the world, the time will have arrived when, according to the prophecy of the Apocalypse itself, the message "sealed up" (see verse 4 of this chapter) therein is to be unsealed and interpreted so that it can be understood. Thus will St. John "prophesy again", as foretold that he "must", in the eleventh verse of this same chapter. His words will become a clear, vital, and profoundly important message to this age, showing clearly in their order all the steps in progress which individuals and the race must take in order to reach the final goal of the demonstration of life wholly spiritual, harmonious and eternal.

INTRODUCTION

Present Work Compared With Previous Commentaries

The first discerning interpretation of any portion of Revelation that the author of this Study has read was made by Mrs. Eddy in her chapter on "The Apocalypse", in Science and Health with Key to the Scriptures. In that chapter, however, she attempts an exposition of only a very limited portion of the Book, though she correctly illustrates the general method by which all of it is to be rightly interpreted.

The author has read the work of many of the best known commentators upon the Apocalypse, but has found among all these scarcely the proverbial "two grains of wheat in a bushel of chaff" in the way of what seems to him a correct exposition. He has also read several recent expositions, not widely known as yet, and has derived from these a number of valuable suggestions, acknowledgment for which will be made at the proper places in the body of the book. In preparing this work, the author has carefully consulted the Greek text, with the aid of the best lexicons, also the best known modern translations, and has considered variations in the original manuscripts from which the standard Greek texts are compiled.

The Spiritual Point of View

The author of this Study has had an advantage, enjoyed by no commentator whose work he has read, namely, the knowledge of Christian Science, by which he has gained a sense of the spiritual significance of the writings of John in the light of divine Principle. It is evident to him that John, as the disciple of Jesus, had the spiritual point of view which has been again brought to human thought in Christian Science; and that no person who has not this spiritual point of view can interpret or understand much of John's symbolism. The interpretation given in this Study must therefore differ in many places from that given by all who are unacquainted with Christian Science.

Suggestions Requested

The author has made an honest endeavor to bring to the entire text of the Book the Christ-light which dawns anew in Christian Science, and which Mrs. Eddy has shown her students how to use in her interpretation of vital parts of the Book; and these Notes are made available to other students of the Bible at the earnest request of many who have read portions of them in manuscript, and with the single purpose and hope that they may be helpful to them as they have been to the author in his endeavor to profit by St. John's remarkable writing, and thus attain to more of that Mind "which was also in Christ Jesus." The Notes are not intended to be taken dogmatically, or to be considered the final word as to the best interpretation of any given text. No doubt the interpretation, or the form of expression, can be improved at many points, and readers are free to exercise their thought to that end. The author would be especially glad of any suggestions which any one may have to offer. The Notes are given out with the hope that they may stimulate thought and inquiry with regard to a portion of the Scriptures, the meaning of which seems obscure to the great body of Bible readers, but which is very rich in practical spiritual teaching, the author's sense of which has been already stated. With respect to the importance of its subject matter, its marvelous insight into deep and hidden things, its practical value when understood, and withal its literary excellence and brilliancy, it is doubtful if another human document of equal length can compare with the Revelation of St. John the Divine.

Literary Form of Apocalypse Described and Outlined

The literary form of the Book is undoubtedly that of a drama. John may very likely have gotten the suggestion for this literary form from the Greek poets, with whose plays he was doubtless familiar. The subject of the drama of the Apocalypse may be plainly stated as follows:

The Drama of the Struggle between Good and Evil upon the Field of Human Consciousness, and of the Final Triumph of Good.

While John's thought seems to have been much centered upon general and sometimes upon outwardly visible movements and effects produced by the struggles between good and evil in human consciousness, yet he does not treat less specifically of the individual problem, and the reader who would derive the greatest practical benefit and spiritual uplift from the study of Revelation will keep constantly in mind that there can never be outward effects except through the workings of mental causes, and that there can be no general mental movements in the human realm except as individual thought, on the part of large numbers, takes part in and becomes the basis for these movements. Most of the struggles which John depicts are now in process, and, accordingly, if we would profit by the instruction and the warnings which he sets so vividly before us, and escape the terrible penalties for wrongdoing which he so forcefully emphasizes,—and there is no realizing of good nor escape from suffering unless one does profit by instruction and warning like that which he gives,—we shall take heed to ourselves personally with regard to every phase of the struggle between good and evil which he describes, and have a care that we are numbered every day and hour among the soldiers of the Christ rather than among the followers of Satan. Indeed, the development of every human consciousness epitomizes all of the most important struggles which are engaged in by mankind as a whole on its way up to God, and whatever conflicts John depicts as taking place on the fields of humanity as a whole, the reader may find going on in his own consciousness if he will but look thoughtfully within; and so all the lessons of the Book are of most vital practical value to him who "hath ears to hear".

Notes on Specific Subjects

Note 1. *No Dead Line.* It is interesting and important to note that there is practically no "dead line" in the Book of Revelation. St. John recognises the saints "here" and the saints "there" or "beyond", as all of one company, following Christ. For the most part, he absolutely ignores the experience called death as much as he ignores the experience called sleep. The drama is carried on above the level of such low lines of demarcation. Cattle are separated from each other by fences, but birds pay no attention to them, flying back and forth and freely intermingling without regard to the fences. So the mental activities dramatized in the Apocalypse for the most part transcend the dividing line called death, except to speak of it in connection with the two resurrections in chapter 20. We, too, can practically ignore the low fence called death in our activities of thought and feeling, if we elevate our consciousness to a plane sufficiently high above the earth,—above materiality in thinking.

Note 2. *Use of Numbers.* Numbers are usually employed in the Apocalypse in a symbolical rather than in a literal sense. The writer has not made an exhaustive original study of the symbolical use of numbers in the Bible, but, on the authority of those who have, the following brief summary is presented.

"*One,*" "*two*" and "*three*" seem to be Spirit-signs, mostly used, when used symbolically, with reference to a member of the Trinity,—Father, Son, or Holy Spirit. "One" and "three" seem never to symbolize evil, and "two" rarely so, though, occasionally, it presents a sense of division and opposition, thus suggesting satanic activity.

"*Four*" seems to be a world-sign, signifying "worldly" or "pertaining to the earth," or to humanity. It also signifies all of the class mentioned. For example, "Four winds of the earth" are *all* winds,—*all* destructive forces of evil. The "beasts" (better translated "living creatures") about the throne, described in the fourth chapter of Revelation, being numbered "four", indicates that that which they symbolize was formerly in the service of the world.

"*Five*" appears to be used as the symbol of government, usually God's government of man, though the number is sometimes used in association with evil, suggesting the government of evil.

"*Six*" seems to be, in the Apocalypse at least, a satan-sign. It falls short of "seven", which is a Sabbath-sign, the sign of completion. So "six" is the sign of short-coming, apostasy. Some writer whose name the author has been unable to learn has written: "Everything satanic is six. . . . Notice that the luke-warm church of Laodicea is reproved with six words of reproof—luke-warm, wretched, miserable, poor, blind and naked. The unrepentant people of the sixth trumpet have six idols, and the people who follow this 'false prophet' are also of six kinds, 'the small, the great, the rich, the poor, the free, and the bond.' The number of the beast is 666."

"*Seven*", as already indicated, is the Sabbath-sign. It is particularly the sign of completeness and of work finished. When used symbolically it stands for *all* of the class mentioned.

"*Eight*" is the symbol of that which is "new" in contrast with the preceding.

"*Nine*" is the symbol of intuitive wisdom.

"*Ten*", as used in the Apocalypse, would seem to be taken as *the multiple of "five"*, carrying with it the "opposition" sense of "two" (2 x 5), and is used in connection with the asserted authority or government of evil, as, for instance, the "ten horns" of the beast.

"*Twelve*" is the symbol of that which is close to God and manifests His government.

"*A thousand*" indicates a large but indefinite number, just as, on returning from a meeting, we might say, "There were a thousand people present", meaning, not exactly a thousand, but a large number. It is also regarded as a symbol of spiritual conquest. See comment on chapter 2, verse 7, in the pages following.

"*144,000*" probably takes its symbolic meaning from the numbers of which it is a multiple (12 x 12 x 1,000). It indicates a large but indefinite number under the manifest government of God.

Note 3. *Chronology.* The numbers used in connection with chronology in the Apocalypse are all symbolical, instead of literal.

"*Ten days*", mentioned in chapter 2:1, may be explained as follows: One of the constellations in the zodiac (though not one of the twelve major "signs of the zodiac") is "Draco", the dragon. "*The dragon*" is one of the Apocalyptic symbols for satan. In its yearly journey through the heavens (that is, as it appears), it takes the sun ten days to pass through the constellation "Draco". Hence, *"ten days"* is dragon-time, and stands for the period of the reign of satan.

"*Five months*", mentioned in chapter 9:5, may be interpreted in the following manner. It is stated that men are to be tormented *"five months"* by *"locusts"*, which are symbols for evil emissaries of satan. Locusts live and are active only during the five summer months. Hence, *"five months"* well indicates the full period of their activity, and stands for *locust-time;* that is, for the entire period of the activity of satanic influences; so the period *"five months"* is the same as that indicated by *"ten days"*.

"*Time, times, and half a time*", "*forty and two months*", "*one thousand and two hundred and three-score days*"; that is, 3½ years, 42 months, 1260 days, which are exactly equivalent, reckoning thirty days to the month,—these are the time expressions most frequently used in the Apocalypse. Their symbolic value is determined from the fact that 3½ years is just half of *"seven"* years; that is, of *all* years, or of *all* time, as contra-distinct from eternity, which is the opposite of time, as "eternity" refers to the spiritual and changeless sense of things, while "time" refers to the material and destructible sense of things. This period of 3½ years is invariably mentioned in connection with the activity of satan or some of his manifestations. Hence, this period is also satan-time. It indicates that the Apocalypse teaches that, during about one-half of humanity's experience in the material or time-sense, satan will seem to be in the ascendency in the affairs of the world*; but that,

*Note.—If it seems to any reader startling, and beside the mark, to regard the present time as within the period of apparent satanic ascendency, let him consider the following fact as a sample of present conditions:

The law of the City of Chicago requires that saloons and all restaurants in which liquor is sold shall close at one o'clock in the morning. In December, 1912, it got rumored abroad that these places were going to keep open on New Year's Eve until three o'clock, with the consent of the Mayor and the Police Department, in order that the drunken carousals might go on unchecked. The clergymen of the city got together, and, after due deliberation, three hundred of them went in a body to the City Hall to protest against any such infringement of the law. The Mayor absolutely refused to see this delegation, representing the Christian forces of the city. This Mayor is not regarded as being personally a bad or intemperate man; but he evidently felt that, whenever it came to a test, the forces of evil in the city were stronger than the forces of righteousness, and, as a politician, he stood with what he regarded as the stronger force. The saloons and restaurants remained wide open on New Year's Eve, and it was found impossible to make a successful prosecution of the Mayor or anyone else for this open, premeditated and willful violation of the law. This is a fair sample of what might occur at the present in any of the great cities of the world, and in many of the smaller ones.

The following, written in 1913 by Mr. Bernard Shaw, may be somewhat overdrawn, but it is largely to the point, nevertheless:

> "When I travel about Europe," he says, "and see Germany studded with colossal images of the man of blood and iron, the latest being also the highest and most irresistibly suggestive of Dagon and Moloch; when I read the recent history of the triumphs of Mars in Tripoli, Morocco and the Balkan states; when I see compulsory military service rapidly becoming universal and Mars achieving miracles of submarines and aeroplanes in a few years, whilst Christ cannot in as many centuries get rid even of such a blazing abomination as the mixed general workhouse, I really cannot see how anyone can allege that Christianity has gained an inch since the crucifixion.

after that, Christ will reign in harmony during an equal period, before the sense of matter is finally destroyed; in other words, that the period before the millennium commences will be about equal to that which follows the commencement of the millennium and ends with the destruction of the material sense of heaven and earth.

"Three days and a half", mentioned in chapter 11:9, is half of *seven* days, half of *all* days, half of all time, and symbolizes the period of satanic ascendency, the same as the time periods or symbols which we have been considering.

"Half an hour", mentioned in 8:1, refers to the latter half of the time period, and is synonymous in meaning with *"a thousand years"*.

"A thousand years", the millennial period, mentioned in chapter 20, is doubtless a "round number", indicating a long period of time, after discord has been overcome, in which harmony will reign supreme among men still dwelling in material sense, in fulfilment of that portion of the Lord's prayer which reads: "Thy kingdom come. Thy will be done, *in earth* (the human-sense realm) as it is in heaven (the spiritual realm)". Probably *"a thousand years"* stands for about the same length of time as "3½ years", "five months", and "ten days", though these three latter are satan-signs, while "a thousand years" is, in this connection, a Christ-sign, and symbolizes the period of spiritual conquest and victory which is to follow the period of apparent satanic ascendency.

Note 4. *Adherence to Principle.*

(a) The attempt is made in these Notes, so far as possible, to conform to the requirements of the absolute and eternal truth, that God is "of purer eyes than to behold evil and cannot look upon iniquity", and that "God is light, and in Him

---

"If one were to dramatize the world movement of the struggle between Christ and Mars, Christ is down and out, despised and rejected of men; spat upon, nailed up and laughed to scorn."

When Christ shall have become ascendent among men, such things as these cannot occur.

is no darkness at all". This divine Principle of being was surely known to St. John (See I John, 1:5); nevertheless he does not seem to have tried to express himself in harmony with this Principle, but rather from the standpoint of human appearance, in the working out of humanity's problem.

(b) In this interpretation, God is regarded as absolute Mind, and there will not be attributed to Him thoughts and deeds which can belong only to a mediatorial consciousness, more or less highly spiritual, but still short of the absolute. This mediatorial consciousness is spoken of as "the Christ-consciousness", and often as "higher understanding", or some equivalent phrase.

(c) Further, God is not represented as purposely approaching men, either directly or through Christ or angels, as is often stated in Revelation; but the fact of men's approach to God through the Christ-consciousness or through their perception of angelic ideas is set forth instead.

(d) God and Christ and the angels of God are not represented as inflicting punishment or other evil upon men; but, instead, the fact is set forth that ignorance and sin are automatically and necessarily excluded from harmony, just as darkness is necessarily excluded from light, evil being by its very nature confined to its own realm of discord, where it must of necessity punish itself.

Note 5. *No God of Wrath.* The Authorized Version, and all the modern translations that the author has consulted, save one, represent God and Christ and the angels of God as being *angry* at the wicked, and as meting out *wrath* to the wicked. This is due to a mis-translation of what seems the evident sense of the original Greek. There are two Greek words which the various translators have rendered "wrath". They are *orgê* and *thumos*. The author does not deny that "wrath" is sometimes a legitimate rendering for these words, everything depending upon the connection in which they are used.

Liddell & Scott's Greek Lexicon gives as primary definitions of *orgê*, "*natural impulse or propension, disposition, nature, heart.*" Hence, the *orgê* of God would represent His nature, that is, Love and its activity. To be sure, the divine *orgê* is destructive of evil, and is feared and hated by those who desire to cling to evil; nevertheless, the world connotes a very different state of divine consciousness and activity from that indicated by the word "wrath".

As previously quoted, the Scripture declares, that God "*is of purer eyes than to behold evil, and cannot look upon iniquity.*" God knows nothing of evil or evildoers, and does not consciously deal with them in any way. But when divine Love is reflected in human consciousness, where it assumes a mediatorial character, it takes the form of great desire and strenuous activity to save men from their sins and to destroy evil. Spiritual love never desires or strives to punish men for the sake of punishing them. If mediatorial love ever does inflict penalties or deprivations upon men, it does so only as a last resort to effect their reformation, or to prevent them from harming others, having previously tried every gentle and persuasive means to this end. The authorities of ecclesiastical organizations have often imposed penalties upon members of such organizations for wrong-doing, for the purpose of punishing them; but they were not reflecting the divine *orgê* in doing so, but were reflecting satan, if the infliction of punishment was their primary purpose.

Other meanings of *orgê* than the fundamental ones above given fit exactly upon the exercise of mediatorial divine love, as above described. The word is derived from the verb *orgaô*, which means, primarily, to swell with passion, and connotes, among other meanings, the frenzy of sexual love. In its reversed higher sense, it indicates mediatorial divine love in a perfect frenzy of desire to propagate righteousness and to save men from evil. *Orgê* is closely related by derivation to the Greek *orgia*, from which is derived our English word "orgy", suggesting that the divine *orgê* (nature), when reflected in human consciousness, takes the form of mediatorial love that is nothing short of *riotous* in its evangelizing and saving work.

The Greek and Latin languages had a common origin; and the older verb which came, in time, to be pronounced among the Greeks *orgaô* came, among the Latins, to be pronounced *urgeo;* and from this verb is derived our English word "urge", which suggests that *orgê* conveys the idea of the *urgency* of mediatorial divine love in its desire to save, thus reënforcing the interpretations already given.

No single English word will adequately translate the Greek *orgê*, but the phrase, *"divine impulse of Love, overcoming evil"*, gives the exact sense in which it is always used in the New Testament.

Thumos should be translated, not "wrath", but "ardor" or "enthusiasm". It connotes, not anger from God or from those in His service, but the *ardor* of mediating love to enforce the will of God, who *is* Love.

Evil-doers are often made to suffer, but, strictly speaking, it is not the enforcement of the power of God that makes them suffer. The power of God, as applied by men, either absolutely destroys evil, as when light destroys darkness, in which case there is nothing to be punished; or else good simply stands as a wall of adamant against the advance of evil and at a certain stage of its advance automatically turns it back upon itself to punish with its own discord those who may be enmeshed in it.* There is no discord in good with which to punish evil; for in good all is harmony.

Note 6. *Salvation from Evil.* Revelation frequently seems to speak of men as though they were or could be permanently identified with evil. This Interpretation holds to the fact that "the wicked" are evil thoughts and influences, not permanently identified with men. The false beliefs of human sense constitute the "mortal men", who must disappear or be "lost" in proportion as the true sense of man is gained. All that is true in human sense constitutes the appearing of

---
*"Science and Health," 543:1; 569:21-28.

immortal man, who is forever safe. Evil in all its phases is to be destroyed, but all human beings are to be saved out of evil. Saith the Christ, "And I, if I be lifted up from the earth, will draw all men unto me"; and St. Paul wrote of God, that He "will have all men to be saved and to come into the knowledge of the truth", and "As in Adam all die, so in Christ shall all be made alive." The last "all" is certainly as inclusive as the first.

The one phrase in the original Greek of the Apocalypse that indicates the duration of punishment or discord is *eis aionas aionôn,* which is rendered literally in the margin of the Revised Version "unto ages of ages", which probably indicates the exact sense,—namely, that evil will be manifest and its followers will be punished *for a very long period,* even as long as satanic activity endures, but there is nothing to indicate that this period will be *endless,* or that any human being who in part follows evil for a time will follow it during the whole of this period. The sense would rather seem to be that during this period punishment will be endured by different men successively, each suffering as long as he remains enmeshed in evil, and no longer. The Greek scholars of the world are now quite generally agreed that there is no word or phrase in the Apocalypse, used in connection with evil or punishment, which legitimately signifies endless duration. The lake of fire and brimstone is to be regarded as a symbol of the final absolute destruction of evil by the fire of the Holy Spirit, mediatorial divine love, rather than as a place of *endless* torment.

Much of the Apocalypse is written from the standpoint of human experience rather than of strict metaphysical fact, and this should be remembered in connection with every passage where the text seems to assert or imply that God sends His angels or others to punish evil or evil-doers, or that Christ punishes evil or evil-doers, or that some human beings are to be saved as such, while others are to be eternally lost as such. Along these lines the translation in the Authorized Version is very misleading.

Note 7. *Use of the word "Heaven".* In most cases in the Apocalypse, St. John uses the term "heaven" as synonymous with the mental realm, either personal or general, where the forces of good and evil are still contending. For instance, in the 12th chapter, he sees the dragon, satan, *"in heaven"*. So, except in the 21st chapter, and perhaps occasionally elsewhere, as can be determined by the context, when John speaks of "heaven" he means either his own consciousness or else the mental realm of humanity which has not yet worked out its problem, and he does not mean the realm of absolute Spirit and harmony.

Note 8. *Form and Emphasis.* Several modern students of the Revelation, including the author, are convinced that it is cast in a distinct dramatic form, though, of course, not intended for presentation on a stage. It has, *in form,* a definite "cast of characters", and has the principal features and figures of the universe of nature as "stage settings", and also a "prologue", seven distinct "acts", and an "epilogue".

However, though the literary *form* of the book is dramatic, it is not dramatic in the succession of events. In a true drama, the events in each act succeed in point of time those of the preceding act; but in the Apocalypse the events or movements depicted or symbolized in the several parts of the book which have the literary form of acts,—these events or movements do not, for the most part, succeed each other, but take place coincidently. In fact, in several of the "acts" the whole course of the struggle between good and evil is sketched through from the beginning of the Christ-activity to the end of evil, though each of these "acts" treats of a different *phase* of the struggle. However, in a general way,—but only in a sense that is distinctly large and general,—there is a progress of action, and especially of the intensity of action, as the thought of the book unfolds; and in the closing chapters there is a distinct maturing and finishing of the various lines of action symbolized in the earlier "acts". Though the *form* is dramatic, the impression upon the mind of the reader, who gets the *thought* of the book as a whole, is more epic than dramatic. In the Modern Reader's Bible, Professor Moulton says:

"The Revelation of St. John is in literary form a 'rhapsody', . . . a new literary form made of the fusion of all other literary forms in one. . . . In the Hebrew rhapsody, while all literary forms are fused together, it is usually the dramatic form that is most prominent; in St. John's revelation the prevailing impression is that of epic succession of incidents, as narrated by the seer.

"This revelation is a Vision, falling into seven 'visions', as in the case of *Zion Redeemed,* or Zachariah's Revelation; the seven parts are, however, continuous, one developed out of the other, with no break: the distinction is one of analysis. It is most important for the interpreter to divest his mind of all idea of succession in time. As with Isaiahan rhapsodies, the relation of these seven parts is not that of temporal succession; each is complete in itself, and a complete presentation of the whole from one side. The connection of the seven is logical. . . . Like the sections of Isaiah's *Vision of Judgment,* the succession of parts may suggest graduation of intensity, and a new vision may be the climax of that which has preceded."

Use of the Charts

As is the case with everything else about the Apocalypse, the facts regarding its literary structure are not very evident upon the surface, but an understanding of them is essential to a full and clear comprehension of its meaning. The skeleton of the human body is not in itself attractive, yet the body would not be very useful or attractive without it; nor can the form of the body and the relation of its parts be well understood, without an understanding of its frame; nevertheless, he who should devote the major portion of his attention to an understanding of the skeleton would miss the larger and more important part of what is to be known about the body. In like manner, it seems to be necessary, in an interpretation of the Apocalypse, to give an analysis of its literary form, and that in some detail, by means of charts, etc., also calling attention to some few other facts of a non-spiritual character. This intellectual side of the presentation should be regarded by the reader as a sort of "John the Baptist, crying in the wilderness, Prepare ye the way of the Lord, make his paths straight". It is to be thought of merely as an aid to a fuller and more accurate understanding of the spiritual teaching, and the reader should avoid any possible danger of centering his thought so much upon what is said about the structure, and the like, as to miss the force of the spiritual teaching,—teaching which is surely as valuable for the solution of problems now pressing upon men, individually and collectively, as any ever written.

The most graphic and easily comprehended presentation of the literary structure is given on the large chart inserted at the end of the book. Although this chart presents the skeleton of the drama, it should not be regarded as merely a skeleton. The *unities of meaning* between symbols and phrases widely variant in form, which it discloses, are more clearly and graphically brought out in the chart than in any other way. By means of it, the different phrases and symbols, being thus placed side by side, are made to interpret each other, and the underlying unities of thought constitute some of the most inspiring and spiritually valuable lessons of the book. The author believes that many hours can profitably be spent in the study of this chart in connection with the text of the Apocalypse. The reader is recommended to spend several moments in glancing over the chart before reading further in this book. It will readily be noted from an examination of the chart that all the actors on the side of good are manifestations of the one Mind, the one good, God, and so are one at the root; and all the actors on the side of evil are manifestations of evil mentality, the one evil, the devil, and so are also one at the root.

There are several minor characters or actors on the side of good and on the side of evil which are not mentioned in the

Cast of Characters, but which are classified in the chart under the different "acts".

In a drama on the stage, not all the characters usually appear in all the acts, and it is seldom that they all appear in any one act; but any given actor appears at least in one act, perhaps in two or three, perhaps in all the acts, according to his importance in the drama. So it is in the presentation of this great world-drama.

In a drama on the stage, usually the actors frequently change their clothing, and sometimes disguise themselves so that they are not easily recognized as really carrying out the same purpose in different acts. So in this world-drama, the various actors appear under frequently varying titles, and frequently in such different offices as not readily to be recognized as the same in the different acts.

The key to the literary structure, and largely to the interpretation, of Revelation may be given in two important statements:

1. *Every character on the side of good will be found to be counterfeited and opposed somewhere in the drama of the Book by an exactly corresponding evil character. More than this, every important act or movement on the side of good will be found to be similarly counterfeited and opposed on the side of evil.*

2. *It seems very clear, after close study, that St. John wrote this Book on the assumption that after Christ Jesus had disappeared in the Ascension, he would be, and in St. John's day had already begun to be, reincarnated as the impersonal Christ in the Christian church, and that, as incarnated in the church, he would, in conquering the world, go through a kind and order of experiences almost exactly duplicating the leading experiences of Christ Jesus during his earthly ministry.*

Note 9. *Accuracy of Text and Translation.* As the author will have occasion to call in question, rather frequently, the accuracy of the translation given in the Authorized Version, and, in some cases, that given in any other translations that he is acquainted with, and as he will sometimes have occasion to call in question the correctness of the several Greek texts upon which modern translations are based, and as some of his readers will probably be unfamiliar with questions of text and translation, it may be helpful to such readers, if, before the work of commenting upon the text of the Book is begun, the author shall state the reasons which give him a right to critically review both the established Greek texts and all existing translations, making changes whenever he can show sufficient cause for doing so.

First, with regard to the matter of translation. Among those who have had even a little experience in rendering one language into another, it is a well known fact, that any given sentence in one language can usually be given several translations into another language, each of which is literally and grammatically correct, though practically only one translation can correctly present the thought which the author of the original sentence desired to express. The question, then, is, how to know which one of the several possible literal translations ought to be chosen. This is always a question of judgment on the part of the translator, and the determining factor with him is, what the general idea of the writer of the original sentence on the point which it brings out, and what the sense of the immediate context of that sentence, require. Accordingly, on general principles, other things being equal, the translator who best understands the thought of an author as a whole will best translate him at points where there is possibility of doubt. In translating, knowledge of vocabulary, grammar, syntax, and rhetoric are very important; but acquaintance with an author's point of view and general system of thought are often quite as important on the part of the translator or even more so. It may not be amiss to give one or two specific instances.

A German student of English translated a passage (Matt. 26:41) from German into English, as follows:

Der Geist ist willig; aber das fleisch ist schwach,
The ghost is ready; but the meat is feeble.

It should be rendered,

"The Spirit is willing; but the flesh is weak".

The first of these translations is just as correct from a literal and grammatical standpoint as the second. Nevertheless it utterly misses St. Matthew's meaning.

The sleeper was evidently disturbed in his dreams.
The sleeper, fortunately, did not leave the rails.
The sleeper under the east end of the building was badly decayed.

Whoever should try to render these three English sentences into any other language, proceeding on the assumption that the word "sleeper" had the same meaning in each sentence, would get very curious and ludicrous results. In the first sentence, *the context* shows us that the word means *a person asleep;* in the second sentence, *the context* shows that the word means *a railroad car in which people sleep;* in the third sentence, *the context* shows that the word means *the sill of a building.* This illustration will serve to indicate the *importance of the context* in determining the meaning of words for translation or otherwise.

Second, with regard to the Greek text. There could be little question about this, if St. John's original manuscript were in existence and available; but it is not, and scholars are obliged to depend upon copies of copies, more or less remote from the original. There are many ancient copies, and they do not agree among themselves at many points, showing that the copyists were sometimes careless, and sometimes inserted words or phrases to suit their own thought of what the text should say. Consequently, modern scholars have no absolute assurance of the reading of St. John's original manuscript at various points, but must compare the various copies, and use their own judgment as to which reading is correct at any given point. By so doing, several modern Greek texts have been published, which are regarded highly, and which are made the basis of translation for modern versions. The Authorized Version was translated in the time of King James First of England (1611), using as a basis previous English translations, which in turn were made from a Latin manuscript, which had been translated from the Greek in the 4th century.* Being a translation of a translation of a translation the Authorized Version is more especially liable to contain errors.

In selecting what is probably the original form in which St. John wrote a given sentence, a correct knowledge of his general point of view and system of thought is just as important as it is in the matter of translation.

Other things being equal, the man who has the best understanding of St. John's general concept of religious things will make the best selection among variant readings in establishing the Greek text as a basis for translation. Consequently, the writer of these Notes feels at liberty to question the standard Greek texts at any point where he can show sufficient cause for doing so from an enlarged knowledge of St. John's general thought, or from the context, and to make changes thus indicated, when there is authority in some ancient manuscripts for the readings which he adopts.

*See "How We Got Our Bible," by J. Patterson Smyth.

NOTES BY THE READER

NOTES BY THE READER

PROLOGUE

1 *"The Revelation of Jesus Christ, which God gave unto him, to show unto his servants things which must shortly come to pass; and he sent and signified it by his Angel unto his servant John.*

2 *Who bare record of the word of God; and of the testimony of Jesus Christ, and of all things that he saw.*

3 *Blessed is he that readeth, and they that hear the words of this prophecy, and keep those things that are written therein; for the time is at hand."*

"Jesus Christ"

"Jesus Christ". When we come to see fully what these words mean, they will be found to designate the central figure, if not the all-in-all in one sense, of the book which we are to study and interpret.

"The revelation (Greek *apocalypsis,* "unveiling") *of Jesus Christ"*, on a little reflection, will be seen to mean the same as *"the testimony* (Greek, *marturian,* "witnessing") *of Jesus Christ"* (verse 2). The phrase, *"the testimony of Jesus"*, is also used in verse 9, modern scholars being agreed that *"Christos"* (Christ) should be omitted from the Greek and English texts. In verse 10 of chapter 19, St. John tells us that the phrase *"the testimony of Jesus"* means *"the spirit of prophecy"*. *"The spirit of prophecy"* is evidently that highly developed spiritual factor or manifestation in human mentality which discerns, first of all, the eternal and fixed order of truth and good, and perceives fully the false claim of error, and then is able to foresee how truth and error will react upon each other in the field of human experience, and the general course of events which will follow in consequence, ending in

the final destruction of error and all its manifestations. Hence, according to St. John's own definition, it is this prophetic consciousness which is meant by the words *"Jesus Christ"*, rather than, or possibly in addition to, that which pertains to the earthly history or personal mentality of Jesus of Nazareth, although this personal sense of the words *"Jesus Christ"* is the only one which the average reader of Revelation has been inclined to consider.

Here, the important and interesting question naturally suggests itself, How could the words *"Jesus Christ"* come to be used in a sense so seemingly different from their apparently natural significance? To answer intelligently requires a bit of analysis.

The Christ, like the Father, of whom he is the perfect reflection, *"is of purer eyes than to behold evil, and cannot look upon iniquity."* Hence, the absolute Christ can have no recognition of human needs and human problems, and could not, therefore, apply the divine power to meet those needs. This can be done by a mediatorial mentality, which can clearly discern the spiritual power of Truth and good on the one hand, and the ignorance, sin, discord and limitation of humanity on the other, seeing the nothingness of the latter in the light of Spirit, and thus intelligently applying the power of God to the destruction of evil. A unique degree of this mediatorial mentality was a distinguishing mark of Jesus of Nazareth. He taught and demonstrated that mentality for something over three years in Palestine, and then he overcame the flesh, ascended above the belief in matter, effectually denied his mortal self, and his human personality vanished; for he had fully *"put on Christ."* But this mediatorial mentality has remained, in greater or lesser measure, in Christ's human church, and among many people outside of any formally organized church. It was this mentality which rendered Jesus of Nazareth of so much significance to the world. He himself said: *"The flesh profiteth nothing: the words that I speak unto you, they are Spirit, and they are life."* Indeed, it was because it was foreseen that he would have this remarkable spiritual endowment that he was given the name *"Jesus"*. *"Thou shalt call his name JESUS: for he shall save his people from their sins."* (Matt. 1:21). As Thayer's Greek Lexicon suggests, among the Jews of that century the word *"Jesus"* had come to mean *"Saviour"*, although by derivation it originally meant the same as *"Joshua"*, *"God-helped"*. The word *"Christ"* (Greek, *christos*) means *"anointed"*. Hence, the words *"Christ Jesus"*, or *"Jesus Christ"*, mean *"anointed Saviour"*, or *"God-blessed Saviour"*. In the Apocalypse, and in most places in the New Testament, these words are used in this derivative sense, not with regard to the human personality of Jesus of Nazareth, but with regard to the mediatorial mentality which has remained among men to this day, in accordance with its promise: *"Lo, I am with you alway, even to the end of the world."*

Without this mediatorial mentality, men could not find their way to the understanding and demonstration of eternal harmony, or "heaven", or to that knowledge of God which is the true and everlasting consciousness or life. Hence, John 17:3 could be correctly paraphrased as follows:

This is life eternal, that they might know thee the only true God, and the way-shower (Jesus Christ, the mediatorial mentality) which thou hast sent.

Thus, when Jesus uttered these words, he was not referring to anything that could be regarded as his own personality, but to a universal spiritualized consciousness among men, which Moses and Isaiah, for instance, expressed in large measure, of which Jesus himself in his own time was the exponent, and which was and is to remain in the world forever, until *"the former heaven and the former earth have passed away, and there shall be no more sea"*, because the eternal heaven and the eternal earth, which are wholly spiritual, shall have been demonstrated. *"And when all things shall be subdued unto him, then shall the Son also himself be subject unto him that put all things under him, that God may be all in all"*; that is, the mediatorial consciousness will vanish when the human problem is entirely worked out, and so the mediator is no longer required as a factor. This spiritual mentality itself declared that it antedated Jesus of Nazareth in the words: *"Before Abraham was, I am."*

Paul's word in Gal. 3:28 might be legitimately paraphrased:

There is neither Jew nor Greek, there is neither bond nor free, there is neither male nor female: for ye are all at one in the mediatorial mentality (Christ Jesus), the mentality which is aspiring after and struggling for eternal truth and good.

The words *"Jesus Christ"* also properly connote *"the spirit of wisdom"*, which not only knows the absolute truth, but knows in what measure it should be given to humanity at any given stage of its advancement, and knows how to practically administer the truth, the law of God, to the best advantage in any human situation. This *"spirit of wisdom"* long antedated Jesus of Nazareth. For instance, we read in Proverbs:

"Doth not wisdom cry? and understanding put forth her voice? Receive my instruction, and not silver; and knowledge rather than choice gold. The Lord possessed me in the beginning of his way, before his works of old. I was set up from everlasting, from the beginning, or ever the earth was. Now therefore hearken unto me, O ye children: for blessed are they that keep my ways, For whoso findeth me findeth life, and shall obtain favor of the Lord. But he that sinneth against me wrongeth his own soul."

It was this *"spirit of wisdom"* which led Moses to put a veil over his face (Exodus 34:29-35), not only to efface as much as possible his own personality, but because the glory of his countenance was more than the people could bear; that is, he could not wisely unveil to them the full measure of truth which he had received from God in the mount of spiritual exaltation.

It was this *"spirit of wisdom"* which is eloquently described in the first five verses of the 11th chapter of Isaiah and in the entire 8th chapter of Proverbs.

It was the *"spirit of wisdom"* which led Jesus of Nazareth to say to his disciples: *"Cast not your pearls before swine, lest they turn and rend you"*, and also: *"Unto you it is given to know the mystery of the Kingdom of God; but unto them that are without, all these things are done in parables, that seeing they may [seem to] see, and not perceive, and hearing they may [seem to] hear and not understand."*

It was the *"spirit of wisdom"* which as *"a voice from heaven"* said unto St. John: *"Seal up those things which the seven thunders uttered, and write them not."* (Rev. 10:4).

Jesus himself effectually settled any question as to the mediatorial Christ being identical with the mental or physical personality of Jesus of Nazareth. In Matt. 22:41-45, he is recorded as saying to the Pharisees:

"What think ye of Christ [the anointed one]? Whose son is he? They say unto him, the son of David. He saith unto them, How then doth David in spirit call him Lord, saying, The Lord saith unto my Lord, Sit thou on my right hand, till I make thine enemies thy footstool? If David then call him Lord, how is he his son?"

If, therefore, we will dissociate the words *"Jesus Christ"*, or *"Christ Jesus"*, from our thought of the corporeality, or earthly history, or personality of Jesus of Nazareth, and think of them as connoting all that may be signified by the terms *"mediatorial mentality"*, *"way-shower"*, *"anointed Saviour"*, *"prophetic consciousness"*, *"the spirit of prophecy"*, and *"the spirit of wisdom"*,—or simply such Biblical terms as *"the Christ"*, *"the Holy Spirit"*, *"the Holy Ghost"*, *"the Comforter"*, *"the Spirit of Truth"*, we shall have a correct sense of *"Jesus Christ"*, as the term is used in presenting the title figure of the Apocalypse. In Science and Health, Mrs. Eddy speaks of this mediatorial consciousness as "divine Science or the Holy Comforter", and says further: "Jesus demonstrated Christ; he proved that Christ is the divine idea of God—the Holy Ghost, or Comforter, revealing the divine Principle, Love, and leading into all truth."

The Apocalypse is the setting forth in images and symbols of practically the whole content of the most highly illuminated prophetic consciousness,—of all that it sees of the fixed order of good and of the details of the false claims of evil, and of the struggles between the different phases of good and evil in human experience, and of the final issue in the struggle.

In this sense, the Book is *"The* Revelation *of* Jesus Christ"; but there is no article before *apokalypsis* in the Greek, and the words "Jesus Christ" do not convey anything like the correct impression to the average reader; and yet a translation should convey the correct impression as nearly as it can be made to do so within the limits of a translation, without attempting to make a paraphrase of it.

Perhaps the best we can do as a translation for the first three Greek words of verse 1 is: *A revelation from Jesus Christ,*—which is perfectly permissible, since *Iêsou Christou* may be regarded as what the grammarians call a "genitive of the source."

The author feels entirely confident that St. John, when rightly understood, does not mean to suggest that the revelation came to him from a Christ who was verbally dictating to him, or who appeared to him as an outward or outlined vision. To be sure, a literal interpretation of verse 17 of chapter 1, and other verses, would seem to indicate to the contrary, but it is perfectly in keeping with an experience that many seers have had that St. John should have been temporarily stunned by an inward vision of things of great and lofty significance; and the phrase *"he laid his right hand upon me"* would be a common Jewish figurative expression for, He mentally laid hold upon me with the impulsion of his inspiration and authority. As it seems to the author, the Christ who gave this revelation to John is to be identified with John's own illuminated consciousness of Truth and Good in their relation to the affairs of the world. This mediatorial consciousness or Christ, on its divine side, was from God, and the elements of truth and good in the revelation God gave to it (or him); and this mediatorial Christ in the consciousness of John caused the revelation to take form in signs and symbols in the human phase of his mentality, and it was then outlined in writing, and thus brought to the attention of all men, many of whom are not yet sufficiently spiritual to receive this message in its entirety from the mediatorial Christ in their own mentalities without some detailed indication to guide their thought and investigations.

Any person who has been obliged to struggle mentally to gain a clear understanding of some difficult line of thought in philosophy or theology has probably many times had the experience of having the truth which he sought come to him clearly, first of all, in terms of an illustration, and he has probably imparted his understanding, thus gained, to others by means of this same illustration. There seems little doubt that, while the prophetic consciousness impelled John, and thus "commanded" him, to write the Book of Revelation, he was nevertheless obliged to struggle severely to gain a clear comprehension of the ideas which he was to embody in the Book. The whole of the 5th chapter would seem to substantiate this view, and especially verse 4: *"And I wept much, because no man was found worthy to open and to read the book, neither to look thereon"*,—referring to the content of the revelation, which first appeared to John as a "sealed" book. As St. John mentally struggled to gain a mastery of the lines of thought, which he at first saw but vaguely, though perceiving their great importance, they were gradually revealed to his consciousness in the terms of illustrations,—but not such illustrations as would come to a western student in the twentieth century. To such a student, comparisons originating from his knowledge of natural science, or of incidents or descriptions in modern literature or the classics, would be most apt to suggest themselves. St. John knew little of natural science, but his thought was saturated with an intimate knowledge of the sacred literature of the Jews, mostly embodied in what we now call the Old Testament,—a literature filled with images and symbols of a kind peculiar to the modes of thought of western Asiatics, and the meaning of which was well known to John. Hence, when this illuminated understanding came to him, it naturally took form in modifications of the Old Testament imagery and symbology.

Says Prof. Moulton, in The Modern Readers' Bible:

"The most important thing in connection with the symbolism of St. John is a point of literary effect, which further seems in the poem itself to be indicated as extending beyond poetic form into the underlying spiritual interpretation. This is that the symbolism of Revelation is the symbolism of Old Testament prophecy revived; the symbolic ideas being not merely revived, but at the same time varied, massed together, and intensified. Indeed, very few, if any, of St. John's symbols are drawn from any other source. Considered from the literary side this is the device of 'echoing', which distinguishes all 'classical' poetry,—the special line of poetic succession in which each poet makes new creations out of detailed reminiscences of the poetry of the past. But in the present case this is much more than a literary device. *The testimony of Jesus is the spirit of prophecy*: one of the leading thoughts of St. John's work is that the mysteries of the old dispensation find their solution and fulfilment in the new: similarly, the forms of ancient prophecy combine to make the symbolic setting of the supreme revelation."

These facts enable us to more fully understand the significance of the verb *esêmanen,* "he signified", in verse 1. It literally means that the revelation came to John in terms of "signs",—that is, images and symbols,—instead of in literal language.

Scholars are quite generally agreed that John intends the first two verses of chapter 1 as a title, or as "headlines", for the Book, and Professor Moulton in his Bible, above referred to, prints these two verses, and the third verse, which is closely connected with them in thought, as "headlines", or almost as a "poster", announcing the Book. He gives to the three verses a whole page, in display type, breaking them into lines as follows:

The Revelation
of
JESUS CHRIST
which God gave him to show unto his servants, even the things which must shortly come to pass
And he sent and signified by his Angel
unto his Servant
John
who bare witness of the word of God and of the testimony of Jesus Christ, even of all things that he saw

Blessed is he that readeth, and they that hear the words of the prophecy, and keep the things which are written therein:

FOR THE TIME IS AT HAND

None of the movements and events forecast in the Apocalypse seem as yet to have been wholly fulfilled for the world in general, but most of them are in process of being fulfilled, with the end still in the indefinite future. If the phrase, "things which must shortly come to pass", be a correct translation, and if it refer to the movements and events above mentioned, then St. John has not been found to be a true prophet in one respect, unless the word "shortly" can properly be taken to connote an indefinite number of thousands of years; but the words above quoted are not the only correct translation of the Greek *ha dei genesthai en tachei.** A little consideration

---

*Note.—If questions of text and translation are uninteresting to a reader who is unacquainted with Greek, he may merely read through paragraphs involving such discussions to catch the general drift of the argument, and give close attention only to the conclusions reached. The writer would avoid these technical discussions, were it not for the fact that his sense of the text and its meaning forces him, at times, to take positions that are radical departures from former received standards, and, in such cases, the writer must justify the positions taken to such readers as are scholars in Greek.

will show that the phrase *en tachei* ("shortly") has a close relation in thought to the clause, *ho gar kairos eggus* ("*for the time is at hand*"), at the end of verse 3. It has not proven true that "the time was at hand" to the world in general for the *events and movements* forecast in the Apocalypse. Hence, if we are to regard St. John as a truly inspired prophet,—and there is every reason to believe that he is,—we must look for some other legitimate translation for *genesthai*. This is an infinitive from the verb *gignomai,* which has the general meaning "happen", or "be born" (see Liddell & Scott), but is much more indefinite in its meaning than many verbs, so that the precise shade of its meaning usually has to be determined from the context or connection in which it is used. Things can be born mentally as well as physically; i. e., they can *be revealed.* An examination of the whole line of thought in these three verses, taken in connection with a knowledge of the Book as a whole—and bearing in mind that these verses are a virtual title for the Book,—makes it seemingly clear that the meaning of *genesthai en tachei* is *unfold quickly,* or possibly, *unfold by quickening.* The sense is, that the things shown unto the servants of God are to be *revealed* to them quickly, but it should not be taken that these things are to "come to pass" quickly for those who know Him not or for the world. The fact is, that when any portion of spiritual knowledge, or knowledge about things involving the operation of spiritual forces, is gained at all, it is gained "quickly", by immediate perception. The phrase is probably equivalent in meaning to the sentence beginning on line 23, page 504, of Science and Health, by Mary Baker Eddy: "The rays of infinite Truth, when gathered into the focus of ideas [gathered into consciousness], bring light instantaneously, whereas a thousand years of human doctrines, hypothesis, and vague conjectures emit no such effulgence." The Apocalypse, rightly understood, is filled with suggestions for practical conduct, which, though they are usually in the *form* of suggestions or implications, have the *force* of *commands* to the consciousness of one who recognizes their source and their importance. *"The time is at hand"* (verse 3) for the servants of God *"that read and hear [comprehend] the words of this prophecy"* to *"keep [hold in thought and obey] those things [the virtual commands] which are written therein"*; but there is nothing in the whole situation to suggest that *"the time is at hand"* for the movements and events forecast in the prophecy to happen to the world at large.

Practically a conclusive proof that the foregoing line of reasoning is correct, is to be found in the comparison of the clause,

ha dei genesthai en tachei from verse 1, of chapter 1, and
ha mellei ginesthai meta tauta from verse 19 of the same chapter.

An examination of the context makes it practically certain that the two pronouns, *ha,* refer to the same "things". If so, the two Greek infinitives cannot be regarded as having the same meaning in the two clauses, although from a literal standpoint they might be made to mean the same; for, to render them both "come to pass", as the Revised Version does, makes St. John speak of the same things as coming to pass "quickly" (*en tachei*) and "hereafter" (*meta tauta*). But it is entirely reasonable that certain movements or events should *be revealed* quickly to the prepared consciousness, but actually transpire or *come to pass* "after that" (the literal rendering of *meta tauta*), or more slowly, for the whole world.

It is important to note in this connection that the antecedent revealing to the servants of God of the things which must later come to pass becomes in large measure the proximate cause of those things coming to pass in the personal experience of God's servants and in the world at large, at least the more quickly, since it enables the servants of God to work according to the pattern, thus more directly and intelligently enforcing His law. God's law becomes manifest in the world only in the measure that human beings apprehend and enforce it; hence it is highly important to rapid progress that men should foreknow the order of advancing demonstration and experience as well as the final goal to be attained.

"He sent and signified it by his Angel unto his servant John." The Greek is: "Esêmanen aposteilas dia tou aggelou autou tō doulō autou Joannê." The literal meaning of *esêmanen* is "he showed by signs", which is nearly the derivative sense of the English "he signified" (from the Latin *signum,* a sign, and *facere,* to make). Taking into account our knowledge of the Book as a whole, the sense evidently is "he showed by images and symbols."

There is no proof from a grammatical standpoint as to the subject of the verb *esêmanen;* but the sense seems to require *theos,* rather than *Jêsou Christou* for the subject; and the latter is evidently synonymous with *aggelou.* In other words, Jesus Christ (the prophetic consciousness) is God's angel or messenger through whom He communicates the message to His servant John. This is the more probable, since *"Jesus Christ"* is unquestionably spoken of as an "angel" many times in later portions of the Book.

Taking these various facts into consideration, we may safely adopt the following as a correct translation of verses 1-3:

A revelation from Jesus Christ (the prophetic consciousness), which God gave him, to show unto His servants the things which must unfold (be revealed) quickly (i. e., to His servants, not necessarily to the world). And He (God) signified them (by imagery and symbols), commissioning His Angel (the mediatorial Christ) to impart them to His servant John, who bore witness to the Word of God and to the testimony of Jesus Christ (the mediatorial Christ), even of all things that he saw.

Foldout lout

Page(s):

_____

Has this book Been ok Been

NOTES BY THE READER

SECTION I

MESSAGES TO THE SEVEN CHURCHES

(Chapter 1:4—3:22)

The Impersonal Christ, through John, sends letters of commendation, reproof, warning, exhortation, encouragement and promise to seven churches of Roman Asia, which are wholly symbolical

In this section, which may be referred to as the first act of the drama, the structural relation of which to the Book as a whole will be spoken of later, we have introduced as characters:—

God, under various titles.
Christ, under various titles and descriptions.
The Holy Spirit, as "the seven Spirits which are before His throne," identical with "the seven stars" and "the angels of the seven churches."
Satan.
Balaam, as the false prophet.
False Apostles, False Jews, Followers of Balaam and the Nicalaitanes, as apostles of Satan.
The Seven Candlesticks, as the Spiritual Woman or Spiritual Church.
Jezebel, as the Carnal Woman or False Church.

CHAPTER I

Introduction

Verse 4 *John to the seven churches which are in Asia: Grace be unto you, and peace, from him which is, and which was, and which is to come; and from the seven spirits which are before his throne;*

5 *And from Jesus Christ, who is the faithful witness, and the first begotten of the dead, and the prince of the kings of the earth. Unto him that loved us, and washed us from our sins in his own blood,*

6 *And hath made us kings and priests unto God and his Father; to him be glory and dominion for ever and ever. Amen.*

As will be made evident later on *"the seven churches of Asia"* symbolize the seven chief faculties of the human mind assembled for instruction by *"the seven angels,"* or the seven chief manifestations of the Christ-mind, which are spoken of in verse 4 as *"the seven Spirits which are before the throne,"* and in verse 16 as *"seven stars."* To be sure, churches in seven cities in Roman Asia are specified, but historians say that in some of these cities there was no Christian church up to the latest time at which St. John could have written the Apocalypse, and that in one of these cities there never has been, to this day, a Christian church,—a fact which goes far to prove the symbolical character of these seven churches.

"The first begotten of the dead". The mediatorial consciousness, *"Jesus Christ"*, the offices of which are discussed at some length in the Prologue, alone has triumphed over death, and no other order of consciousness ever will thus triumph. When we fully attain the "mind in Christ Jesus", which Paul exhorted us to have, we shall also gain the victory over death.

"Washed us from our sins, in his own blood,"—that is, through the agency of his own life and love, of which "blood" is the symbol.

"And hath made us Kings and Priests unto God and his Father." Literally, And hath made us a kingdom,—priests unto God and his Father.

It is interesting to note the *seven* phrases in verses 5, 6, descriptive of the character and offices of the Christ, symbolizing the *completeness* of his manifestation of God.

Verses 7, 8 *"Behold, he cometh with clouds; and every eye shall see him, and they also which pierced him: and all kindreds of the earth shall wail because of him. Even so, Amen. I am Alpha and Omega, the beginning and the ending, saith the Lord, which is, and which was, and which is to come, the Almighty."*

"With clouds". This phrase seems to be used here as a symbol of Christ's future exaltation and glory, since it is immediately stated that *"every eye shall see him"*. "Clouds" are often a symbol of partial obscuration, indicating that spiritual things are more or less hidden from human sense.

The Coming of the Message

Verses 9, 10 *"I, John, who also am your brother, and companion in tribulation, and in the kingdom and patience of Jesus Christ, was in the isle that is called Patmos, for the word of God, and for the testimony of Jesus Christ. I was in the Spirit on the Lord's day, and heard behind me a great voice, as of a trumpet."*

"In the isle that is called Patmos." In its symbolic sense "Patmos" would denote withdrawal from material consciousness, or into a sense barren of thoughts and feelings of a fleshly order, *i. e.*, withdrawal into spiritual consciousness, or the Holy Spirit. It seems to be used in the same sense as the word "wilderness" in chapter 12. The Authorized Version translates the Greek *thlipsis* in this text "tribulation", but its primary meaning is *pressure*. In the phrase "for the word of God", the Authorized Version gives the word "for" as a translation for the Greek *dia,* the meaning of which is indefinite, and has to be determined by the context. It is here used in the sense of "because of". So far as the author knows, all students and expositors of the Book have supposed that John was driven by persecution into Patmos, an island in the Mediterranean, or was exiled there by the government, on account of his stand for Christianity. The author is convinced, however, that the meaning of the verse is that the impulsion of the Christ-mind upon the consciousness of John drove him into the realm of Spirit. The verse would thus be better translated:

"I, John, who also am your brother and companion in the stress and ruling and patient persistence of the Christ-mind [the spirit of prophecy], was in the island called Patmos [that is, was in the Spirit], because of the word of God and the testimony of Jesus" [because of the impulsion of "the spirit of prophecy"].

Verse 10 *"On the Lord's day"*. This does not refer to either the first or the seventh day of the week, but to the spiritual consciousness; so that the phrase evidently means, *I was in the Spirit* (with no reference to any particular time). *"A great voice, as of a trumpet"*, doubtless symbolizes the Holy Spirit, or the prophetic consciousness.

Verse 11 *"Saying, I am Alpha and Omega, the first and the last: and, What thou seest, write in a book, and send it unto the seven churches which are in Asia; unto Ephesus, and unto Smyrna, and unto Pergamos, and unto Thyatira, and unto Sardis, and unto Philadelphia, and unto Laodicea."*

"I am the Alpha and Omega, the first and the last." The sentence which these words translate does not occur in authoritative Greek texts, and need not, therefore, be interpreted. However, in verse 17, the Christ is represented as declaring: *"I am the first and the last."* This evidently means, not that the Christ is "the beginning and the end", but the all-inclusive. The third verse of chapter 1 of John's Gospel might well be translated, All things came into being (or expression) *in* him (the Word, the Christ); and *apart from him* (that is, outside of him) nothing came into being (or expression). In Romans 11:36, we read: "For of him, and through him, and to him, are all things." These, and numerous other passages of Scripture, rightly translated and understood, teach that the Christ, the divine Word, is synonymous with the complete order of the divine manifestation. For instance, 1 Cor. 8:6, translated in keeping with this thought, would read: "But to us there is one God, the Father, of whom are all things, and we in Him, and one Lord Jesus Christ, *in* (not "by") whom are all things, and we in him". The Greek preposition *dia* cannot be translated "by" without forcing it out of its natural meaning, as the Authorized Version has undoubtedly done in this text, and in the one previously quoted from the Gospel of John, and also in Eph. 3:9, which would better read, Who created all things *in* (Jesus) Christ. Col. 1:16 should read: For *in* (not "by") him were created all things. The Greek in this verse is "en autǫ", and the Revised Version translates the phrase *"in him"*.

Verses 12, 13 *And I turned to see the voice that spake with me. And being turned, I saw seven golden candlesticks; and in the midst of the seven candlesticks one like unto the Son of man, clothed with a garment down to the foot and girt about the paps with a golden girdle.*

"Seven golden candlesticks." Verse 20 informs us that these are *"the seven churches"*, and the first clause of verse 13 gives us to understand that the Christ-mind *pervades* (is *"in the midst of"*) those churches. It has already been suggested that *"the seven churches"* are the human consciousness, considered in the seven chief phases of its activity. Conclusive proof of this fact will appear in the discussion of chapters 2 and 3. The nature of the churches and their relation to their "angels" may be represented succinctly as follows:

The Churches and Their Angels

The *Church in Ephesus* is human consciousness in the attitude of *Attention*,* and its *Angel* is the Christ-mind acting as *Spiritual Aspiration, "Soul."*

The *Church in Smyrna* is human consciousness acting as *Reason*, and its *Angel* is the Christ-mind acting as *Spiritual Reason, "Principle."*

The *Church in Pergamos* is human consciousness acting as *Will*, and its *Angel* is the Christ-mind as the *Executive Mind, "Life."*

The *Church in Thyatira* is human consciousness acting as *Intuition*, and its *Angel* is the Christ-mind as *Spiritual Intuition, Direct Cognition, "Mind."*

The *Church in Sardis* is human consciousness acting as *Love*, and its *Angel* is the Christ-mind acting as *divine Love, "Love."*

The *Church in Philadelphia* is human consciousness acting as *Sense of Reality*, and its *Angel* is the Christ-mind acting as *Perception of Reality, "Truth."*

The *Church of the Laodiceans* is human consciousness as *Sense of Substance*, and its *Angel* is the Christ-mind acting as *Perception of Substance, "Spirit."*

(With acknowledgment to Mr. James M. Pryse for suggestions in connection with the presentation above given, and to Mrs. Mary Baker Eddy for the terms in quotation marks.)

---

*The use of capitals for the names of the mental equivalents of "the churches of Asia" is not intended to indicate that these mental equivalents are synonyms for deity, but indicates their relative importance.

From the absolute standpoint *"Perception of Reality"* and *"Perception of Substance"* are the same; but in human experience they are not coincident. For instance, the majority of mankind will admit that God is real, but it is hard to persuade most men that God (Spirit) is substance. So in analytical classification, that activity of the Christ mind which leads the human consciousness into the perception of substance should be distinguished from that activity which leads it into the perception of reality. But *in the absolute* all these seven activities of the Christ mind are one Mind.

The Christ being *"clothed with a garment down to his foot, and girt about the paps with a golden girdle"*, probably indicated him in a priestly office. One expositor has said that his wearing the girdle at the breasts, instead of at the waist, shows him as a priest engaged in active service rather than as merely ready for service.

Verse 14 *"His head and his hairs were white like wool, as white as snow; and his eyes were as a flame of fire."*

"His head and his hairs, white like wool, as white as snow" may indicate majesty and holiness, probably, also, eternity. *"His eyes as a flame of fire"* denote the power of the Christ, of Truth, to penetrate and search all hearts, and to uncover and destroy evil.

Verse 15 *"And his feet like unto fine brass, as if they burned in a furnace; and his voice as the sound of many waters."*

"His feet like unto fine brass, as if they burned in a furnace." A literal rendering of the original Greek would read as follows: His feet like to *chalko-libanon*, as *it* were melted in a furnace. Liddell and Scott's Greek Lexicon says that, although *chalkos* means specifically *copper*, it has the general meaning of *metal*. *Libanos* is the Greek name for "the frankincense-tree", a gum tree. The word is certainly allied in derivation with the verb *libazô*, which means "to run out in drops", as that is the way that gum usually exudes from a tree. These facts indicate that this Greek phrase should be trans-

lated: *His feet were like to metal which runs in drops, as though it had been melted in a furnace;* and the metal referred to is evidently quick-silver, or mercury, which, among the Greeks, was held sacred to Hermes, the messenger of the gods, celebrated for his supposed swiftness in flight. This fact was, of course, perfectly familiar to John, and to practically all educated men of his time, since, as already indicated, the Greek language and literature were the source and avenue of practically all the culture of the known world of that time. Evidently, therefore, the reference here should be taken to indicate the swiftness or the omnipresence of the Christ, which thought is not adequately presented in the authorized translation, "like unto fine brass, as if they burned in a furnace".

"His voice as the sound of many waters" may indicate that he expresses the consciousness of the multitudes of the redeemed. In chapter 17:15, St. John defines "waters" as "peoples, and multitudes, and nations, and tongues". This interpretation would indicate the Christ as being the head of the true church and as being synonymous with the Holy Spirit.

Verse 16 *"And he had in his right hand seven stars: and out of his mouth went a sharp two-edged sword: and his countenance was as the sun shineth in his strength."*

His having *"in his right hand seven stars"* indicates his expression of the seven chief manifestations of divine Mind. The *"sharp two-edged sword"* going *"out of his mouth"* suggests the militant character of the truth in human consciousness, and its power to distinguish and separate between good and evil. It may also suggest the affirmation of truth and the denial of error, as the means of overcoming the latter. The former purifies the mind; the latter destroys evil thoughts and manifestations.*

---

*"This sharp sword, with two edges, which the saints 'joyful in glory' use, is the denial of the evil, or unreal, and the affirmation of the good, by means of which the human 'consciousness' is purified."—"Life Understood," page 140.

"His countenance as the sun shineth in his strength" doubtless indicates the lordship, the over-ruling character and rank of the Christ.

The fact that, in verses 13-16, *nine* phrases are employed in describing the Christ may be intended to indicate him as *intuitively* wise, the Greek equivalent of which, *epistêmôn*, (the sum of the numerical values of its letters being taken), represents the number 999. The *seven* phrases used in describing the Christ in verses 5 and 6, might serve to indicate him as the *crucified one,* the sum of the numerical values of the letters of the Greek word *stauros,* meaning the cross, being 777. It is the more probable that something of this kind is implied, because St. John, in chapter 13:18, gives the symbolical numerical value 666 to "the beast", whose number, he says, "is the number of a man", evidently meaning material sense. The numerical value of the letters of the Greek *hê phrên* (the lower mind or the mind of fallen or mortal man), is 666.*

Words of Encouragement and Command

Verse 17 *"And when I saw him, I fell at his feet as dead. And he laid his right hand upon me, saying unto me, Fear not; I am the first and the last."*

"And when I saw him, I fell at his feet as dead". The effect of beholding the unveiled glory and power of the Christ upon one who still had anything of the mortal about him would be almost to destroy his mortal sense of life, much as darkness is destroyed when exposed to the light. *"No man can look upon the face of God, and live".* It was as when the children of Israel could not look upon the unveiled face of Moses, after he had been in the Mount with God, for the glory of his coun-

---

* Note 1.—The author is indebted to Mr. Pryse for suggestions as to these numerical values.

Note 2.—"VICARIVS FILII DEI," written over the Pope's chair, foots up the number 666, if the sum of the Roman values of the letters is taken. The letters A, R, S, E and F have, of course, no numerical values.

tenance, or as when Paul saw the Christ on his journey to Damascus, and "fell to the earth" (Acts 9:4), and was temporarily stricken blind.

The phrase, *"I am the first and the last"* is interpreted under verse 8, *quod vide*.

Verse 18 *"I am he that liveth, and was dead; and, behold, I am alive for evermore, Amen; and have the keys of hell and of death."*
"I am he that liveth, and was dead; and am alive forevermore."

At the start, the human consciousness is "dead to the truth," or the truth is "dead" to it; but as the human consciousness becomes instructed in the truth in a thorough-going way, the truth "liveth" in that consciousness to which it formerly "was dead," and is "alive for evermore" therein. Jesus taught that "eternal life" *is* the knowledge of God (Truth) and of His Christ (reflected truth). *Vide* John 17:3.

His having *"the keys of hell and death"* probably denotes his power to raise the dead, and save them; in other words, denotes that he has the solution of the problems of hell and death.

Verses 19, 20 *"Write the things which thou hast seen, and the things which are, and the things which shall be hereafter; the mystery of the seven stars which thou sawest in my right hand, and the seven golden candlesticks. The seven stars are the angels of the seven churches: and the seven candlesticks which thou sawest are the seven churches."*

These verses are more closely connected in thought with the next chapter than they are with the verses preceding; and it would have been fortunate if chapter 2 had been made to begin with verse 19 of chapter 1.

There are no chapter or verse divisions in the original manuscripts. The divisions in the Authorized Version and other texts and translations depend upon personal judgment.

CHAPTER II

Messages to the Churches

I. To the Church in Ephesus (2:1-8)

Verse 1 *"Unto the angel of the church of Ephesus write; These things saith he that holdeth the seven stars in his right hand, who walketh in the midst of the seven golden candlesticks."*

The message is introduced by the words: *"Unto the angel of the church of Ephesus write."* All of the translators and expositors with whom the author is acquainted endorse this general form of statement, and all seem to agree that the meaning is, that John is directed to write to the angel of the church of Ephesus; but there is no way in which this meaning can be made to harmonize with the rest of the letter. If the term "angel" be interpreted to mean the *pastor* of the church, then it is the pastor who is commended, rebuked, exhorted, etc. Moreover, it is doubtful whether the churches in St. John's day had pastors in the modern sense. If the term "angel" be taken to mean a manifestation of the Christ-mind, which the author understands to be the true interpretation, then it seems foolishness for the Christ to direct John to write to one of the phases of his (Christ's) own Mind.

The Greek from which this sentence is translated is as follows:

"Tǫ aggelǫ tǫ en Ephesǫ ekklesias grapson."

The first three words are in the dative case, and there is no reason why this construction should not be what the grammarians call "the dative of interest or advantage", and this is what the whole context (the final determining point in translation, among different renderings which are grammatically correct) requires. In this case, the rendering should be:

For (in behalf of, as the amanuensis of) the Angel, write.

The article "tǫ̂" is repeated after the noun,—a very common Greek usage, to indicate emphasis by suggesting, though not actually making, repetition of the noun.

It is also important to note that there is no article before *ekklesias,* as there would be if a specific church, instead of a symbolical one, were referred to.

Taking these facts into consideration, the Christ is represented as saying to John:

For the Angel, the one of a church in Ephesus, write.

The messages to all the other churches should doubtless commence in similar fashion, since some of the ancient Greek manuscripts retain the same form of expression for the introductory sentence in the case of the letters to all of the seven churches.

Other manuscripts, which are followed by the Westcott and Hort, Souter, and Oxford-Cambridge texts, change the third word of the sentence from "tǫ̂" to *tês,* or omit it altogether, in the case of the introductory sentences of the letters to some of the churches. For instance, these texts give:

"Kai tǫ̂ aggelǫ̂ tês en Philadelphiạ ekklesias grapson,"— rendered:

And for the Angel of the church in Philadelphia, write.

But there is no certainty that the manuscripts which give this reading, or the texts based upon them, are correct on this point. The apparent necessities of the context would indicate that they are not, and where the indications of the context are strong, the context should be the determining factor, not only on a question of translation, but in deciding a disputed question as to the text itself.

The Christ, who holdeth within his power all the seven manifestations of divine Mind, and who is active in all phases or states of right consciousness,—this Christ, in the attitude of Spiritual Aspiration, which is the only true and right attitude, addresses the human consciousness in the attitude or activity of *attention,* and says to it:

COMMENDATION

Verse 2 *"I know thy works, and thy labor, and thy patience, and how thou canst not bear them which are evil: and thou hast tried them which say they are apostles, and are not, and hast found them liars."*

"I know thy works, and thy labor and thy patience"; that is, I know that, as attention, you are always busy,—always working, even harder than necessary if you worked rightly, and always persisting. *"And how thou canst not bear them which are evil"*; that is, I know that, on general principles, thou canst not bear wicked men. It is true that the human consciousness always hates wickedness, and wicked people, in the abstract. For instance, no theatre audience will applaud the hero more warmly or hiss the villain more vigorously than one that is made up of criminals, if they be allowed to give free rein to the expression of their feelings. Well-nigh every person will tolerate meanness in himself, but is very much disinclined to tolerate it in anyone else. *"And thou hast tried them which say they are apostles, and are not, and hast found them liars."* In the long run, the human consciousness detects frauds, and unmasks those who claim to be worthy spiritual teachers and guides, but are not.

It is quite possible that *"them which are evil"* and the false *"apostles"* here spoken of refer to activities of the false or "carnal" mind, which is "enmity against God", and which even the human consciousness finds it difficult to *"bear"* with, and which, sooner or later, it detects as being false witnesses.

Verse 3 *"And hast borne, and hast patience, and for my name's sake hast labored, and hast not fainted."*

The human consciousness has always toiled, with ceaseless patience, and often in the face of much persecution, for the truth,—both to discover truth, and to serve that which it believed to be the truth.

REBUKE

Verse 4 *"Nevertheless I have somewhat against thee, because thou hast left thy first love."*

The human consciousness has always given some attention to Truth and Spirit; but it ought to give *all* its attention to God, Spirit. Because it does not, it has left its first love, its primary duty.

EXHORTATION AND WARNING

Verse 5 *"Remember therefore from whence thou art fallen, and repent, and do the first works; or else I will come unto thee quickly, and will remove thy candlestick out of his place, except thou repent."*

The human mentality is exhorted to take heed that it is apostate from its high duty, and to turn about and render its primary and only legitimate service. Then the human consciousness is warned that, unless it does give its attention to spiritual things, it will soon cease to be a light bearer. Christ is represented as saying that he will take its light away from it, but this form of statement is a concession to the human viewpoint. The light of life is never "taken" away from any man, or away from humanity as a whole; but men, by failing to give their attention to the true light, gradually lose sight of it, until finally they exclude themselves from it almost wholly.

ADDITIONAL COMMENDATION

Verse 6 *"But this thou hast, that thou hatest the deeds of the Nicolaitanes, which I also hate."*

The Nicolaitanes were a sect, widely spread over Asia Minor in St. John's day, which practiced sexual immorality in many vile forms under the name of religion. There has always been a tendency among men to deify and worship the bodily senses and activities; yet, on the whole, the human consciousness has always condemned and turned against such pseudo-religion and unclean practice.

FINAL EXHORTATION AND PROMISE

Verse 7 *"He that hath an ear, let him hear what the spirit saith unto the churches; To him that overcometh will I give to eat of the tree of life, which is in the midst of the paradise of God."*

"He that hath an ear, let him hear what the Spirit saith unto the churches;" that is, let him who has sufficient discernment to understand the hidden meaning of this message, heed it.

"To him that overcometh will I give to eat of the tree of life, which is in the midst of the paradise of God." The one who heeds this message, and overcomes the difficulty of giving his attention to spiritual things only, or very largely so, is The Conqueror, who is named in Greek, *Ho nikôn.* If the sum of the numerical value of these Greek letters is taken, the result is 1000, which is therefore, the symbol of conquest, or completion of labor. It is more than likely that, for this reason, the period of "a thousand years" is specified in chapter 20 as the period of the reign of complete harmony on the earth,—the so-called millennium. Only those who have proven to be conquerors can have part in the millennium. Over such, "the second death", the final destruction of evil, has no power, St. John tells us; for there is nothing evil in them to be hurt or destroyed. He who conquers his attention, who brings it into the undivided service of God, is promised immortality, *"the tree of life, which is in the midst of the paradise of God."*

II. To the Church in Smyrna (2:8-11)

For the angel, the one of a church in Smyrna, write:

"These things saith the first and the last, which was dead, and is alive."

In the 8th chapter of John's Gospel, the Christ is represented as speaking through Jesus of Nazareth, saying, *"Before Abraham was, I am"*. He also said, *"Lo, I am with you alway, even to the end of the world"* (that is, to the end of material sense). The Christ *is,* before material sense appears, and *is,* after it disappears,—the eternal idea of the Father. He became incarnate in Jesus who was crucified, but the Christ was and is forever alive.

The church in Smyrna seems to symbolize *human reason;* and its angel is *Spiritual Reason,* reason which always takes Spirit at its premise. "Reason" is not to be here understood in the loose sense in which the word is sometimes employed, as being synonymous with the content of consciousness, but in the strict sense of being that mental faculty which draws conclusions from major and minor premises, stated or implied, Though human reason often takes material premises,—and, speaking analytically and strictly, it is not in the province of reason to choose its premises, but merely to act upon those premises presented to it by other mental faculties,—it is usually correct in the conclusions which it draws, granted that the premises are correct. So, in a sense, reason is as nearly infallible as any human faculty, and in its strict province of drawing conclusions from premises, it has been very little corrupted. Accordingly, the church at Smyrna receives very little in the way of rebuke or warning from its Angel.

COMMENDATION

Verse 9 *"I know thy works, and tribulation, and poverty, (but thou art rich) and I know the blasphemy of them which say they are Jews, and are not, but are the synagogue of satan"*

The reason is always at work; it is put to many severe trials; and, in so far as it is asked to work upon a material basis, it is poor indeed; but it has the privilege of working upon a spiritual basis, and so is potentially rich.

"Jews" are supposed to be "chosen people", those initiated into "the secret place of the Most High". Those who *"say they are Jews, and are not"*, are those who pretend to be spiritual initiates and true teachers, but are not, and so belong to the congregation of satan.

EXHORTATION

Verse 10 *"Fear none of those things which thou shalt suffer: behold, the devil shall cast some of you into prison, that ye may be tried; and ye shall have tribulation ten days: be thou faithful unto death, and I will give thee a crown of life."*

It has been already explained, in the Note on Chronology in the Introduction, that *"ten days"* refers to the period which it takes the sun to pass through the constellation "Draco", one of the minor signs of the zodiac. "Draco" means *dragon,* one of the apocalyptic symbols of "the devil and satan". Hence, *"ten days"* means *dragon-time,*—the period of the apparent ascendency of satan in the world of humanity. During this period, human reason will be partly in bondage to the claim that it must work from material premises, and so will be *"in prison";* nevertheless, in its technical sense, it is of God, cannot be destroyed, and need not fear anything. It will be faithful to its work, even to the death of the body, and beyond, and will have the "crown of life",—that is, right service and continued being.

PROMISE

Verse 11 *"He that hath an ear, let him hear what the Spirit saith unto the churches; He that overcometh shall not be hurt of the second death."*

"He that overcometh shall not be hurt of the second death." The man who has learned to reason from spiritual premises, and from such premises only, has become so purified from error that the final destruction of error, "the second death" (Rev. 20:14), will not find anything in him to wrench away, and so he cannot be "hurt of the second death."

III. To the Church in Pergamos (2:12-17)

For the Angel, the one of a church in Pergamos, write:
"These things saith he which hath the sharp sword with two edges."

Rightly understood, *Will* is the active manifestation of Mind, and it is also the executive faculty of the right reasoning of the human mind. Because of its executive character, this Angel, this manifestation of the Christ-mind, is represented as carrying the two-edged sword, symbolical of the militant power and of the victory of Truth. The sword is the offensive or fighting weapon, as distinguished from defensive armor.

COMMENDATION

Verse 13 *"I know thy works, and where thou dwellest, even where Satan's seat is: and thou holdest fast my name, and hast not denied my faith, even in those days wherein Antipas was my faithful martyr, who was slain among you, where Satan dwelleth."*

The human will is ever at work. When, as is often the case, it is set up in opposition to divine Will, it is in a special sense the activity of satan, satan's chief agent. Hence, the human will is spoken of as dwelling "where satan's seat is". As we shall see later, the rule and authority set up by human will, when not in accord with God's will, is connoted or included in the symbols of the "black horse and his rider" (6:5, 6) and of "a beast, rising up out of the sea, having seven heads and ten horns, and upon his horns ten crowns, and upon his heads the name of blasphemy. . . . And the dragon [satan] gave him his power, and *his seat,* and great authority."

The human consciousness tenaciously holds fast to the name of Truth, and does not deny, but always affirms, its belief in Truth, and that it is a follower of Truth,—which, to a large extent, it is; but, even at its best, it has usually been in the condition of "certain disciples" in Ephesus, to whom Paul said, "Have ye received the Holy Spirit since ye believed? And they said unto him, We have not so much as heard whether there be any Holy Spirit." Among these professed followers of Christ, Truth, the Holy Spirit was dead, so far as they were concerned; or, to be more exact, they were dead to the Spirit. Likewise, the human consciousness, though holding fast the name of Truth, and not denying faith therein, is usually dead to the spirit of Truth. Now, the spirit of Truth is the only wholly *faithful witness* of Truth. (*Faithful witness* is a more correct translation than "faithful martyr", the Greek word *marturos* meaning *witness* more often than *martyr*.) As usual, St. John did not choose to make his real meaning evident, unless the reader has the spiritual viewpoint from which he would know what St. John might be expected to mean under given circumstances. Accordingly, he does not speak of "the faithful witness" as the Holy Spirit, since this would make his meaning more evident, and might furnish a clew to the interpretation of the rest of the symbolism of these letters to the churches, which he intentionally disguised for reasons already named. So he here speaks of the faithful witness as "Antipas", with the evident intent of leading the uninitiated reader into a supposition that the witness to which he refers was some human being in the church at Pergamos, who had suffered martyrdom. But historians have no record of any such person; and, having discovered that "the churches in Asia" are themselves symbols of forms of mental activity, and that their Angels are symbols of forms of Mind-activity, we may naturally expect that the term "Antipas" refers, not to a person, but to another form of Mind-activity. Then the question arises, Why this particular word,—a word which occurs nowhere else in the Greek language so far as is known. To the author, it seems most likely that it is compounded from the Greek words *anti* and *pas,* which compound may be rendered *in place of all,* signifying that the "spirit of Truth" may stand as a "faithful witness" in place of all other manifestations of consciousness. The Holy Spirit is "slain" in human consciousness, whenever and wherever unregenerate human will is set up as a ruler and chief executive. So Antipas is spoken of as being "slain . . . where satan dwelleth".

REBUKE

Verses 14, 15 *"But I have a few things against thee, because thou hast there them that hold the doctrine of Balaam, who taught Balac to cast a stumbling block before the children of Israel, to eat things sacrificed unto idols, and to commit fornication. So hast thou also them that hold the doctrine of the Nicolaitanes, which thing I hate."*

These verses are sufficiently self-interpretative, except to call attention to the fact that the human will, and men under its influence, are often found serving the lowest and most unworthy ends, instead of serving God. Also, the human consciousness often partakes of false doctrines as mental food, and thus feeds itself upon mental influences which have been offered in service to false gods (false standards of good). Thus does the human mentality, in symbolic language, *"eat things sacrificed unto idols"*, and thus, also, it manifests loyalty to that which is not God, and so it *"commits fornication."* Hence the need of this rebuke.

EXHORTATION AND WARNING

Verse 16 *"Repent; or else I will come unto thee quickly, and will fight against them with the sword of my mouth."*

The human consciousness is here warned, that unless it turns from its evil practices, the Christ will quickly appear in a militant attitude, fighting against these evils with the utterance of truth; and the human consciousness will suffer, if it is still clinging to evil.

PROMISE

Verse 17 *"He that hath an ear, let him hear what the Spirit saith unto the churches; to him that overcometh will I give to eat of the hidden manna, and will give him a white stone, and in the stone a new name written, which no man knoweth saving he that receiveth it."*

He that "overcometh" is he that resists all temptation to exercise his will in opposition to the divine Will. He who succeeds in doing so will be given the privilege of mentally feeding upon spiritual truth, which is *"the hidden manna"*, and to know which is eternal life. "This is life eternal, that they might know thee, the only true God, and . . . Christ, whom thou hast sent." "Man shall not live by bread alone, but by every word that proceedeth out of the mouth of God." "He that eateth of this bread [spiritual truth, the hidden manna] shall live forever."

To the conqueror is also promised *"a white stone."* In St. John's time, voting was done by means of white and black pebbles, as it is still in many secret societies. To be given the right to use the voting pebble, was to invest with citizenship. The white pebble was the sign of an affirmative vote. Accordingly, the conqueror is here promised citizenship in the kingdom of God.

When Jacob wrestled with the angel and prevailed, attaining the spiritual vision which he sought, he was given the *new name* "Israel". When Simon discerned that Jesus represented the Christ, the Son of the living God, he was given the *new name* "Peter". Likewise, it appears, that to each of us, when we are "born again", and enter Christ's realm, will be given a *new name;* for we have become "new creatures in Christ, old things have passed away."

The voting pebble is the symbol of our *character* as citizens of the kingdom of God, and our "new name" is to be written in the voting pebble, the "white stone"; that is, in our spiritual character. The true significance of the term "name" in such a connection is *nature* or *character.* For instance, when we are exhorted to "believe on the *name* of Christ", the meaning is that we are to have faith in the *nature* or *character* of Christ. When Christ directs us to rejoice because our *names* are written in heaven, the meaning is, that we are to rejoice because we have acquired the spiritual *nature* or *character.* So, the conqueror is given "a new name" automatically, by the fact that he has attained a new character, and by that same fact he automatically attains citizenship in the kingdom of God, symbolized by "the white stone."

Other interesting facts concerning the "white stone" are these: In various regions of the East, it was a custom for two people, entering into a covenant or other close relation with each other, to take a white pebble and engrave a word or name on it, and then break it in two so that a part of the word should be on each portion. Then one of the pieces of the stone was given to each party. Neither part of the stone, by itself, would show the whole word, and no two pieces of stone would match, or fit together perfectly, except the two parts of the one stone. Christ is represented as entering into this intimate kind of a covenant with his true followers. The Commentator Wordsworth has this to say:

"In ancient courts of justice, the acquittal of the criminal was declared by a majority of white stones, cast into the judicial urn. Christ, the Redeemer of the World, and judge of quick and dead, will pronounce the acquittal of him that overcometh. The white stone is not only a stone of acquittal, but is a *tessera* of citizenship, and a passport of admission to the spiritual banquet of the life eternal in the heavenly Jerusalem. The name which Christ will give is a *new* name, promised by ancient prophecy (Isaiah 62:2), but revealed under the gospel by him who 'maketh all things new', and admits to the *new* Jerusalem, and enables to sing the *new* song, and it is a name which Christ says that no one knows except the receiver, perhaps with an allusion to the practice above noticed, by which it was provided that no one could use the *'tessera hospitalitatis'* (an invitation to a social function), except the party to whom it belonged, and because no one can enter Christ's presence by means of the merits of others; everyone must give an account of himself to God, and be rewarded according to his own works."

NOTES BY THE READER

IV. To the Church in Thyatira (2:18-29)

For the Angel, the one of a church in Thyatira, write:

"These things saith the Son of God, who hath his eyes like unto a flame of fire, and his feet are like fine brass" (*"liquid metal,"* instead of *"fine brass,"* is correct).

The Angel of this church is the Christ-mind in its activity as *Spiritual Intuition, Direct Cognition, Knowledge without Reasoning Process, "Mind"*. Its clear, powerful discernment is symbolized by *"eyes like unto a flame of fire"*, and its swiftness in perceiving truth is symbolized by *"feet like liquid metal"* (mercury). The translation "fine brass" is incorrect, and the mercury is symbolical of swiftness, as explained in the comment on verse 15, of chapter 1.

The church in Thyatira seems to symbolize the human consciousness in its activity as intuition. The human mind gets direct evidence of many so-called physical facts and phenomena, without reasoning process, and without effort, and is prone to trust the validity of the evidence thus gained; but, as manifest in the vast majority of persons, the human mind has little direct cognition of metaphysical realities, and is disposed not to trust the validity of the impressions which it does receive from the spiritual realm. However, there are some human mentalities which are strongly aware of receiving impressions which do not come either through the avenue of physical sense or of reasoning processes, and these mentalities are often strongly disposed to trust and to act upon the impressions thus received. In ordinary speech, such people are said to be "intuitive". The impressions which they get may be either with regard to physical facts, or with regard to the mental states or motives of others, or with regard to what should be done in a given situation, or with regard to absolute spiritual realities.

Of course, the only true intuition is the perception of absolute metaphysical reality. On the human plane, what is called intuition is valuable and commendable in proportion as it grades up toward this absolute ideal,—in other words, in proportion as its activity is inspired and controlled through conscious relation to and reliance upon the divine Mind. When the human faculty of intuition becomes a channel for impressions received through the subconscious and lower psychic mental realms, it is distinctly apostate from its "high calling of God in Christ Jesus."*

---

*On the subject of direct perception of the states of mind of other persons, and of intuitive knowledge of events, past, present, or future, in ways that seem abnormal or out of the usual order to ordinary human consciousness, Mrs. Mary Baker Eddy says, in "Science and Health" (page 83, commencing at line 25): "There is mortal mind-reading and immortal Mind-reading. The latter is a revelation of divine purpose through spiritual understanding, by which man gains the divine Principle and explanation of all things. Mortal mind-reading and immortal Mind-reading are distinctly opposite standpoints, from which cause and effect are interpreted. The act of reading mortal mind investigates and touches only human beliefs . . . The ancient prophets· gained their foresight from a spiritual, incorporeal standpoint, not by foreshadowing evil and mistaking fact for fiction,—predicting the future from a groundwork of corporeality and human belief. When sufficiently advanced in Science to be in harmony with the truth of being, men become seers and prophets involuntarily, controlled not by demons, spirits, or demigods, but by the one Spirit. It is the prerogative of the ever-present, divine Mind, and of thought which is in rapport with this Mind, to know the past, the present, and the future."

On page 128 of "Life Understood," Mr. Rawson presents as a test to distinguish between right and wrong intuitive action (sometimes called "psychic" when referring to direct but unusual knowledge of what is transpiring on the human plane) the following: "Whenever a person obtains abnormal results, he is bringing them about in the wrong way, if he at the same time loses any of his ordinary powers even for a moment or two"; that is, if, in order to exercise abnormal perception, he goes into what is called a "trance." When Jesus read the thoughts of others, he was in full possession of his ordinary faculties, and that will be the case with us, whenever we are exercising "immortal Mind-reading."

The use of intuition should in no sense be discouraged; yet, thus far in human development, the exercise of this faculty is so liable to be clouded (as is the exercise of all other human faculties which are at the root expressions of divine Mind), and the presentations which it receives are so liable to come from lower rather than higher sources, that it is not wise to trust too absolutely what is intuitively received or felt, until the presentations have been tested in other ways. Whether a given impression is from Truth or from error can only be determined, thus far in human experience, by subjecting the mental presentation to careful intellectual examination and comparison, and more especially by the repeated test of practical experience. If a given mental presentation, when translated into the realm of action, proves, in the long account, to result in good, that fact may be taken to validate the perception. On the other hand, if the perception, in the long run, proves practically worthless or harmful in the field of experience, it is thus shown to have been a presentation through the counterfeit of true intuitive action, no matter how sure the person who received the impression may have been that it was of divine origin. For our present discussion, intuition may therefore be defined as that activity of the human consciousness whereby it is convinced that certain things are true, even if it cannot give a clear intellectual account of the reason therefor.

It may be said to *feel* that things are thus and so, even if it cannot, for the time being, prove it by an intellectual process. Humanity as a whole has held to the main facts of the Christ-teaching, and has acted to a considerable degree upon the assumption that they are facts, even when the conditions of human thought were such that it was impossible to prove, by intellectual processes, the validity of these facts. But the human consciousness has also accepted as true and worthy many things which are not true, and has done this in a pseudo-intuitive manner, without adequate intellectual investigation. Accordingly, in the exercise of its faculty of taking direct impressions, human consciousness deserves both commendation and rebuke.

COMMENDATION

Verse 19 *"I know thy works, and charity, and service, and faith. and thy patience, and thy works; and the last to be more than the first."*

To perceive that this statement is a true one with regard to the human consciousness, one has only to consider how, by intuition, it has held to religious truth during the last three hundred years, at a time when human learning, vaunting itself as natural science, was saying that Spirit and strictly spiritual things are "unknowable", if not impossible.

During this period when so many of the learned men of the world were promulgating materialistic doctrines, it is well known that women, as a class, were much more loyal to religion, and to the church as its institution, than were men as a class. The reason for this is to be found in the fact that women, as a class, are much more guided in their thought and activity by the intuitive faculty than are men, who are likely to be more controlled by the results of reasoning than they are by what is to be learned through direct cognition. Indeed, many men are inclined to doubt whether there is any such method of gaining knowledge that is at all trustworthy. But, more and more, intuition is coming to be recognized, even among men, as being the most important avenue of truth for the human consciousness. The author recently heard a prominent man say in a public address, that, when he was a young man, he used to scoff at a woman's "Because"; but that, in later years, he had learned to attach more importance to this unreasoned reason than to the rationalistic processes which he had formerly regarded as the one reliable means of arriving at trustworthy conclusions. He said that, when a woman says, "Because", she is unable to state the reason for her conviction, simply because she arrived at it by direct cognition, and not by any reasoning process. However, the *dictum* which she announces, is, in general, not therefore less valid, but more so, than as though she knew, just at the time, what reasons could be marshalled in favor of such a *dictum*.

As a matter of interest, the reader will note, that even the natural scientists are no longer asserting that Spirit and spiritual things are either unknowable or impossible. In fact, most of them are now asserting that natural science, within its own domain, can never furnish an adequate interpretation of the universe or of the facts of human life or of ultimate reality, and that such interpretation must be looked for in the realm of metaphysics, that is, in the realm of religion. Natural science is not religious, and never can be; but men who study natural science can also be students of religion and believers in religion, as most of the leading natural scientists now are. Natural science, at its best, can clear the way for men to become religious, through showing, as it has already done, that so-called knowledge on a material basis is not ultimate knowledge.

The Angel prophesies that intuition, or direct perception of reality, is to play a larger part in human mental activity in the future than it has in the past, and the trend of events seems to bear out the prophecy. The gentleman above mentioned said that it is his belief, that all the real knowledge,—that is, knowledge that stands the test of long continued experience,—that mankind has ever gained, has been perceived, little by little, through direct cognition,—though it has been afterwards examined and verified through reason and rational processes. He also said, that he looks to intuition alone to point out the path of progress in the future.

REBUKE

Verses 20-23 *"Notwithstanding I have a few things against thee, because thou sufferest that woman Jezebel, which calleth herself a prophetess, to teach and to seduce my servants to commit fornication, and to eat things sacrificed unto idols. And I gave her space to repent of her fornication; and she repented not. Behold, I will cast her into a bed and them that commit adultery with her into great tribulation, except they repent of their deeds. And I will kill her children with death; and all the churches shall know that I am he which searcheth the reins and hearts; and I will give unto everyone of you according to your works."*

Jezebel, in the Old Testament story, was the wife of Ahab, and was a wicked sorceress. It would not be amiss to read in this connection the accounts of this woman, which are given in the two books of Kings. In the Revelation, John uses her name to symbolize that activity of satan which tries to counterfeit, on the plane of human experience, the activity and works of spiritual intuition, thus deceiving the human consciousness, and leading it into harmful lines of activity. Among such harmful procedures are to be noted spiritualistic and mediumistic practices, and the activities of the so-called subconscious mind in general, when its agency is invoked to perform unusual and occult works. The extremely emotional states of consciousness, resulting in conditions of unconsciousness and trance, which are aroused in the meetings of some so-called religious sects, are also counterfeit activities, and are connoted under the symbol Jezebel. All who cultivate and partake of such emotionalism and psychism *"commit fornication"*, or become apostate from God, with this wicked activity of evil mentality. Those who do so are cast into beds of sickness, and endure great tribulation, and, as a rule, are brought to an earlier death, and are all the time sinking deeper into moral death. To know the truth through direct cognition is to eat the bread of life. The reading of the human mind through higher intuition, as when "Jesus knew their thoughts", is not to be condemned; but to mentally feed on the teachings of false psychism is to *"eat things sacrificed unto idols"*.

PROMISE

Verse 24 *"But unto you I say, and unto the rest in Thyatira, as many as have not this doctrine, and which have not known the depths of satan, as they speak; I will put upon you none other burden."*

As intuition or direct cognition leads to the knowledge of God, and to the highest form of spiritual knowledge and practice, so, by reversal, the attempted deification of the lower elements in the human mind, making them workers of wonders and miracles, and thus leading human thought away from God, the true source of men's instruction, healing, and regeneration, —this psychic belief and practice are the most misleading, and therefore the wickedest, of all forms of human activity, and are rightly characterized as *"the depths of satan"*. To those who keep free from such wicked activity it is promised that they will not have heavier burdens to bear than those they have borne already,—with the implication that it will prove otherwise with those who try to escape from the ills they already have by invoking the aid of this false prophetess, who is but the symbol for all those activities of the human mind known as hypnotism, mesmerism, mental suggestion, emotional trance, occultism, etc.

EXHORTATION

Verse 25 *"But that which ye have already, hold fast till I come."*

That is, such true knowledge as you have, hold on to until you attain full knowledge,—until you come into the experience of "the Spirit of truth . . . which shall guide you into all truth."

PROMISE OF REWARD

Verses 26-29 *"And he that overcometh, and keepeth my works unto the end, to him will I give power over the nations: and he shall rule them with a rod of iron; as the vessels of a potter shall they be broken to shivers: even as I received of my Father. And I will give him the morning star. He that hath an ear, let him hear what the Spirit saith unto the churches."*

The victor in this line of endeavor attains the Christ-mind, which does have power over the nations, and will eventually rule them according to an inflexible law of truth, under which any resistance that they may offer will *"be broken to shivers"*, as a piece of pottery is when it is struck with a rod.

The clearness and beauty and purity of the Christ-mind, which the victor will attain, is well symbolized by *"the morning star."*

CHAPTER III

Messages to the Churches (Continued)

V. To the Church in Sardis (3:1-6)

For the Angel, the one of a church in Sardis, write:

"These things saith he that hath the seven Spirits of God, and the seven stars."

The church in Sardis symbolizes the human consciousness in its activity as *love;* and its Angel is the Christ-mind in its activity as divine *Love.* Love seems to be universally regarded as the one word which most fully characterizes God. Said St. John, "God is love". And St. Paul said, "Love is the fulfilling of the law." Hence, the Christ-mind, in its activity as Love, is said to have *"the seven (all) Spirits of God, and the seven stars";* that is, it sums up in itself all spiritual ideas. The human consciousness naturally manifests but relatively little love that is really spiritual; hence, in this phase of its activity the Angel finds little to commend, but starts the message with a

REBUKE

Verse 1 *"I know thy works, that thou hast a name that thou livest and art dead."*

The human consciousness thinks that its natural affection, —the love for near relatives and friends,—is spiritual, and it thinks that it has love for God which is spiritual; but the idea of God, or good, that it loves is usually much removed from a correct idea of God as pure Spirit. Hence, neither its love of God or men is really spiritual, though the human consciousness thinks it is. Hence, concerning love in the human consciousness it is said, *"Thou hast a name (a reputation) that thou livest, and art (really) dead."* That which is not true or spiritual love is but false love, and this is really not love at all, just as false or counterfeit money is not money at all. If there is no spiritual love in human consciousness, then love is "dead" in it.

EXHORTATION

Verses 2, 3 *"Be watchful, and strengthen the things which remain, that are ready to die: for I have not found thy works perfect before God. Remember therefore how thou hast received and heard, and hold fast, and repent."*

In these words, recognition is made that there is some element of spiritual love in the human consciousness, and that it has received and is capable of understanding right instruction in this activity. It is exhorted to nurture with great care such elements of spiritual love as it has, lest they die out, and to bear in mind such true instruction as it has received, and hold fast to it, and to "repent" or turn from its lower or fallen ways.

WARNING

Verse 3 *"If therefore thou shalt not watch, I will come on thee as a thief, and thou shalt not know what hour I will come upon you."*

This may be taken to mean, that if the human consciousness is not faithful to spiritual love and to the service of higher things, it may seem to deaden what is called "the conscience"; but when this is outraged to too great an extent, or neglected too long, it is liable to assert itself powerfully at some most unexpected time, and bring the individual, or a whole community, into terrible remorse and mental upheaval, often resulting in very painful consequences.

COMMENDATION

Verse 4 *"Thou hast a few names even in Sardis which have not defiled their garments; and they shall walk with me in white: for they are worthy."*

There are a few of human kind who have not been governed, at least predominantly, by a lower sense of love. These *"have not defiled their garments."* They are pure, and so are said to walk with the Christ *"in white."*

There are some activities, reflected from God, within the human consciousness (though not in "mortal" consciousness) which are always pure. Probably the verse really refers to these, even more than to any particular human men or women.

Historically, Sardis was a center of Venus-worship. There was a temple of Astarte there, another name for the Venus idea. This was doubtless the reason why Sardis was chosen to symbolize the love-activity of the human consciousness. If we knew all the peculiarities concerning the six other cities mentioned, there might be an equally evident reason why they were selected as symbols.

PROMISE

Verse 5 *"He that overcometh, the same shall be clothed in white raiment; and I will not blot out his name out of the book of life, but I will confess his name before my Father, and before His angels."*

He who succeeds in directing his love-activity into spiritual channels thereby acquires true or eternal consciousness or life, and his name or character cannot be removed from *"the book of life"*, but his name or *character* is "confessed" or present before the Father, and before, or in the presence of, all right ideas.

VI. To the Church in Philadelphia (3:7-13)

For the Angel, the one of a church in Philadelphia, write:

"These things saith he that is holy, he that is true, he that hath the key of David, he that openeth, and no man shutteth; and shutteth, and no man openeth."

This is a description of the Christ-mind in its activity as *Perception of Reality* and *Authoritative Judgment*. Such perception is holy and true, and it was "the key" by which David unlocked many of the mysteries of the kingdom of heaven. What this perception once opens or brings to human consciousness, no man can close: and what it "shutteth", or suppresseth as false, no man can make true. The church in Philadelphia symbolizes the human consciousness in its *sense of reality*, which is quite as often a false sense as a true one.

COMMENDATION

Verses 8-10 *"I know thy works: behold, I have set before thee an open door, and no man can shut it; for thou hast a little strength, and hast kept my word, and hast not denied my name. Behold, I will make them of the synagogue of Satan, which say they are Jews, and are not, but do lie; behold, I will make them to come and worship before thy feet, and to know that I have loved thee. Because thou hast kept the word of my patience, I also will keep thee from the hour of temptation, which shall come upon all the world, to try them that dwell upon the earth."*

The opportunity of the human consciousness to know reality is an ever-present one; it is *"an open door, and no man can shut it."* The perception of reality has *"a little strength"* in human consciousness, and that consciousness has kept the *"word"* reality as a very important word, and has never denied the importance of that name or idea, but has always cherished it.

"Jews" are supposed to be *"chosen people"*, those who have received, and have chosen to obey, spiritual instruction, and who, consequently, are fitted to be spiritual teachers. They are supposed to be perceivers of reality. If any pretend to be

"Jews" in this sense, but are not, they are automatically excluded by divine law from the realm of harmony, and so are confined to the realm of discord, *"satan"*, and are made to be *"of the synagogue of Satan"*. If such, through false pretenses, have gained exalted places among men, and have seemed to be in a position to scoff at and look down upon true spiritual teachers, true perceivers of reality, these false teachers shall, nevertheless, in time be humbled, and shall be brought to the feet of the true teachers for instruction and aid. Very often today those who hold high places in the estimation of men on the basis of a teaching about reality which is untrue fall into sickness which they are unable to cure, and then resort to those who have a true perception of reality for aid, and receive the same.

Those who hold to the true sense of reality will be safely kept in the hour of trial, which is constantly coming in the world of human experience, putting to the test those who dwell in material sense, the false sense of reality. These do not safely abide the test, but have to be "converted" to a true sense of reality, before they can gain harmony.

EXHORTATION

Verse 11 *"Behold, I come quickly: hold that fast which thou hast that no man take thy crown."*

The Christ-mind as *Perception of Reality* does *"come quickly"* to human consciousness,—so "quickly"; that it is always present, even though unrecognized: The true sense would be better conveyed, perhaps, by the words, I come *living*. The idea is the same as in the case where the Christ is represented as coming "to judge the quick (living) and the dead." The perception of that which *is real* comes to the human mentality *"by quickening"*.

The human consciousness is exhorted to hold fast to so much perception of reality as it has, in order that its reward be not taken away.

PROMISE

Verse 12 *"Him that overcometh will I make a pillar in the temple of my God, and he shall go no more out: and I will write upon him the name of my God, and the name of the city of my God, which is new Jerusalem, which cometh down out of heaven from my God: and I will write upon him my new name."*

He who gradually gains the perception of reality becomes, in the measure that he does so, a consciousness which is established in Truth and good, a part and parcel of the larger Christ-consciousness, and is included in humanity's spiritual consciousness worshiping God, which is the true church or temple, in which he becomes a pillar, and outside this spiritual consciousness, after he has entered in, he goes no more. Being borne into this higher and true sense of reality, he is "born again", and becomes, more and more, "a new creature in Christ", and gradually receives a new nature, a *"new name"*, which is the name or character of *"the city of God"*, and this is the spiritual consciousness, the *"new Jerusalem"*, a quality of consciousness *"which cometh down out of heaven from God."*

NOTES BY THE READER

VII. To the Church of the Laodiceans (3:14-22)

For the Angel, the one of a church in Laodicea, write:

"These things saith the Amen, the faithful and true witness, the beginning of the creation of God."

This is a description of the Christ-mind in its activity as *Perception of Substance*. The true sense of substance, the perception of substance as Spirit instead of as matter, is the most difficult of all attainments for the human mentality; and so this activity of the Christ-mind, this angel of the human consciousness, is spoken of as *"the Amen"*; that is, *the final*. This angel is also a *"faithful and true witness."* Since the creation of God must spring from substance, and since substance really is Spirit, the Christ-mind as Spirit is spoken of as *"the beginning (the source) of the creation of God."* The word *archê* may be correctly translated as "ruler", "over-lord", as well as "beginning". The church of the Laodiceans symbolizes the human consciousness in its activity as *sense of substance*. The human mentality has less of true perception, is less what it ought to be, in this activity than in any of the others mentioned. Hence, the church of the Laodiceans receives no commendation, but only rebuke, warning, exhortation, and a promise.

REBUKE

Verse 15 *"I know thy works, that thou art neither cold nor hot: I would thou wert cold or hot."*

The human consciousness is disposed to recognize both Spirit and matter as substance, and thus tries to serve two masters. It makes the ridiculous and self-defeating blunder of trying to render mental allegiance to two contradictory senses of substance at the same time,—in other words, tries to call both of two diametric opposites "real." Lukewarm water is nauseating, while hot water and cold water are not. The mental attitude of the thorough-going materialist, who affirms that matter is the only substance, is more respectable and tolerable from a logical standpoint than is the attitude of those who affirm that both Spirit and matter are real.

WARNING

Verse 16 *"So then because thou art lukewarm and neither cold nor hot, I will spew thee out of my mouth."*

Such vacillating, divided, illogical mental allegiance or service is automatically rejected from the Christ-mind, and so is remanded to the realm of discord.

EXHORTATION

Verses 17-20 *"Because thou sayest, I am rich, and increased with goods, and have need of nothing; and knowest not that thou art wretched, and miserable, and poor, and blind, and naked; I counsel thee to buy of me gold tried in the fire, that thou mayest be rich; and white raiment, that thou mayest be clothed, and that the shame of thy nakedness do not appear; and anoint thine eyes with eyesalve, that thou mayest see. As many as I love, I rebuke and chasten: be zealous therefore, and repent. Behold, I stand at the door, and knock: if any man hear my voice, and open the door, I will come unto him, and will sup with him, and he with me."*

The human consciousness thinks it is rich in its sense of matter under various pleasing forms, and is inclined to think that it has no other need than matter, if it can have enough of it, of the right kind. It does not appreciate that *true riches* are *desirable states of consciousness,*—namely, love, joy, and peace, that these can be obtained only from Spirit, God, and that, lacking these, it is *"wretched, and miserable, and poor, and blind, and naked"*, no matter how many material "goods", so-called, it may have. The Christ-mind counsels the human consciousness to obtain from it, as Spirit, that sense of substance and good which neither fire nor any other agency can destroy, that it may indeed be rich; and it counsels the human consciousness to robe itself in righteousness, which is to be obtained from Spirit, not from matter, that it may be truly clothed. Otherwise, to a discerning sense, the shame of its nakedness will appear, no matter how fine the material raiment. Often ones sees a woman whose body is carefully clothed with fine raiment; but the nakedness of her irritability, fretfulness, fearfulness, frivolity, impurity, uncharitableness, and the like, lays perfectly open to any beholder. She needs *"white raiment, that she may be clothed, and that the shame of her nakedness do not appear."* The white robe of the truth will not merely cover up such mental poverty and wickedness, but will destroy them. The understanding of Spirit as substance is the *"eye-salve"* with which we should anoint our mental vision, in order that we may be able to see truly.

The true perception of substance, including the perception of all good, is constantly knocking at the door of every man's consciousness. It is always at hand, ready to be learned, just as is the multiplication-table. If any man will open the door of his consciousness, by divesting his mind of preconceived false opinions, and by becoming teachable as a little child, all truth and good will come into his consciousness and experience, and make itself at home with him.

PROMISE

Verse 21 *"To him that overcometh will I grant to sit with me in my throne, even as I also overcame, and am set down with my Father in his throne."*

The Christ manifests the authority of God, and he who conquers through the Christ-mind shares the authority of the Christ.

88 NOTES BY THE READER

A REVISED TEXT AND SUGGESTIVE PARAPHRASE

If the author's earnest study of the Apocalypse in the light of the Principle and teaching of Christian Science, coupled with a critical examination of the fundamental sources of knowledge about the Book, has availed anything, it has done so, first of all, in giving a more accurate sense of the Greek text at certain points, and a better translation of that text, both at those points where changes in the Greek text have been shown to be necessary, and at certain other points where the sense of the Greek has not been correctly apprehended by many translators. It therefore seems to the author that it is due those who have carefully perused his rather voluminous Interpretative Notes, and who have satisfied themselves that the positions assumed on points of text and translation are well taken, that the results of the work along this line should be summed up in a presentation of an English text or translation which embodies the interpretative conclusions at which we have arrived. In attempting to meet this need, the author has before him the choice of amending existing translations, or of making a practically new one. Compared with the work of interpretation which is presented in this book, the labor of making a new translation would not be great, but while the changes in translation which have been noted are of vital importance, they are few in number, and do not seem to call for an addition to the already rather numerous modern translations, or to warrant asking the reader to consider the Apocalypse in a literary dress different from that with which he is reasonably familiar, except at such points as may be necessary.

Accordingly, the author has decided to present in this volume the Revised Version of the Apocalypse, amending words, phrases, and clauses where necessary, and clearly indicating the portions thus amended by italicizing them, and then presenting in parentheses the portions of the text of the Revised Version for which emendations are substituted.

It also seems due to the faithful reader of these Notes, who has taken the time to study them with care, that there should be presented in brief compass, and in a form for ready reference, the results of this effort at interpretation in a statement essentially as compact as the text itself. Thus the student, when he so desires, can quickly turn, when he wishes to refresh his memory, to the plain, condensed interpretation of any given verse,—having previously satisfied himself as to the correctness of the interpretation by a careful study of the extended Notes which were presented for his consideration first of all.

Such a condensed interpretation, the author here presents in the form of a "Suggestive Paraphrase", printed, for the convenience of the reader, parallel with the amended translation upon which it is based.

This paraphrase is not to be taken dogmatically, nor is it to be considered the final word as to the best interpretation of any given text. The author could have paraphrased many verses in quite a different wording, which would have conveyed about the same idea, and perhaps equally well. No doubt the interpretation, or the form of expression, can be improved at various points, and readers are free to exercise their thought to this end. The author would be especially glad of any suggestions which anyone may have to offer. The paraphrase is intended to be just what is indicated in the title, *suggestive,* with the hope that it may stimulate thought and inquiry with regard to a portion of the Scriptures, the meaning of which seems obscure to the great body of Bible readers, but which is very rich in practical spiritual teaching.

The paraphrase is not offered as a substitute for the original, but as a help in adapting Jewish modes of thought and figures of speech to modern western idioms and forms of expression, thus rendering the original more easily understood. *When the original can be read understandingly, it is much more poetic, vivid, interesting and moving* than this paraphrase or any other modern statement of the same ideas can be. It is hoped that the readers of the paraphrase will read the original, not less but more frequently than formerly, and it is confidently expected that this will be the result. With respect to the importance of its subject matter, its marvelous insight into deep and hidden things, its practical value when understood, and withal its literary excellence and brilliancy, it is doubtful if another human document of equal length can compare with the Revelation of St. John the Divine.

Before beginning to read the paraphrase, the student is requested to again refer to Note 5, of the Introduction, entitled: "Adherence to Principle". The points to be specially borne in mind are, that the paraphrase will endeavor to avoid representing God as knowing evil, or as consciously approaching or dealing with mortal sense. The issue is wholly confined to "the suppositional warfare between truth and error", as Mrs. Eddy has phrased it (S. & H., p. 288), between the right idea and false belief within the arena of human consciousness.

PROLOGUE

Chapter I

Amended Revised Version

1 *A* (The) Revelation *from* (of) Jesus Christ, which God gave him, to shew unto *His* (his) servants · the things which must shortly *be revealed* (come to pass): and he sent and signified it by *His* (his) angel unto *His* (his) servant John; 2 who bare witness of the word of God, and of the testimony of *Jesus* Christ, even of all things that he 3 saw. Blessed is he that readeth, and they that hear the words of the prophecy, and keep the things which are written therein: for the time is at hand.

Suggestive Paraphrase

A revelation of the things made known in the prophetic consciousness, which emanates from God, to show unto His servants the things which must quickly unfold to them: and He revealed these things in images and symbols to His servant John; who bare record of the Christ of God, and of the things made known by the mediatorial consciousness, even of all things that he saw. Blessed are they that read with understanding the words of the prophecy, and keep in mind and are governed by the things written therein: for to them the time is at hand.

SECTION I
MESSAGES TO THE SEVEN CHURCHES

Chapter I. Introductory

Greeting to the Churches

Amended Revised Version

4 John to the seven churches which are in Asia: Grace to you and peace, from him which is and which was and which is to come; and from the seven Spirits which are before his 5 throne; and from Jesus Christ, who is the faithful witness, the firstborn of the dead, and the ruler of the kings of the earth.

Suggestive Paraphrase

Greetings from John to humanity in its every form of mental activity: May you have grace from the eternal God; and from all the manifestations of infinite Mind; and from the spirit of prophecy, which is the faithful witness, and the only order of consciousness which has made a demonstration over death, and which is the rightful lord of all the powers of the world.

Ascription of Praise

Unto him that loveth us, and loosed us from our sins 6 by his blood; and he made us to be a kingdom, to be priests unto his God and Father; to him be the glory and the dominion for ever 7 and ever. Amen. Behold, he cometh with the clouds; and

Unto the impersonal Christ whom we love and who cleanses us from our sins through his life of love; and hath made us a kingdom of priests in the service of God, his Father; to him be ascribed glory and dominion forever and ever. Amen. Behold, he is to be exalted in the mental realm; and all men must take account of

Amended Revised Version	*Suggestive Paraphrase*
every eye shall see him, and they which pierced him; and all the tribes of the earth shall mourn over him. EVen so, Amen.	him, even those which have sought to destroy him, and this Christ-mind will cause all the dwellers in material sense to mourn. So let it be.
8 I am the Alpha and the Omega, saith the Lord God, which is and which was and which is to come, the Almighty.	I am the origin and the completion, the summation of all things, saith the Lord God, the everlasting and Almighty.

The Coming of the Message

9 I *John*, your brother and partaker with you in the *stress and over-ruling and patient persistence which are in Jesus Christ* (tribulation and kingdom and patience which are in Jesus), was in the isle that is called Patmos, for the word of God 10 and the testimony of Jesus. I was in the Spirit on the Lord's day, and I heard behind me a great voice, as 11 of a trumpet saying, What thou seest, write in a book, and send it to the seven churches; unto Ephesus, and unto Smyrna, and unto Pergamos, and unto Thyatira, and unto Sardis and unto Philadelphia, and unto Laodicea.	I *John*, who am the brother of you who are servants of God, am partaker with you in the stress and compulsion and unremitting service which are characteristic of the prophetic consciousness in its service of God. I was in exile from material sense, because of the demands of truth and of the spirit of prophecy; and I was in spiritual consciousness in the timeless world, the Lord's day, and I unexpectedly received a great spiritual impulse directing me, What thou perceivest, write in a book, and address it to the human consciousness as expressed in Attention, Reason, Will, Intuitive Sense, Feeling, Sense of Reality, and Sense of Substance.

A Vision of the Redeemer

12 And I turned to see the voice which spake with me. And having turned I saw seven golden candlesticks; 13 and in the midst of the candlesticks one like unto a son of man, clothed with a garment down to the foot, and girt about at the breasts with a golden girdle. And 14 his head and his hair were white as white wool, white as snow; and his eyes were 15 as a flame of fire; and his feet like unto *liquid metal* (burnished brass), as if it had been *melted* (refined)	And I examined the source and character of the spiritual impulse directing me: and as I did so, I beheld seven mental light-bearers; and their ruler, which pervaded them, was the Christ-mind, completely robed in righteousness and engirt with holiness, as a High-Priest to God. Majesty and exceeding holiness are beheld of all who perceive this Christ-mind; and it manifests unlimited penetration and ability to discern between good and evil; and it is characterized by exceeding swiftness, even omnipresence; and its utterance is the voice of all wisdom, or ever the world was.

I : 16-II : 3   TEXT AND PARAPHRASE   95

Amended Revised Version

in a furnace; and his voice as the voice of many waters.
16 And he had in his right hand seven stars: and out of his mouth proceeded a sharp two-edged sword: and his countenance was as the sun shineth in his strength.

Suggestive Paraphrase

And from this Christ-mind proceed seven great lights: also the word of Truth judging the world and smiting error: and its glorious manifestation is commanding and prevailing. enlightening the world.

Words of Encouragement and Command

17 And when I saw him, I fell at his feet as one dead. And he laid his right hand upon me, saying, Fear not; I am the first and the last,
18 and the Living one; and I was dead, and behold, I am alive for evermore, and I have the keys of death and
19 of Hades. Write therefore the things which thou sawest, and the things which are, and the things which shall come to pass here-
20 after; the mystery of the seven stars which thou sawest in my right hand, and the seven golden candlesticks. The seven stars are the angels of the seven churches: and the seven candlesticks are seven churches.

And I was stunned by the character and magnitude of the vision. But the prophetic consciousness laid hold upon me with the impulsion of its inspiration and authority, saying, Fear not; I am the world-enduring mediatorial Christ, dead to mortal sense, and yet forever alive, and with me is the solution of the problems of death and hell. Write therefore the things that you perceive, both those that are now in evidence and those that must come to pass hereafter. The seven candlesticks are emblematical of the seven chief activities of human sense, which are to receive instruction from the seven corresponding activities of the mediatorial Christ-mind, which are symbolized as seven stars.

Chapter II. Messages to the Churches

The Letter to a Church in Ephesus

1 *For* (To) the angel of *a* (the) church in Ephesus write: These things saith he that holdest the seven stars in his right hand, he that walketh in the midst of the seven golden candle-
2 sticks: I know thy works, and thy toil and patience, and that thou canst not bear evil men, and didst try them which call themselves apostles, and they are not, and
3 didst find them false; and

In behalf of the Christ-mind as Spiritual Aspiration address instructively human consciousness in its activity as Attention.
These things saith the Christ-idea, who is the light-bearer of the world and is active in all phases of the human consciousness: The human mentality toils long and patiently, and will not long give attention to men known to be evil. and, in the long account, detects religious impostors. It is a seeker after truth, and will patiently bear all things for the sake of

Amended Revised Version

thou hast patience and didst bear for my name's sake, and hast not grown weary.
4 But I have this against thee, that thou didst leave
5 thy first love. Remember therefore from whence thou art fallen, and repent, and do the first works; or else I come to thee, and will move thy candlestick out of its place, except thou repent.
6 But this thou hast, that thou hatest the deeds of the Nicolaitans, which I also hate.
7 He that hath an ear, let him hear what the Spirit saith to the churches. To him that overcometh, to him will I give to eat of the tree of life, which is in the Paradise of God.

The Letter to a Church in Smyrna

8 And *for* (to) the angel of *a* (the) church in Smyrna write:

These things saith the first and the last, which was
9 dead, and lived again; I know thy tribulation, and thy poverty (but thou art rich), and the blasphemy of them which say they are Jews, and they are not, but are a synagogue of Satan.
10 Fear not the things which thou art about to suffer: behold, the devil is about to cast some of you into prison, that ye may be tried; and ye shall have tribulation ten days. Be thou faithful unto death, and I will give thee the crown of
11 life. He that hath an ear, let him hear what the Spirit saith to the churches. He that overcometh shall not be hurt of the second death.

Suggestive Paraphrase

what it believes to be truth; but it does not know that Spirit and its ideas are the only truth, and so it is apostate from its prime allegiance. It is exhorted to seek to serve Spirit only, lest, if it continue to give attention to material things, it should suddenly come into judgment, and lose such perception of truth as it already has, thus ceasing to be a lightbearer.

But this is in the favor of the human consciousness as a whole, that it hates indecent and licentious practices. He that has sufficient spiritual discernment, let him understand and heed what the Spirit says to human sense. To him who overcometh ignorance and evil the Christ will give that understanding of Truth which is eternal life in the midst of all the joy and harmony of God.

And for the Christ-mind as Principle address instructively human consciousness in its activity as Reason.

These things saith the once incarnate Christ which triumphed over death. I know the trials and the poverty of attainment of human reason (though when governed by Principle it is rich), and I know the blasphemous teachings of those who claim to reason according to Spirit, but do not, serving satan instead. Reason need not fear the outcome of any of the trials which are before it, though satan will hold it partially in bondage in trying to totally enslave it, and its testing time will last during the whole period of satanic ascendency. Be faithful to God, even if you are tried to the point of seeming death, and I will give you eternal life. He that hath sufficient spiritual discernment, let him understand and heed what the Spirit saith to human sense. He that overcometh evil shall not be hurt during the final destruction of evil which is called the second death. (See 20:14.)

The Letter to a Church in Pergamum

Amended Revised Version

12 And *for* (to) the angel of *a* (the) church in Per-
13 gamum write: These things saith he that hath the sharp two-edged sword: I know where thou dwellest, even where Satan's throne is: and thou holdest fast my name, and didst not deny my faith, even in the days of Antipas my witness, my faithful one, who was killed among you, where Satan
14 dwelleth. But I have a few things against thee, because thou hast there some that hold the teaching of Balaam, who taught Balak to cast a stumbling block before the children of Israel, to eat things sacrificed to idols, and to commit forni-
15 cation. So hast thou also some that hold the teaching of the Nicolaitans in like
16 manner. Repent therefore; or else I come to thee quickly, and I will make war against them with the
17 sword of my mouth. He that hath an ear, let him hear what the Spirit saith to the churches. To him that overcometh, to him will I give of the hidden manna, and I will give him a white stone, and upon the stone a new name written, which no one knoweth but he that receiveth it.

Suggestive Paraphrase

And for the Christ idea as Executive Intelligence address instructively human consciousness in its activity as Will.

These things saith the mediatorial Christ which is the executive of Truth: The human will is often the chief agent of satan when in the service of selfish desire and ambition; yet the human mind has always held fast the name of truth, and, on the whole, has not denied the letter of the Christ-teachings, even when it was wholly lacking in the Spirit thereof,—the Holy Spirit, which is the only true and faithful witness. However, the human will deserves rebuke because it tolerates and fosters mental tendencies and dispositions to sexual promiscuousness, to take part in the practices of mediumship and divination and the worship of false gods, and to depart from the true faith. It also tolerates and does not sternly cast out the vile thoughts and practices of mortal mind. Unless the human mind repents of such looseness of thought and conduct, it will come suddenly and unexpectedly into judgment and suffering. He that hath sufficient spiritual discernment, let him understand and heed what the Spirit saith to human sense. To him that overcometh sin I will give the understanding of Truth which is hidden from the world; and I will give him citizenship in the Kingdom of God and a new character, which is spiritual, which only those who gain it can know and appreciate.

The Letter to a Church in Thyatira

Amended Revised Version

18 And *for* (to) the angel of *a* (the) church in Thyatira write:
These things saith the Son of God, who hath his eyes like a flame of fire, and his feet are like unto *liquid metal* (burnished
19 brass): I know thy works, and thy love and thy faith and ministry and patience; and that thy last works are
20 more than the first. But I have this against thee, that thou sufferest the woman Jezebel, which calleth herself a prophetess; and she teacheth and seduceth my servants to commit fornication, and to eat things
21 sacrificed to idols. And I gave her time that she should repent; and she willeth not to repent of her
22 fornication. Behold, I do cast her into a bed, and them that commit adultery with her into great tribulation, except they repent of
23 her works. And I will kill her children with death; and all the churches shall know that I am he which searcheth the reins and hearts: and I will give unto each one of you according
24 to your works. But to you I say, to the rest that are in Thyatira, as many as have not this teaching, which know not the deep things of Satan, as they say; I cast upon you none other
25 burden. Howbeit that which ye have, hold fast till I
26 come. And he that overcometh, and he that keepeth my works unto the end, to him will I give authority
27 over the nations: and he

Suggestive Paraphrase

And for the mediatorial Christ as Spiritual Intuition address instructively human consciousness in the exercise of its Intuitive Faculty.

These things saith the Christ-mind, which has clear, penetrating discernment, and is swift in carrying messages of wisdom: The human consciousness through its intuitive sense has held to and kept alive in the human realm the word of Truth with much labor and love and faith and service and patience in the face of much opposition, and its loyal labors are increasing. On the other hand, the human mind tolerates sorcery, mediumship, and occultism, which claim to be legitimate prophecy, and which deceive and seduce those who seek to exercise true intuition into false and misleading activities and into the study of psychism and its phantom worship. Plenty of opportunity is given human sense to turn from such counterfeits of true intuitive perception, but it has refused. In consequence, this occultism becomes a realm of discord and weakness, and those who practice it ultimately fall into great tribulation except they repent. They often fall into moral or physical death, or both. By bitter experience, if in no other way, every phase of the human consciousness will learn that the Christ-mind is the searcher of hearts and the administrator of exact justice. But those who have no part in these studies and practices, which are the very depths of satan, will not be tried more severely in the battle of life than by the experiences which they have already endured. Such true knowledge as it has the human consciousness should carefully hold to until it attains full knowledge; and he who obeys this precept will attain that consciousness which has authority over the nations and will ulti-

II : 28-III : 6 TEXT AND PARAPHRASE

Amended Revised Version

shall rule them with a rod of iron, as the vessels of the potter are broken to shivers; as I also have received of my Father: and 28 I will give him the morning 29 star. He that hath an ear, let him hear what the Spirit saith to the churches.

Suggestive Paraphrase

mately rule over them by an inflexible law, overcoming all opposition and breaking it to pieces,—even as the Christ-mind receives authority and power to rule from the heavenly Father: and he that overcomes will gain that mediatorial perception which is the harbinger of the full day of Spirit.

CHAPTER III. MESSAGES TO THE CHURCHES (CONTINUED)

The Letter to a Church in Sardis

1 And *for* (to) the angel of *a* (the) church in Sardis write:

These things saith he that hath the seven Spirits of God, and the seven stars: I know thy works, that thou hast a name that thou liv-2 est, and thou art dead. Be thou watchful, and stablish the things that remain, which were ready to die; for I have found no works of thine fulfilled before my 3 God. Remember therefore how thou hast received and didst hear; and keep it, and repent. If therefore thou shalt not watch, I will come as a thief, and thou shalt not know what hour I will 4 come upon thee. But thou hast a few names in Sardis which did not defile their garments: and they shall walk with me in white; for they are worthy. 5 He that overcometh shall thus be arrayed in white garments; and I will in no wise blot his name out of the book of life, and I will confess his name before my Father, and before his 6 angels. He that hath an ear, let him hear what the Spirit saith to the churches.

And for the Christ-mind as the manifestation of divine Love address instructively human sense in its exercise of love.

These things saith the Christ-idea which embraces the seven chief manifestations of God, acting as the guiding angels of human thought. Love that is true is reputed to be exercised by the human mind, but that mind is virtually dead to spiritual love, which alone is true. Humanity should take great care to firmly fix in consciousness that spiritual love which it has so nearly lost, since it has brought none of its attainments to perfection as measured by the standard of God. It should bear in mind the things which it has been taught, and hold fast to them, and turn from its evil ways; otherwise it will be brought to a reckoning and to punishment at a most unexpected time. There are a few who have not fallen into sin in their exercise of love. They dwell with the Christ in purity; for they are worthy. He that overcometh the perverted sense of love shall live in purity; and he shall be numbered among the everliving, and shall know God and all His manifestations, and shall be honored of Him. He that hath sufficient spiritual discernment, let him understand and heed what the Spirit saith to the human sense.

The Letter to a Church in Philadelphia

Amended Revised Version

7 And *for* (to) the angel of *a* (the) church in Philadelphia write:
These things saith he that is holy, he that is true, he that hath the key of David, he that openeth, and none shall shut, and that shut-
8 teth, and none openeth: I know thy works (behold, I have set before thee a door opened, which none can shut), that thou hast a little power, and didst keep my word, and didst not
9 deny my name. Behold, I give of the synagogue of Satan, of them which say they are Jews and they are not, but do lie; behold, I will make them to come and worship before thy feet, and to know that I have loved
10 thee. Because thou didst keep the word of my patience, I also will keep thee from the hour of trial, that hour which is to come upon the whole world, to try them that dwell upon the earth.
11 I come quickly: hold fast that which thou hast, that
12 no one take thy crown. He that overcometh, I will make him a pillar in the temple of my God, and he shall go out thence no more: and I will write upon him the name of my God, and the name of the city of my God, the new Jerusalem, which cometh down out of heaven from my God, and mine
13 own new name. He that hath an ear, let him hear what the Spirit saith to the churches.

Suggestive Paraphrase

And for the mediatorial Christ-mind as Perception of Reality instructively address the human consciousness in its activity as Sense of Reality.
These things saith the Christ-idea, holy and true, the order of understanding by which David discerned Truth, which reveals reality so that no man can hide it from the true seekers, and yet covers it so that no false mortal sense can see it. The mediatorial Christ-mind knows the activity of human sense, and sets before it a great opportunity which is never withdrawn. It has a little spiritual strength, and has kept the letter of the Christ-teaching, and has not disowned his name. Those who claim to be initiated into spiritual things when they are not are automatically remanded by the Christ-mind to a portion among the wicked. Their sins and the consequences thereof shall cause them to be humbled before the true perception, which they shall know is loved by the Christ. Because human sense has held fast to the message of Christ resolutely, he will save it from destruction during the trial and judgment that shall come upon all materiality. The truth comes to the human consciousness suddenly. It should hold fast all the truth and good which it has, that it may not lose its reward. The truth will make him that overcometh falsehood a great power in the redemptive order of Truth, from which he shall never be separated; and he shall be known as a follower of God, and as a dweller in the realization of God, which is the true and eternal city, to which men mentally rise as they learn of God; and because they have been born again, they shall have a new character.

The Letter to a Church in Laodicea

Amended Revised Version

14 And *for* (to) the angel of *a* (the) church in Laodicea write:
These things saith the Amen, the faithful and true witness, *the ruler of* (the beginning of) the creation
15 of God; I know thy works, that thou art neither cold nor hot; I would that thou wert cold or hot. So be-
16 cause thou art lukewarm, and neither hot nor cold, I will spew thee out of my
17 mouth. Because thou sayest, I am rich, and have gotten riches, and have need of nothing; and knowest not that thou art the wretched one and miserable and poor
18 and blind and naked: I counsel thee to buy of me gold refined by fire, that thou mayest become rich; and white garments, that thou mayest clothe thyself, and that the shame of thy nakedness be not made manifest; and eyesalve to anoint thine eyes, that thou
19 mayest see. As many as I love, I reprove and chasten: be zealous therefore, and re-
20 pent. Behold, I stand at the door and knock: if any man hear my voice and open the door, I will come in to him, and will sup with him,
21 and he with me. He that overcometh, I will give to him to sit down with me in my throne, as I also overcame, and sat down with
22 my Father in his throne. He that hath an ear, let him hear what the Spirit saith to the churches.

Suggestive Paraphrase

And for the mediatorial Christ as Perception of Substance address instructively the human Sense of Substance.

These things saith the Christ-idea, which is absolute and final, the faithful and true witness, the overlord of the creation of God.

The mediatorial Christ knows the content of human sense, that it has no overruling zeal for either Spirit or matter, and heartily desires that it were placed definitely on one side or the other. The Christ rejects an indifferent consecration, which assumes his name, and yet often dishonors it. Because human sense thinks itself to be rich in material goods and to be in need of nothing, whereas, in truth, it is desperately poor, both mentally and outwardly, it is earnestly exhorted to gain through the Christ the only true and indestructible substance, that it may indeed be rich,—rich in righteousness, the only garment that will not wear out and that covers nothing to be ashamed of; and to sharpen its understanding with spiritual discernment, that it may be able to perceive truly. Whoever loves the Christ-mind is rebuked for his sins and is instructed thereby. The truth is omnipresent, and so is knocking at the door of every man's consciousness. If any man recognizes this fact, and takes the truth in, he becomes at one with it.

Whoever overcomes the sense of matter shall share the power and authority of Christ, even as Christ Jesus overcame the flesh and now shares the power and authority of God. He that hath sufficient spiritual discernment, let him understand and heed what the Spirit is revealing to the human sense.

(Continued on Page 155.)

Foldout

Page(s):

_____

Has this book Been

NOTES BY THE READER

THE SEVEN ANGELS OF THE BOOK OF REVELATION

These Angels are introduced in the Apocalypse as Angels of the Churches, Angels of the Trumpets, Harvest-Angels, and Angels as Angels of the Vials. Apparently, these Angels are different offices they fill, four sense in which these four different offices. They are rather forms of manifestation to the Christ-Mind of the activities of the human consciousness corresponding to the seven Angels. The human consciousness is instructed and reformed by these Angels.

Description of the Angels	Symbol	Belief in matter	Spiritual
Angels to the Churches (1 Act)	The Churches, and the forms of opposition to the Angels of the Churches.	Forms of opposition to the Angels of the Trumpets and Vials (Acts 2 and 5)	
		Forms of opposition to the Angels of the World-Harvest (2 Act)	Rewards to those who obey the message of the Angels, and thus "Overcome."
			Immortals

105

THE SEVEN ANGELS OF THE BOOK OF REVELATION

These Angels are introduced in the Drama of the Apocalypse as Angels of the Churches, Angels of the Trumpets, Harvest Angels, and Angels of the Vials. They are the same seven in these four different offices.

These Angels are chief forms of manifestation of the Christ-Mind. The "Seven Churches of Asia" symbolize seven activities of the human consciousness corresponding to the seven Angels as just defined. The human consciousness is instructed and reformed by these Angels.

Description of the Angels	The Churches and forms of opposition to the Angels in the Churches (Act 1)	Forms of opposition to the Angels of the Trumpets and Vials. (Acts 3 and 6)	Forms of opposition to the Angels of the World-Harvest. (Act 5)	Rewards to those who obey the message of the Angels, and thus "Overcome"
Spiritual Perception, Attention to Spirit. "Soul"*	*Symbol*, Ephesus. Physical sense Attention to matter. "Sense"	Belief in matter. Materiality, Sensuality. *Symbol,* "The Earth".	Earth-dwellers (14:6). Materiality.	Immortality (Tree of Life) *Attributes,* Strength
Spiritual Reason, Spirit as Premise. "Principle"*	*Symbol,* Smyrna. Human Intellect. Matter as premise. "Discord"	Sensuousness, Psychic sensuality. *Symbol,* "The Sea".	Beast-worship (14:9). Idolatry.	True Being, (Crown of Life) *Attributes,* Skill.
Will, Mind in Action and in Execution. "Life"*	*Symbol,* Pergamos. Human Will. "Dwellers at Satan's seat." "Death"	Emotions, Human love and hatred *Symbol,* "Rivers and fountains of waters."	Not mentioned	Spiritual power and knowledge (Hidden manna and voting pebble) *Attribute,* Force.
Spiritual Intuition, Knowledge without Reasoning. "Mind"*	*Symbol,* Thyatira. Worldly Prudence. Carnal knowledge and conduct. "Mortal mind"	Human wisdom. "The wisdom of this world." *Symbol,* "Sun, moon and stars" darkened.	Dwellers in Babylon	Dominion over all Promises. (The Rod of Iron) *Attributes,* Dominion, Wealth, Thanks.
Divine Love. "Love"*	*Symbol,* Sardis. Impurity, Sensuality. "Hate"	Fleshly desires and their consequences. *Symbol,* "A fallen star".	Not mentioned	Eternal Bliss (Book of Life) *Attributes,* Praise, Ruling
Perception of Reality "Truth"*	*Symbol,* Philadelphia. False doctrine. False teaching. "Error"	Idolatry. *Symbol,* "The Euphrates".	Not mentioned	Freedom from Temptation and Apostasy Pillar in temple *Attributes,* Honor, Deliverance
Perception of Substance The full Proclamation of Truth. "Spirit"*	*Symbol,* Laodicea. Lukewarmness, Divided allegiance "Matter-belief"	Every form of evil and error. *Symbol,* "The air".	"The wine of the earth."	Christ, the Spiritual Body (Throne of God) *Attributes,* Glory, Authority

With acknowledgment to the writings of Mr. James M. Pryse for some of the material in the first and last columns of the chart.

*With acknowledgment to Mrs. Mary Baker Eddy for these terms, each of which corresponds in meaning to the phrases printed immediately above it.

NOTES BY THE READER

Eternal Bliss (Book of Life), Attributes, Ruling	Not mentioned	Freshly desires and consequences, Symbol, "A fallen star"	Synagogue, Impurity, Sensuality	Divine Love
Redemption and Sanctification of People, Afflictions, Honor, Deliverance, Christ, the Spirit and Body (God), Elohim (God), Kindness, Glory, Authority	Constancy (4:1), Eternity care & benedicum	Pride, Apostasy, Sensuality, Worldliness, "Free-to-serve" ones, "The Synagogue of Satan"	[illegible], Division between sensual & material, "Error"	Perception of Truth, [illegible], Proclamation of Truth, "Spirit"

With forgiveness for some for error. M. Three is Mr. Robert Eddy that just and last compares the four in the material in -corres which does seek for same, of which indebted or persecuted their above indirectly swats

SECTION II
THE VISION OF THE SEVEN SEALED LETTERS
(Chapter 4:1—8:1)

After Christ Jesus had nearly finished instructing his personal disciples, he took Peter, James and John into the (mental) mount of transfiguration, and showed them a wonderful vision. "And as they came down from the mountain, Jesus charged them, saying, Tell the vision to no man, until the Son of man be risen again from the dead." (Matt. 17:9.) Likewise, after the impersonal Christ has told John to write letters of instruction to his impersonal disciples, the churches, he takes John into the mount of vision and shows to him the wonderful scene depicted in chapters 4 and 5.

CHAPTER IV

A Vision of the Millennium, the Reign of the Holy Spirit

This Fourth Chapter and a Portion of the Fifth Describe all Redeemed Humanity in the Act of Worshipping God

In this vision St. John gives us a full presentation of the condition which will prevail in the entire realm of human mental activity when the struggle between good and evil is nearly finished. This 4th chapter is a forevision of that period of humanity's spiritual development which, in chapter 20:1-4, is spoken of in the place and order where it actually will come to pass. This is the period in which satan (discord) will be "bound" or suppressed for a long period, spoken of by St. John as "a thousand years." Because the Latin word for a thousand is *mille,* and the Latin word for a year is *annum,* this "thousand-year" period of harmony among men on the earth is spoken of in Christian literature as "the millennium". How St. John knew that such a period will occur, and how we may know that it will, will be made clear in the comments on the last acts of the drama. Why this forevision of the millennium is given to John at this point in the drama, and is given by him to us, will be considered in the comment on chapter 5.

The imagery and symbolism of these chapters appear to be extremely materialistic, but, as we shall see later, it is impossible to interpret them materially if we take into account *all* of the details which they present.

Verse 1 *"And after this I looked, and behold, a door was opened in heaven: and the first voice which I heard was as it were a trumpet talking with me; which said, Come up hither, and I will shew thee things which must be hereafter."*

The meaning of this whole verse is equivalent to: And I was seized with a powerful mental impulse, which awakened me to a new and higher vision, giving promise of a fore-knowledge of future development.

Throughout the New Testament, the term "heaven" is practically synonymous in meaning with the word "consciousness", and it will illumine the significance of many passages of Scripture to substitute the one term for the other. For instance, the phrase *"a door was opened in heaven"* is equivalent to, A door was opened in (my) consciousness. In the Lord's Prayer, the phrase *"Our Father which art in heaven"* should be interpreted as meaning, Our Father which art in consciousness.

Verse 2, 3 *"And immediately I was in the spirit: and, behold, a throne was set in heaven, and one sat on the throne. And he that sat was to look upon like a jasper and a sardine stone: and there was a rainbow round about the throne, in sight like unto an emerald."*

These verses may be interpreted as follows: And immediately I had a spiritual vision; and I saw divine Mind reigning in spiritualized or redeemed consciousness. And I perceived the majesty and justice of God: and I perceived that mercy,—that is, love ultimating in final peace for mankind,—is characteristic of God.

The human consciousness is itself, or should be, a "throne" for divine Mind, God. The many-hued jasper or opal may be taken to symbolize the majesty or glory of God, and the blood-red sardine stone may be taken to symbolize God's justice. The "rainbow" is the conventional Biblical symbol for the ceasing of a storm, or of rest after conflict. The fact that the rainbow is spoken of as being "emerald" or green in color,—green being of all colors the most restful to the eye,—emphasizes the idea of peace which the symbol of the rainbow is intended to convey.

Verse 4 *"And round about the throne were four and twenty seats: and upon the seats I saw four and twenty elders sitting, clothed in white raiment; and they had on their heads crowns of gold."*

This verse introduces a passage extending to the end of the 8th verse, which is a description of the Holy Spirit, the redeemed human consciousness in the service of God, the description being suggested by numerous symbols, most of which seem strange to western thought. The reign of the Christ or of the Holy Spirit in human consciousness is synonymous with the millennial period or experience. It is almost impossible for the writer to describe the mental paths by which he finally arrived at the interpretation of the passage included in verses 4-8, and it would be tedious and fruitless for him to do so, if he could. When one studies a puzzle-picture, turning it first this way and then that, in order to discover the concealed figure, after he has discovered it, he could scarcely remember all the different angles at which he held it while he was looking for the figure, nor could he give any definite reason why he had not seen it sooner; for, when seen, it is perfectly evident, though wholly hidden up to the instant that it is seen. If it were important for another to see the hidden figure in the picture, the thing for the discoverer to do would be to simply show the other the outlines of that figure. Once the other had seen it, he would need no arguments to convince him that it was there, and no arguments to convince him what animal or other object the hidden picture was intended to represent.

This passage in verses 4-8 is distinctly a mental puzzle-picture, in which the hidden figure is the Holy Spirit. The writer believes that all that is necessary to enable any reader to see this fact is for him to be shown the mental outlines of the figure, regardless of the processes by which the writer discovered it; but the reader may have to wait until all the outlines presented in the entire five verses have been shown before he clearly sees and is wholly convinced. It is the *ensemble* that is convincing, rather than the separate parts considered by themselves; and it needs the vision of the whole in order to see the significance of the several parts,—just as, in finding the hidden figure in a puzzle-picture, one could probably not see clearly the head or a foot until he saw the whole figure.

For the present, the reader will largely have to take the writer's mere statement for the fact that the *"four and twenty elders"* are to be considered collectively as symbolizing the Holy Spirit. There is not enough detail to the symbolism concerning these "elders" to make it possible to determine with certainty in what specific capacity they were thought of by John as a figurative presentation of the Spirit, though of the general meaning there can be no doubt. After many hours of consideration at many and various times, it seems to the author most probable that these "elders" were thought of by John as symbolizing the *leading ideas* or *manifestations* of Mind, such as liberty, justice, changelessness, purity, and the like, the number "twenty-four" (a multiple of "two" and "twelve") signifying that these ideas *are* manifestations of Mind (see Note 2 of the Introduction), having no special significance in its literal numerical sense,—that is, the number of right ideas or manifestations is not to be considered as being limited to "twenty-four" in number.

It may be that these "four and twenty elders" were thought of by John as representing the twelve patriarchs or heads of tribes of the Old Testament and the twelve apostles of Christ, regarded as heads of his church, which is to include all mankind, Gentiles as well as Jews; but, in this case, the patriarchs and apostles are to be considered representatively as standing for *all* Jews and Gentiles, indicating that they will all come into the service of God.

The phrases *"clothed in white raiment"* and *"on their heads crowns of gold"* indicate that these "elders" are free from sin and are crowned with the authority of God.

Verse 5 *"And out of the throne proceeded lightnings, and thunderings, and voices: and there were seven lamps of fire burning before the throne, which are the seven Spirits of God."*

The "lightnings" symbolize the enlightening quality of the Holy Spirit and the swiftness or immediateness of its judgments; the "thunderings" signify the majesty and power of the Spirit, and the "voices" its intelligence and evangelizing character. *"The seven lamps of fire burning before the throne"* which are spoken of as identical with *"the seven Spirits of God"* are the seven chief manifestations of the Christ-mind, which have been described and discussed at length in the comment on the Angels of the Churches in Section I.

Verse 6 *"And before the throne there was a sea of glass like unto crystal."*

In this first clause of verse 6, the redeemed human consciousness, the Holy Spirit, is again presented under the figure of "a sea of glass like unto crystal", symbolizing the fact that this spiritualized consciousness, in its absolute loyalty to Truth, will be changeless and immovable as glass, and transparent as crystal, because it will contain nothing which will need to be concealed.

Verse 6 (second sentence) *"And in the midst of the throne, and round about the throne, were four beasts full of eyes before and behind.*

7 *"And the first beast was like a lion, and the second beast like a calf, and the third beast had a face as a man, and the fourth beast was like a flying eagle.*

8 *"And the four beasts had each of them six wings about him; and they were full of eyes within: and they rest not day and night, saying, Holy, Holy, Holy, Lord God Almighty, which was, and is, and is to come."* *

In the verses of this passage is given a piece of imagery which seems to have perplexed students of Revelation more than any other part of the book. The author has read nearly a score of different interpretations of what St. John is supposed to have meant by this passage,—interpretations given by expositors recognized as having been men of scholarly attainments; yet none of these, as it seems to the author, have clearly apprehended what the interpretation of this passage from a wholly spiritual point of view enables us to see.

The key to what seems to the author to be the right interpretation is given by the fact that these *"four beasts"* (better translated, as in practically all modern translations, *"four living creatures"*) are represented as being *"in the midst of the throne, and round about the throne"* (which is a fair and exact rendering of the Greek text); that is, they are represented as having exactly the same position as the four and twenty elders (see verse 4) and as "the Lamb", or the Christ (see verse 6 of chapter 5). Now, if the "throne" were material, or if the four living creatures or the twenty-four elders were corporealities, the physical law that two or more material objects cannot occupy the same place at the same time would interdict the possibility that the above description could be true. But if the four living creatures be regarded as wholly mental, then they could literally *pervade* both the divine Mind and the redeemed mentalities of the representative elders.

---

* Compare Ezekiel 1:5-25.

We must consider the further fact that these four living creatures, being represented as *"in the midst of the throne"*, are presented as occupying exactly the same mental position as the Christ, who, in verse 6 of chapter 5, is also presented as being *"in the midst of the throne"*. In all Biblical literature there is only one entity represented as being as close to God, the Father, as is Christ, the Son; and that third entity is "the Holy Spirit", which "proceeds from the Father and the Son", and is "one" with the Father and the Son. In all carefully considered theological definitions of the Holy Spirit, it, or he, is represented as being the manifestation of God and the Christ in the consciousness of humanity. These facts, taken together with the fact that the whole chapter is dealing with the relation of redeemed humanity to God, gives us an indication, which we can presently confirm, that the four living creatures are intended to symbolize the redeemed human consciousness, that consciousness in which there is the presence and the rule of the Comforter, the Holy Spirit.

The Holy Spirit, the spirit of Truth in human consciousness, if we are to have a complete account of it, must be regarded from two standpoints,—not only as "coming *down*" from God, in which case it is well symbolized by *"the seven Spirits before the throne"*, but also as "coming *up*" to God, in which case it is aptly symbolized by the four living creatures, as we shall presently see.

"Four" is often used in the Apocalypse and elsewhere in a collective sense. For instance, *"the four winds of the earth"*, mentioned in verse 1 of chapter 7, is an expression manifestly intended to signify *all* destructive forces, or the *one* destructive agency, satan. In addition to the fact that, according to the idiom of his own language, St. John could use the term "four" in this connection without implying a denial of the unity of the manifestation that he was describing, there was a special reason why he should use that term, namely, the fact that, in Hebrew usage, "seven" was a Spirit-sign, while "four" was a world-sign, both signifying *all,* or the totality of what-

ever class or manifestation is being described. Accordingly, *"the seven Spirits of God before the throne"* indicate the *divine* factor in awakened consciousness, the spirit of Truth, while *"the four living creatures"* indicate the *human* factor in *awakened* but not yet fully spiritualized human consciousness, which was formerly in the service of the world rather than of God. Clear thinking requires, however, that we should understand that a world-serving consciousness cannot be *made into* a God-serving consciousness, but that the world-serving factor in human consciousness is being gradually *replaced* by Spirit-serving consciousness, and that finally this replacing process will be complete. However, this replacing process is so gradual that the redeemed human consciousness seems to gradually *come up* from the world-serving plane on the one side, as it actually comes from God, the Spirit-serving plane, on the other side. There being this perfectly evident reason for representing the redeemed human consciousness under the symbol of "four", according to the current Hebrew usage (such usage of "four" in the sense of the total or one being practically invariable), we need not be dissuaded from understanding that the consciousness described by St. Paul as *"the mind that is in Christ"* is here symbolized, either by the fact that *"four"* creatures are mentioned, or that they are apparently mentioned separately in verse 7, in various verses of chapter 6, and in other places in the Book. When the phrases, *"the first living creature", "the second living creature",* and so on, are mentioned, we are to understand one *phase* of the indwelling Spirit, the Comforter, or, more likely, the use of that figure of speech, common in all languages, whereby a part is used as signifying the whole,—as, for instance, when we speak of four ships as "four sail".

These four living creatures are spoken of as *"full of eyes before and behind"*, and as *"full of eyes within"*; that is, as being *composed* of eyes. In Biblical literature the "eye" is very frequently used as the symbol of spiritual intelligence. "The eyes of the Lord run to and fro throughout the whole earth" (2 Chron. 16:9). "The seeing eye the Lord hath made" (Prov. 20:12). God is "of purer eyes than to behold evil" (Hab. 1:13). "The light of the body is the eye" (Matt. 6:22). "The eyes of your understanding being enlightened" (Eph. 1:18). Hence, in terms of the usage of the Jews for centuries, the description of the living creatures as *"full of eyes before and behind and within"* is equivalent to saying that the living creatures are *composed of,* or *wholly manifest,* spiritual intelligence,—which fact exactly confirms the interpretation of the living creatures as being the symbol of spiritual consciousness, the Christ-consciousness or the indwelling Holy Spirit.

In verse 7, we are told that the first living creature was like a lion and the second like a calf, and the third had a man-face, and the fourth was like a flying eagle. One may see at a glance what this imagery means, viz., that the four chief phases of the redeemed human consciousness (the four living creatures considered collectively) are: *moral courage,* symbolized by the lion; *sacrifice* (not slavish obedience, but loving sacrifice), symbolized by the calf, which is the Biblical symbol of priestly sacrifice; *intelligence,* symbolized by the man-face; and *holiness,* symbolized by the flying eagle, which is employed later in the Apocalypse, as we shall see, as a symbol for the Holy Spirit. If one will carefully consider, he will readily perceive that any human being, or humanity as a whole, if exercising moral courage, self-sacrifice, intelligence and holiness, is perfectly equipped for the service of God. It may be that *aspiration* toward God is a more perfect interpretation of the flying eagle than *holiness,* though they are not much different in meaning, especially when considered as a *desire* on the part of humanity. Several expositors have advanced the idea that the four living creatures symbolize moral courage, sacrifice, intelligence and aspiration, but none of them seem to have thought of these four as united, symbolizing the Christ-mind or Comforter in human consciousness.

Lastly, these four living creatures are represented as having *"each of them six wings".* Since all winged creatures in the natural world have only one pair of wings, the fact that each of these living creatures has three pairs,—or twelve pairs among them, considering them collectively,—indicates an exceeding swiftness of flight, so much so, that the possession of this number of wings' may readily be taken to symbolize *omnipresence,* another necessary quality of spiritual consciousness. If some one raises the objection that "six" is the conventional Hebrew satan-sign, it may be answered by saying that, if so, this merely indicates, as in the case of the use of "four", that the human consciousness was formerly in the service of the world and of satan. But, again, if the six wings be considered as *three pairs* of wings, which would be more natural, then we have the use of "three", which was another conventional Spirit-sign,—as, for instance, "the Father, Son, and Holy Ghost, and these *three* are one". In fact, in the conventional usage of the Jews, "three" is the most strongly spiritual symbol known to their language.

While he does not interpret the four living creatures as symbolizing the Holy Spirit manifest in human consciousness, one commentator* makes the interesting suggestion that the twenty-four wings (six each) of the four living creatures are identical with the twenty-four elders. The twenty-four elders, servants or apostles of God and His Christ, are certainly in the service of the Holy Spirit, and might very properly be regarded as "wings" for the promulgation of the Spirit among men; that is, *all* apostles of Christ are wings for the transportation or dissemination of Truth. He also makes the further interesting suggestion that each of the six wings of the living creatures corresponds to one of the six directions in space (represented by the six faces of a cube), and so symbolizes omnipresence,—an interpretation which is exactly in accord with the nature and office of the spirit of Truth.

It may clarify and make practical our understanding of the

---

*Mr. Pryse.

four living creatures, if we consider that collectively they symbolize the aggregate mental activity of those human beings who in all ages have practically demonstrated the healing and saving truth, which Christ Jesus taught, and of those who, today, are proving by their works, in casting out evils and healing the sick, the correctness of their apprehension of Truth, their possession of that Christ-mind which St. Paul declared was to be in us effectually upon this plane of experience.

Verses 9-11 *"And when those four hearts give glory and honour and thanks to him that sat on the throne, who liveth forever and ever, the four and twenty elders fall down before him that sat on the throne, and worship him that liveth forever and ever, and cast their crowns before the throne, saying: Thou art worthy, O Lord, to receive glory and honour and power: for thou hast created all things, and for thy pleasure they are and were created."*

In the Greek, verse nine is introduced by the word *hotau,* which means *whenever,* instead of *"when."* The reason for the assertion made in the verses above quoted is that the *"four beasts"* and the *"four and twenty elders"* are exactly equivalent, both, when considered collectively, symbolized the Holy Spirit or the true church. In the case of the *"four beasts,"* the manifestation of Mind is considered in four broad phases, while in the case of the *"elders"* it is considered in a larger number of more specific phases, which, however, are included in the *"four."* Accordingly, *whenever* the *"four beasts"* do anything the *"four and twenty elders"* are necessarily doing the same thing.

CHAPTER V

The Sealed Book and the Lamb Who Is to Open It

Verse 1 *"And I saw in the right hand of him that sat on the throne a book written within and on the back side, sealed with seven seals."*

John here indicates that the solution of the human problem is known only to God, the Father. Sin so enslaves the human sense that it cannot understand or "unloose" its own problems. In making the assertion given in verse 1, John is making concession to the immaturity of human understanding, as did Jesus, when he said: "But of that day and hour knoweth no man, no, not the angels of heaven, but my Father only". These are *ad hominem* ways of saying that the working out of human redemption can only be rightly understood by a quality of consciousness that is spiritual, that is elevated far above the ordinary materialistic sense of things. God "is of purer eyes than to behold evil, and cannot look upon iniquity". Hence, in the absolute, Mind can have no consciousness of the human struggle with error, since to infinite Truth there is no error, as to light there is no darkness. Yet Mind is the only basis of power which men can effectually apply to overcome evil.

It has been suggested (*) that the phrase *"written within and on the back side"* is to be interpreted as meaning that this book, when first disclosed to humanity, would have an exoteric, outer, or apparent meaning, which many would accept as the real meaning, but that it would also have an esoteric, inside, or hidden meaning,—so effectually hidden, that it is represented as being *"sealed with seven seals"*,—that is, hidden in large part from human understanding.

---
* Mr. Hughes, in "The Revelation."

Verses 2-5 *"And I saw a strong angel proclaiming with a loud voice, Who is worthy to open the book, and to loose the seals thereof? And no man in heaven, nor in earth, neither under the earth, was able to open the book, neither to look thereon. And I wept much, because no man was found worthy to open and to read the book, neither to look thereon. And one of the elders saith unto me, Weep not, behold, the lion of the tribe of Judah, the Root of David, hath prevailed to open the book, and to loose the seven seals thereof."*

The *"strong angel"* of verse 2 fittingly symbolizes one of the higher phases of John's spiritual consciousness. These verses as a whole represent John's method of emphasizing the importance of what he saw, and that it might be disclosed, if a way could be found. The Christ-man is, of course, *"the lion of the tribe of Judah"*, and, being the true selfhood of every human being, he is *"the Root"* of every man, and was *"the Root of David"*. This Christ-man, being "lifted up", or enthroned in the consciousness of John, broke for John the seals of ignorance which had hidden from him the knowledge of the future, even as this same Christ-man, if we lift him up, or attain unto him, will reveal to us all that he revealed to John, —will make known to us "the way of Life".

Verse 6 *"And I beheld, and, lo, in the midst of the throne and of the four beasts, and in the midst of the elders, stood a Lamb as it had been slain, having seven horns and seven eyes, which are the seven Spirits of God sent forth into all the earth."*

The Lamb is, manifestly, the Christ-consciousness, which pervades the spiritual church (which is *"the throne"* of God), *"the four beasts"*, and the consciousness of *"the elders"*, as explained in the comment on chapter 4. *"Having seven horns and seven eyes"* means having *all* the power and knowledge of God, which knowledge and power, considered collectively, is the Holy Spirit, *"the seven Spirits of God"*,—the spiritualized human consciousness in its militant work of saving the world.

Verse 7 *"And he came and took the book out of the right hand of him that sat on the throne."*

This is a figurative way of saying that the Christ-consciousness, operating in John's mentality, was about to reveal *"the things which are, and the things which shall be hereafter"*.

Verses 8-14 *"And when he had taken the book, the four beasts and four and twenty elders fell down before the Lamb, having every one of them harps, and golden vials full of odors, which are the prayers of saints. And they sung a new song, saying, Thou art worthy to take the book, and to open the seals thereof: for thou wast slain, and hast redeemed us to God by thy blood out of every kindred, and tongue, and people, and nation* (All modern authorities agree that the last half of this verse should be rendered: "and hast redeemed to God by thy blood *men* out of every kindred, and tongue, and people, and nation"); *and hast made us* (them) *unto our God kings and priests: and we* (they) *shall reign on the earth. And I beheld, and I heard the voice of many angels round about the throne and the beasts and the elders: and the number of them was ten thousand times ten thousand, and thousands of thousands; saying with a loud voice, Worthy is the Lamb that was slain to receive power, and riches, and wisdom, and strength, and honor, and glory, and blessing. And every creature which is in heaven, and on the earth, and under the earth, and such as are in the sea, and all that are in them, heard I saying, Blessing, and honour, and glory, and power, be unto him that sitteth upon the throne, and unto the Lamb for ever and ever. And the four beasts said, Amen. And the four and twenty elders fell down and worshipped him that liveth for ever and* **ever."**

There is little in this passage that requires comment, except perhaps to say that this is the first of a series of similar chants interspersed in the Book between the different acts, and John probably got the idea of such insertion from the chants in the Greek dramas.

NOTES BY THE READER

CHAPTER VI

The Opening of the Seals

The First Seal

Verse 1 *"And I saw when the lamb opened one of the seals, and I heard, as it were the noise of thunder, one of the four beasts say, Come and see."*

"The Lamb", removing John's ignorance with regard to one phase of what was to be made known, was his dawning spiritual consciousness, and it was also this same spiritual consciousness which was *"as it were the noise of thunder, one of the four beasts saying, come and see"*. Divine Mind, the Christ-consciousness, and the Holy Spirit are indeed "one" in office, and are inseparable in essence. Divine Mind as the Christ makes a revelation to John, and one phase of the Christ-mind or the Holy Spirit (*"one of the four beasts"*) summons John to behold the revelation. The *"thunder"* symbolizes the power and majesty of the message. The phase of the Christ-consciousness which here speaks to John is that *"like a lion"*, and summons John to behold *"the lion of the tribe of Judah"*, the Christ, under a different figure, as we shall see in the next verse.

Verse 2 *"And I saw, and behold a white horse: and he that sat on him had a bow; and a crown was given unto him: and he went forth conquering, and to conquer."*

We here have the Christ-idea, entering upon the conquest of the world, under the figure of a white horse with his rider. In chapter 19:11, we shall find him under the same figure, just in the process of finishing his task. The bow is symbolical of the power of the Christ-consciousness to "shoot" the truth into human consciousness; in other words, it symbolizes the militant attitude of the Christ. The crown is the symbol of his authority.

The Second Seal

Verse 3 *"And when he had opened the second seal, I heard the second beast say, Come and see."*

The Christ-consciousness, in its second phase, that of self-sacrifice ("like a calf"), summons John to behold the first great obstacle which the militant Christ meets in the human consciousness,—namely, self-assertiveness or human will, opposed to self-sacrifice, as we shall see in the next verse.

Verse 4 *"And there went out another horse that was red: and power was given to him that sat thereon to take peace from the earth, and that they should kill one another: and there was given unto him a great sword."*

Wherever human will is set up as governor, there peace departs, and men begin to kill one another. The significance of the symbolism and teaching of this seal is very aptly, though inadequately, illustrated in the career of Napoleon Bonaparte and attendant results, also in the present (1914-1915) wars in Europe and in Mexico. Without doubt, the aggregation of impersonal evil in all its gigantic proportions is most fittingly symbolized by *"the red horse with his rider"*, *"the great red dragon"*, and by *"the horned beasts"* of Revelation. A mere Napoleon or any other person is seen to be a trivial thing indeed when compared to the lust, the false belief, of the world, considered as a whole.

A current number of The Literary Digest (March 6, 1915) gives some excellent examples of the activities of the carnal mind which are symbolized by *the red horse and his rider,* and which *"take peace from the earth";* namely, the attempt at domination by human will, conceit and selfishness under the guise of what is supposed to be "patriotism." Writing in the Berlin *Deutsche Tageszeitung,* Count von Reventlow says:

"Germans will do much more than persevere. They will fight until everything complies with their will—a will that vehemently and without scruple puts all means into its service by which it desires to arrive at its aim."

Writing in the *Frankfurter Zeitung,* Professor von Leyden, of the University of Berlin, declares:

"Germany must and will stand alone. The Germans are the salt of the earth; they will fulfill their destiny, which is to rule the world and to control other nations for the benefit of mankind.....There are the neutral nations....Most of them entertain hostile feelings against Germany. We do not need them. They are not necessary to our happiness nor to our more material interests. Let us ban them from our houses and our tables. Let us make them feel that we despise them. They must understand that they are to be left out in the cold just because they do not merit German approval."*

In the Munich *Neueste Nachrichten,* Dr. Karl Wolff counsels the German people as follows:

"Thou shalt have no other thought than of this war: for its consequences of disaster, if we are vanquished, shall make themselves felt to the third and fourth generation. But it will bear blest fruit unto the tenth generation if we know how to conquer and found the world anew as a German product.

"Thou shalt not take in vain the terrible name of War, neither in gross pleasantry, nor in foolish derision, nor in any way unworthily, by word or picture.

"The German soul shall continue to spread over the world, mighty in its culture, full of understanding, and gathering into the treasure-store of the Fatherland all that all the nations hold as most precious."

Such false ambitions as these started the latest war in Europe, and have started the majority of the wars whose records blacken the pages of human history. Such false ambitions as these are not by any means confined to the

---

* Just as this book is going to press, the author learns that this statement has been discredited, as coming from Professor von Leyden. However, somebody wrote it, and so it illustrates just as well the kind of motive which is the cause of war.

German people. They can be found dominating the hearts and minds of great numbers of Americans, English, French, Russians, Japanese, and of peoples of every nation and race, to a greater or less extent. How aptly did St. John declare, in symbolic language: *"And there went out* [from and in mortal mentality] *another horse that was red: and power was given to him that sat thereon to take peace from the earth, and that they should kill one another; and there was given unto him a great sword."*

The following from an editorial in the *Chicago Examiner* of March 17, 1915, well sums up the situation as to the present war:

"Russia is at war to gain her centuries-old object of seizing Constantinople and welding the Slav peoples into a world-dominating Slav empire.

"Austria is at war to hinder Russia's aggrandizement and to blot out the Serbian and Montenegrin nationalities.

"France is at war to regain prestige and to recover Alsace-Lorraine.

"Serbia is at war because racial and religious antipathies and Russian money and intrigue controlled the assassin who made himself king of that turbulent country by double murder of his royal predecessors.

"Japan is at war because she plots to seize China and exploit the riches and resources of that populous and helpless country in building up a great Asiatic world power.

"Germany is at war because she means to remain the predominating power in Europe.

"And Great Britain is at war because German industry, patience and skill were rapidly taking the trade of the world from British financiers, manufacturers and ship-owners, and events gave Great Britain a chance to destroy that trade competition by a war in which all other parties to the conflict were bound to suffer more loss than Great Britain, no matter which way victory went.

"This war is just like every other European war—a slaughter of the peoples for the benefit and gains of the autocratic and aristocratic classes."

The Third Seal

Verses 5, 6 *"And when he had opened the third seal, I heard the third beast say, Come and see. And I beheld, and lo a black horse; and he that sat on him had a pair of balances in his hand, And I heard a voice in the midst of the four beasts say, A measure of wheat for a penny, and three measures of barley for a penny; and see thou hurt not the oil and the wine."*

The Christ-mind or Holy Spirit, manifest as spiritual intelligence ("face as a man"), summons John to behold the activity of its opposite, materialism and selfish stupidity, as the second opponent to the militant Christ. Material sense and selfishness value things above men, matter above intelligence.

The black horse and his rider may be taken as a symbol for "commercialism" in its selfish and greedy form, in which it would extort, if it could, something like a silver denarius ("a penny" of Bible times, worth in purchasing value in the present day about a dollar, the current day's wage for common labor) for a quart, or ration, (*choenix,* "measure") of wheat, and a denarius for three rations of barley.

We may not be entirely sure what St. John meant by the phrase *"and see thou hurt not the oil and the wine",* since in these words so few details are given that there is practically no basis at all for a satisfactory analysis. Hence, we are thrown back wholly upon a consideration of what our sense of John's thought in general would lead us to expect him to mean in this connection, together with our knowledge of the sense in which the words *"oil"* and *"wine"* are employed in the Scriptures generally, where they are sometimes used literally and sometimes symbolically.

The phrase has been interpreted to mean, "put the oil and the wine out of reach altogether", making the whole sentence equivalent to a declaration to modern common laborers in America:

A quart of wheat for a day's wages, and three quarts of barley for a day's wages; and see that you do not touch butter and milk.

This interpretation is only possible by a very strained translation of the Greek *mê adikêsês,* the natural meaning of which is "hurt not", as in the Authorized Version.

On the whole it seems best not to take *"the oil and the wine"* literally, but symbolically, in a sense in which they are often employed in the Scriptures, denoting faith and inspiration. These words being thus interpreted, the phrase *"see thou hurt not the oil and the wine"* seems to be an assurance from the Holy Spirit *("a voice in the midst of the four beasts")* that mortal sense, in all its selfish and murderous doing, in all its domination and imposition, and in all its long-drawn period of apparent ascendency, will never be able to suppress spiritual aspiration and consecration to spiritual ideals in the human consciousness.

Probably the wheat and the barley should also be taken symbolically, as well as the oil and the wine; in which case, the whole sentence would indicate that the selfish and greedy assertiveness of mortal sense produces in human consciousness a great famine of "the bread of life," of the demonstrable knowledge of God and of His Christ, which is life eternal, but does not cut off the spiritual consecration and inspiration which hold humanity anchored against the tide of materialism until the latter has run its course and become inert.

The experience of humanity in the last eighteen hundred years would seem to justify such a declaration. Until very recently, there has been in all these centuries very little spiritual knowledge of a demonstrable kind,—of a kind which would heal the sick, or effectually and promptly reform the sinner without leaving him to struggle in the throes of human will and which would serve as a reliable basis for overcoming poverty and want; and thus, there has been a famine of "that bread which cometh down from heaven" which actually feeds people in their daily lives; but during all these centuries a degree of inspiration which has kept alive in the human consciousness a vital sense of God and a faithful consecration to the call of religion with a confident expectation of the triumph of good farther on has never been destroyed nor even seriously "hurt".

This would seem to indicate the true import of John's message in this verse. In any case, it may be said with assurance that there could be no material famine, let mortal sense do what it would, unless it first produced a spiritual famine, since to those who are really "rich toward God", a sufficient supply of this world's goods is infallibly "added". Said Christ Jesus: *"Be not anxious, saying, What shall we eat? or, What shall we drink? or Wherewithal shall we be clothed? . . . But seek ye first the Kingdom of God and his righteousness; and all these things shall be added unto you"* (R. V.); and our Lord knew whereof he spake, when he made this declaration.

It would seem that we are now entering upon the period when the black horse and his rider are beginning to be overcome, and when humanity will use and enjoy not only *"the oil and the wine"*, but the *"wheat"* and the *"barley"*, of spiritual life,—when here and now men shall partake of spiritual bread and wine.

The general facts indicating the arrival of such a period are two-fold. *First,* materialism as a theory has run its course. The men most wise in the world's wisdom, the leading natural scientists, have openly confessed that neither matter nor force, nor anything else discoverable in the realm of natural science, furnishes an adequate explanation of the universe or of innumerable activities which the natural scientist daily observes; and so these men are openly turning to an assumed First Cause, God, infinite Mind, as the only sufficient interpretation of the things that are and of the things that live. The collapse of materialism in theory is bound to be followed by the collapse of materialism in practice, since, in the long account, the activities of men are governed by their ideals, though, through the inertia of ignorance and habit, practice lags behind theory as the tides lag behind the moon which causes them.

If the demonstrable truth, made known to humanity in Christian Science, had been active in the human world long enough to have reached and influenced the masses of Europe, the present (1915) war would never have started. It commenced and is being carried on only because the majority have not yet learned that materialism, in all its phases, is false doctrine, and so have continued to be deceived by it, as an inheritance from the ignorance of the past. But if the leaders of human thinking continue to teach that materialism is not the permanent truth and reality of being, and if they teach that the nature of God (Spirit) furnishes the only reliable standard by which to measure thought, feeling and conduct, and if they live, so far as may be for the present and increasingly, in a manner consistent with their teachings, and succeed in influencing the masses of the people to think, feel and act likewise, further wars will be impossible. It may be regarded as certain that as long as materialism is regarded as truth by the great majority of the world's people, wars and famines will periodically occur, but—

Second, the healing of the sick, the reforming of the sinner, and the overcoming of poverty and discord of various kinds, through the understanding and enforcement of the power of God,—these practical works are now being done in every land, and there is every indication of a rapid and more widespread increase of these activities, so that, as indicated above, the author believes that materialism, as a predominant force in the world, will soon be found to have received its death-blow.

NOTES BY THE READER

The Fourth Seal

Verses 7, 8 *"And when he had opened the fourth seal I heard the voice of the fourth beast say, Come and see. And I looked, and behold a pale horse; and his name that sat on him was Death, and Hell followed with him, and power was given unto them over the fourth part of the earth, to kill with the sword, and with hunger, and with the beasts of the earth."*

The Christ with us, manifest as holiness (*"like a flying eagle"*, aspiration after Spirit), summons John to behold its opposite, sensuality, worldly lust, as the third opponent in human consciousness to the militant Christ. This is symbolized by the pale horse and his rider. Sensuality constitutes the chief cause of *"death and hell"* in human experience; and, in the sense of being opposite to Spirit, which is Life and harmony, sensuality is itself death and discord,—"dead" to all that is pure and true. In this 8th verse, sensuality is rightly said to dominate something like a fourth of human activity, and to lead to war and famine and death and persecution. Sensuality and worldliness have repeatedly led rulers to throw followers of the Christ, spiritually minded men, into the arena, to be devoured by "beasts of the earth". On the field of individual experience, sensuality will seem to kill the spiritual life, if it be given sway, with mental conflict ("the sword"), and with a famine of truth and good ("hunger"), and with absolute materialism ("death"), and with animal passion ("beasts of the earth").

In this chapter, we have seen the carnal mind, manifest as human ambition, under the symbol of a red horse with his rider; later, especially in chapter 12, we shall see it as "a great red dragon", symbolizing "that old serpent, the devil and satan". We have seen the dominance of worldly government, human will actuated by greed, under the symbol of a black horse with his rider; later, especially in chapter 13, we shall see it under the symbol of a seven-headed, ten-horned beast. We have seen sensuality under the symbol of a pale horse with his rider; later, especially in chapters 17 and 18, we shall see it under the figure of a woman arrayed in purple and scarlet, "the great whore", Babylon, the worldly city.

AN EXCERPT

The following from the author's pamphlet, "The Cause and Cure of War," was not written with verses 3-8 of chapter VI in view, but seems worth reprinting here as a commentary upon them

When men thoroughly learn the divine nature, and are supremely seeking to live on the higher spiritual planes, they will be less concerned about material luxuries and the gratification of fleshly appetites. Material comfort all men are entitled to, as long as they still dwell in material sense at all; and when all are satisfied with comfort in human living, not seeking material extravagances because their supreme interest and affections are set on things above, there will be plenty of material supplies in every country for all, without need for one country to try to enrich itself at the expense of others. When greed, selfishness, avarice and sensuous pleasures are removed, then each nation can begin to solve the problem of properly distributing its material resources and supplies among its own citizens. Then all will have enough,—all that is needful while they are learning the higher things of Spirit, which is the only legitimate end of human living. If, for instance, in England, the landed aristocracy would give up their shooting preserves and other large tracts held merely for selfish, material enjoyment, so that this land could be distributed among numbers of small farmers, England would not need to worry about maintaining control of the seas lest her food supply might be cut off.* One of the main producing causes

---

*That the above may not seem a mere unwarranted assertion on the part of the author, the following may be quoted from Mr. Frank Harris, long a resident of England, and formerly editor of *The Fortnightly Review,* also of *The Saturday Review:*

"Thanks to the greed of England's landowning oligarchy, she does not produce one-quarter enough food to supply her own wants; this is

of war is, that the ruling classes of many nations not only take to themselves more of the material products of their own countries than is needful to serve their own highest good, but, even in addition to this, bring their countries into war, every now and then, for the purpose of adding to their gains at the expense of other nations. When finally, however, the divine nature comes to rule in the hearts of men, this sort of thing will cease to happen.

There will always be more or less strife and ill feeling among mortals as long as some are ruled by others; yet the necessity for some to hold sway over others will continue until all have reached practically an equal understanding of God and His law. When all are acquainted with and recognize in conduct the supremacy of the divine law, every man will be governed by the law of God and cannot trespass on his brothers' rights. Thus will be removed all need of legislatures, courts, police officers, and every other form of the machinery of government having to do with the regulation of matters of personal conduct. This is divine autocracy or the true democracy.

But this equality in the understanding of God cannot come through material generation or the propagation of the human species, the offspring of the carnal mind. So long as the fleshly mind conceives and embodies its sensual progeny, the machinery of material government and the domination of one human will over another must continue to result in war, pestilence, famine, disease, and death.

---

the Achilles heel of England. . . . Nothing will ever teach the English oligarchy or dissipate their pleasure-sodden dream of perpetual parasitical enjoyment except defeat in war. . . . One-third of England's population is always on the verge of starvation. . . . More than a hundred years ago, Tom Paine declared that nothing would civilize England till the blood of her children had been shed on her own hearths. It will take a defeat in war to wrest the land of England from the lords who stole it and give it back to the people."

The millennium, the period of perfect harmony among men, will appear only when the fact comes to be both theoretically and practically realized, that God is the only creator and Father, and that the only real man,—man in the image and likeness of God, and therefore spiritual,—is already born —eternally borne forth of divine creative thinking. Jesus said: "Call no man your father upon the earth: for one is your Father, which is in heaven" (Matt. 23:9). St. Paul declared: "They which are the children of the flesh, these are not the children of God." If God is the only creator, then those which are not His children are not real or actual men. It is the continued propagation of the mortal or false sense of man that continues the troubles to which humanity is heir. When the spiritual facts of being are understood, it will become apparent to all that man is already born and emanates from God. Error will then cease to usurp God's prerogative of creatorship. When humanity as a whole discerns spiritually God's allness and man as the image and likeness of eternal Life, Truth, and Love, there will be no more death, neither sorrow, nor sighing, for the former false material senses will have passed away.

As recorded in the 20th chapter of St. Luke, Jesus declared: "The children of this world marry, and are given in marriage: but they which shall be accounted worthy to obtain that world, and the resurrection from the dead, neither marry, nor are given in marriage; *neither can they die any more:* for they are equal unto the angels; and are the children of God, being the children of the resurrection." In some apocryphal sayings of Jesus, discovered a number of years ago in a fragment of old manuscript, and which are considered by scholars genuine, it is related that one of the disciples of Jesus asked him, "When will death cease?" His reply was, "When your women cease to bear children."

In proportion as human birth ceases when it shall cease because of increasing spirituality and the consequent suppression of carnality and fleshly impulse in human consciousness, in that proportion death will cease also; so the earth will not be depopulated as a result of the cessation of birth by reason of increased knowledge of God. As Mrs. Eddy has said in "Science and Health" (page 64): "Until it is learned that God is the Father of all, marriage will continue;" but "Spirit will ultimately claim its own,—all that really is,—and the voices of physical sense will be forever hushed."

When the works of the flesh are brought to an end through the increase of spirituality, and children of the flesh or the counterfeit creation no longer appear, then man as the child of God will be more fully revealed on earth. Then will a petition in the Lord's prayer have received its answer, "Thy kingdom come, Thy will be done, on earth as it is in heaven," and the prophecy of Jeremiah will be fulfilled: "And they shall teach no more every man his neighbor, and every man his brother, saying, Know the Lord: for they shall all know Me, from the least of them unto the greatest of them, saith the Lord." This is a forecast of the millennium, also foretold in Revelation 20:1-3, and by Mrs. Eddy, in the following words:

"Mortals can never understand God's creation while believing that man is a creator. God's children already created will be cognized only as man finds the truth of being. Thus it is that the real, ideal man appears in proportion as the false and material disappears. No longer to marry or to be 'given in marriage' neither closes man's continuity nor his sense of increasing number in God's infinite plan. Spiritually to understand that there is but one creator, God, unfolds all creation, confirms the Scriptures, brings the sweet assurance of no parting, no pain, and of man deathless and perfect and eternal." ("Science and Health," p. 69.)

The Fifth Seal

Verses 9-11 *"And when he had opened the fifth seal, I saw under the altar the souls of them that were slain for the word of God, and for the testimony which they held: and they cried with a loud voice, saying, How long, O Lord, holy and true, dost thou not judge and avenge our blood on them that dwell on the earth? And white robes were given unto every one of them; and it was said unto them, that they should rest yet for a little season, until their fellow-servants also and their brethren, that should be killed as they were, should be fulfilled."*

So persistent and subtle is the satanic activity, that it manages to find a field for its operations even in the mentalities of those so wedded to the Christ that they are willing to suffer martyrdom; and so, until the very end of satanic rule, the one evil manages to oppose the Christ even in the camp of his own followers, arguing discouragement and revenge, if it can do nothing more. Discouragement and revenge are very great and subtle hindrances to spiritual progress for those who have not suffered martyrdom as well as for those who have.

As has been said: "Discouragement is the more sinister because it is generally looked upon as harmless. In fable it is told that the devil one night held a sale and offered all his tools to any one who would pay his price. These were spread out for sale, some labeled hatred, and envy, and sickness, and sensuality, and despair, and crime,—a motley array. Apart from the rest lay a harmless-looking, wedge-shaped implement marked 'discouragement'. It was much worn and was priced above the rest, showing that it was held in high esteem by its owner. When asked the reason the devil replied, 'I can use this more easily than any of the others, for so few know it belongs to me. With this I can open doors that I cannot move with the others, and once I get inside I can use whichever of them suits me best' ".*

---
* Wm. R. Rathvon.

While the Apocalypse depicts discouragement and revenge as great hindrances to the complete triumph of the Christ, it seems to indicate, in verse 11, that these sins of the human consciousness are comparatively excusable, since those manifesting these satanic activities are given the "white robes" of purification and pardon, and are recommended to wait patiently until satanic activity has spent its force and is completely overcome.

The Sixth Seal

Verses 12-17 *"And I beheld when he had opened the sixth seal, and, lo, there was a great earthquake;· and the sun became black as sackcloth of hair, and the moon became as blood; and the stars of heaven fell unto the earth. even as a fig tree casteth her untimely figs, when she is shaken of a mighty wind. And the heaven departed as a scroll when it is rolled together; and every mountain and island were moved out of their places. And the kings of the earth, and the great men, and the rich men, and the chief captains, and the mighty men, and every bondman, and every free man, hid themselves in the dens and in the rocks of the mountains; and said to the mountains and rocks, Fall on us, and hide us from the face of him that sitteth on the throne, and from the wrath of the Lamb: for the great day of his wrath is come; and who shall be able to stand?"*

And when the sixth seal was opened, it revealed a mighty disturbance (*"earthquake"*) as about to occur. It revealed that the light of divine Mind (*"the sun"*) would be almost completely obscured from human mental vision, and that the light of the Christ-consciousness (*"the moon"*) would seem to change its character; and that many of those who would try to be Christians (*"stars of heaven"*), making some progress, would not be permitted to become mature in Christian faith and practice, as a result of false doctrine and schism, but would be cast from such heights as they should attain to in the mental realm (*"heaven"*) back into materialism and false belief (*"the earth"*), even as a fig tree casteth off her unripe figs when she is shaken by a mighty wind. And harmony (*"the heaven"*) would depart as a scroll vanishes mostly from sight when it is rolled up; and every established institution of society (*"every mountain and island"*) would be moved out of their places. And the kings of the earth, and the great men, and the rich men, and the generals, and the mighty men, and every slave, and every free man, would be so smitten with consternation, because of the fear of death by war, assassination, or torture, that they would be inclined to hide themselves in the dens and in the rocks of the mountains, and would often do so; and they would be so crazed with fear over the mighty upheavals and devastating strifes that would happen as a result of false doctrine and schism, that they would gladly have the mountains and rocks fall on them, thinking, in their frenzy, that death might hide them from the terrible state of affairs which they would think was resulting from the zealous activity of Christ in warring against human ignorance, false belief, cruelty, tyranny, and general wrong-doing.

When the air is full of dust, as in the hot days in summer, the moon assumes a bloody appearance. So, the phrase *"the moon became as blood"*, in verse 12, suggests that the mental atmosphere of the human consciousness is charged with the "dust" of false belief, thus causing the Christ-consciousness, which really emits mental "light" which is "white" and beautifully clear, to assume in human experience a seemingly bloody and baleful aspect.

As indicated fully in Note 4 of the Introduction, the phrase *"from the wrath of the Lamb"*, in verse 16, would better be translated "from the passion of the Lamb",—that is from the *zeal* of the Christ to overcome evil with good,—which is the sense that should also be substituted for the word "wrath" in verse 17. Many important Greek manuscripts give a plural genitive, *autôn*, instead of the singular, *autou*,—according to which the rendering should be: *For the great day of their passion is come.* "Their" would thus refer both to *"the Lamb"* and to *"him that sitteth on the throne"*. Since divine Love, though not "wrath", is destructive to evil and evil-doers, the wicked very naturally seek refuge *"from the face of him that sitteth on the throne"*, as well as from the zeal of the Lamb, who but reflects the activity of divine Mind.

The activities depicted in this sixth seal find their counterpart in the activities of the two-horned beast or "false prophet", spoken of at length in the last half of chapter 13.

NOTES BY THE READER

CHAPTER VII

A Fore-vision of the First Resurrection

Verses 1-3 *"And after these things I saw four angels standing on the four corners of the earth, holding the four winds of the earth, that the wind should not blow on the earth, nor on the sea, nor on any tree. And I saw another angel ascending from the east, having the seal of the living God: and he cried with a loud voice to the four angels, to whom it was given to hurt the earth and the sea, saying, Hurt not the earth, neither the sea, nor the trees, till we have sealed the servants of our God in their foreheads."*

"After these things". This is a literal rendering of the Greek, where the English idiom would be, "After this."

The *"four angels standing on the four corners of the earth"* may be regarded as the same four which are spoken of in Matthew 24:31, who are to "gather together his (God's) elect from the four winds, from one end of heaven to the other." Compare Matthew 13:39, 41, and 2 Thes. 1:7, 8, where the angels are represented as ministers of God's power.

"The four winds of the earth" (verse 1) seem to symbolize the self-destroying forces of evil. Being from the four points of the compass, they indicate or stand for all the winds there are, and so symbolize all the destroying forces of evil there are.

These destroying forces are represented as being held in check for a time by four good angels, so that they cannot blow destructively on either the earth, or the sea, or any tree, until the servants of God shall be sealed in their foreheads,—the inference being that, after this sealing, the destroying forces will be loosed. In other words, John foresees that at some future period there will be a lull in the conflict between good and evil. This holding of the forces of evil in check cannot be intended to represent a continuing state of affairs in the mental realm, but must refer to some special period of quiescence in the world, such as history has not recorded up to the present time. Taking the customary Apocalyptic interpretation for *"the earth"* and *"the sea"* and *"any tree"*, these three verses forecast a condition when no normal human activity, emotion, or institution is destroyed or *"hurt"*, with the implication, however, that all these are strictly in abeyance, while distinctly spiritual activities are in the ascendency. It should be noted that satanic activities are those which *"hurt"* or bring discord into all normal human functions and activities, both physical and mental,—such as human procreation, digestion, breathing, circulation, secretion, etc., (all of which are symbolized by "the earth"), and such as human love and other normal emotions (which are symbolized by "the sea"), and also those other activities and institutions which are symbolized by "trees". Ultimately, the divine Mind will destroy all these, but it will do so as painlessly as light overcomes darkness; but until the time is fully come for these to be overcome and removed from human activity by the enforcement of divine Mind, that Mind has a tendency to render all these activities strong, normal, and harmonious, while it is only satanic influence, such as temptation to excess and the like, that brings weakness, disease and discord among them. During the period spoken of in the three verses which we are considering, there is to be no discord among these human activities, nor are they to be rendered incapable of use or blotted out of experience, but they are simply to be held to a minimum of activity while the servants of our God are being sealed in their foreheads.

The only period of the type here referred to, indicated in the Apocalypse, and the only like period indicated by a scientific forecasting of the working out of humanity's problem, is that described in chapter 20, verses 1-6, where satan is represented as bound for a thousand years, at the beginning of which those *"that were beheaded for the witness of Jesus, and for the word of God, and which had not worshipped the beast, neither his image"* (20:4), are resurrected (20:5), and *"live and reign with Christ* (that is, with the Truth in consciousness) *a thousand years"*. These saints are not described in the same language as is employed in describing those of chapter

7 (see verses 14-17 of that chapter), but they are probably the same company of saints or redeemed ones, since, in order to be redeemed, men would have to get the victory over every kind of tribulation and temptation. This same company is described in chapter 5, verses 9-12; it is mentioned in chapter 11:18, and this same company is seen (14:1-5) before the judgment and harvest of the world (14:6-20); and yet again (15:2, 4) before the pouring out of the seven last vials. It may be that St. John got from the choruses of the Greek dramas the idea of introducing at frequent intervals this company of the redeemed, with their songs of praise and triumph. The recurring visions of the redeemed, enjoying the fruits of victory, tend to have, in the mind of the reader, an encouraging and uplifting effect, in the midst of the recital of conflicts and woes. For this reason, they have been called "consolatory visions".

The sealing of these servants of God in their foreheads may, and probably does, refer to their resurrection from the dead in *"the first resurrection"* (20:5), which is the special sign of their sainthood and of their redemption. *"Blessed and holy is he that hath part in the first resurrection: on such the second death hath no power, but they shall be priests of God and of Christ, and shall reign with him a thousand years"* (20:6). They are *"sealed in their foreheads"*†; that is, they are given the *demonstrable understanding* that life is eternal, by being resurrected. As further evidence that their resurrection is their sealing, consider Paul's saying in Romans 8:23, which in the Twentieth Century New Testament is rendered: "We ourselves, though we have already a first gift of the Spirit— we ourselves are inwardly groaning, while we eagerly await

---

† Mr. F. L. Rawson suggests with regard to the phrase "sealed in their foreheads" that, in case a man has learned to do mental work on a spiritual basis, one can know this fact "by the brightness and softness of the look in his eye." On the other hand, "the mark of the beast" (chap. 13:16) is the hard metallic look in the eyes and the hard, horny character of the hands."

our *full adoption* as sons—the redemption of our bodies." The authorized version is: "Even we ourselves groan within ourselves, waiting for the adoption, to wit, the redemption of our body". The redemption of the body evidently is the healing of it in the case of sickness, or the resurrection of it in the case of death. This sealing or resurrection takes place while satan is bound. Since, as already indicated, *"the four winds"* (7:1) are *all* of the destroying forces of evil, the holding of them in check is the same as the binding of satan. While satan is bound, it is fair to assume that nothing normally human will be "hurt". But the implication is, that after *"the servants of our God are sealed in their foreheads"*, the winds, the destructive forces of evil, are to be loosed; and in chapter 20:7, 8, we are told that "when the thousand years are expired, satan shall be loosed out of his prison, and shall go out to deceive the nations which are in the four quarters of the earth" (that is, just where the four winds of the earth, of chapter 7:1, are held in check for a time, and are then loosed). The nations are gathered by satan for battle against the saints and the city of God; and so discord and tumult again reign for a time, but finally satan and the forces of evil are overthrown and "cast into the lake of fire and brimstone, where they shall be tormented (Greek, *rubbed against the touch-stone*) day and night for ever and ever"*; that is, they shall be utterly destroyed. After this occurs the second or general resurrection, and then the destruction of the sense of matter, and then full realization of the spiritual city of God as depicted in chapter 21. Questions about the first and second resurrections, the loosing of satan for a season after the millennium, the final judgment, and what occasions these events, will be discussed much more fully in the notes on chapter 20, which see.

The *"angel ascending from the east, having the seal of the living God"* is undoubtedly the Christ, who says to the four

---

* Greek, "unto the ages of the ages"; that is, until the end of time, but *not* in eternity, or "forever."

angels, Do not let the self-destroying forces of evil get loose to make any further disturbance, *"till we have sealed the servants of our God in their forehead."* The four angels are four good angels, not four destructive ones. It is not in their power to *"hurt"*, except in the negative way of letting go their supposed hold upon the self-destroying forces of evil, which they will only do at the proper time in order that evil may go to self-destruction. *"The east"*, being the region of the dawn of material light, symbolizes divine Mind, the Source of spiritual light, from which the Christ *"ascends"*.

"The four angels standing on the four corners of the earth", considered collectively, represent the spiritual factor in human consciousness, enforcing the law of God, the law of harmony, against the *"four winds of the earth"*. These four angels, collectively, represent Immanuel, the Holy Spirit, the militant activity of God and His Christ in human consciousness. Because this human consciousness has formerly been in the service of the world, it is symbolized by the world-sign *"four"*; otherwise, the activity of the divine Mind would doubtless have been here symbolized by *seven* angels, rather than *"four"*. These *"four* Angels" may very properly be considered as synonymous with the "four beasts" of chapter IV, both, collectively, being the Holy Spirit.

Verse 4 *"And I heard the number of them which were sealed: and there were sealed an hundred and forty and four thousand of all the tribes of the children of Israel."*

The *"hundred and forty and four thousand"* surely represent redeemed Israel. The number is symbolic, signifying *the conquerors manifesting God,* and stands for a great host. Ultimately *"all Israel shall be saved"* (Romans 11:26), but some not until the final resurrection. In verse 9, the redeemed from the nations of the Gentiles are spoken of, a *"great multitude".* Ultimately, *all* the Gentiles are to be redeemed. *"This is good and acceptable in the sight of God our Saviour, who will have all men to be saved, and to come unto the knowledge of the truth"* (1 Tim. 2:3, 4), but the complete redemption of many will not be effected until the last judgment, the final separation between truth and error.

Verses 16, 17 *"They shall hunger no more, neither thirst any more; neither shall the sun light on them, nor any heat. For the Lamb which is in the midst of the throne shall feed them, and shall lead them unto living fountains of waters: and God shall wipe away all tears from their eyes."*

Whoever eats of material food and drinks of material water very soon hungers and thirsts again. But whoever thoroughly assimilates divine Truth and Love into his consciousness has them as continuing possessions, which never pass away, which never have to be relearned, but which are always ready in consciousness for use. Since the terms "consciousness" and "life" are practically synonymous, Truth and Love, which are the support of consciousness, are the support of life, and are *"living fountains of waters"*.

The Seventh Seal

Chapter 8, verse 1 *"And when he had opened the seventh seal, there was silence in heaven about the space of half an hour."*

The interpretation of this verse will be made plain a couple of pages farther on. It is omitted here to save repetition.

As stated in the Introduction, it seems very clear that St. John wrote this Book on the assumption that after Christ Jesus had disappeared in the Ascension, the impersonal Christ would be, and in St. John's day had already begun to be, reincarnated in the Christian church, and that, as incarnated in the church, he would, in conquering the world, go through a kind and order of experiences almost exactly duplicating the leading experiences of Christ Jesus during his earthly ministry. This, apparently, was John's basis, at least in part, for the dramatic action of the Apocalypse. We have now arrived at a point where we can illustrate and justify this statement.

Christ Jesus spent a large portion of the earlier part of his ministry in instructing a company of personal disciples. Likewise, the Apocalypse opens by representing the impersonal Christ instructing the impersonal churches, symbolized as seven churches of Asia, through the medium of his servant John. Near the close of his ministry, Christ Jesus took Peter, James and John into the Mount of Transfiguration, and showed them a wonderful vision, concerning which they were commanded to keep silent "until the Son of Man should be risen from the dead." Likewise, after directing John to send letters of instruction to the churches, the impersonal Christ takes John into the Mount of Vision, and gives him a fore-view of the Millennium and of things which are to transpire before it, but represents these things as "sealed" until after "the seventh angel" should have begun to sound his message. Soon after the experience of the Mount of Transfiguration, Christ Jesus had his final struggle with satan, represented in the personal ambition, the greed and selfishness, the materialism, sensuality and false doctrine of the Jewish and Roman authorities, backed up to a large extent by the common people, who were handled by satan against Jesus without knowing what they did. As a result of this struggle, Christ Jesus was seemingly put to death, and his influence was seemingly removed from the sphere of human activity. Likewise, after the impersonal Christ takes John into the Mount of Vision, he is represented, under the symbolism of the seals, as meeting in conflict on the field of human consciousness the same series of satanic influences above mentioned, with the result that, apparently, the Christ-activity is driven out of the field of human consciousness (the sun becomes as black as sackcloth, and the moon becomes as blood, and the stars of heaven fall,—all spiritual light is blotted out), and the impersonal Christ seems to human sense dead. Following his apparent death, Christ Jesus arose, and spent a period of about "forty days" with his disciples, before the Ascension; this was apparently a time of happy association, free from conflict with the world. So, too, following the apparent death of the impersonal Christ, as above described, he is represented as alive and active again in the millennial scene depicted in chapter 7, where he has happy association, free from discord, with his Father and with his disciples. About forty days after his resurrection from the dead, Christ Jesus overcame the flesh and ascended above the sense of matter into the realm of Spirit and eternal peace. Likewise, the opening of the seventh seal, spoken of in chapter 8:1, discloses, though in a somewhat hidden manner, the Christ as finally triumphant over all discord, so that there is *"silence [peace] in heaven [the mental realm] about the space of half an hour"*. An *"hour"* is probably here taken as the symbol of the whole of the time-period, the prophecy being that, during the last half of it, the Christ will rule in "silence" or peace. This is the period of the millennium, immediately following the "first resurrection".

This coming of the impersonal Christ into the field of human consciousness may be considered in several ways. In the first place, the Christ-idea comes into the individual consciousness, tries to instruct it, takes it into the Mount of Vision, shows it wonderful ideals, but meets in the individual consciousness self-assertiveness, selfishness, sensuality and materialism, discouragement and revenge, false doctrine and superstition, and, by the activity of these combined, often seems to be more or less completely driven out, but, in the end, regains a hold upon the individual consciousness and will conquer and save it.

Again, the impersonal Christ comes into the consciousness of the people of some section of the world, with a partial revelation of Truth, and this partial activity of the Christ goes through about the same line of experiences as above described. Such, for instance, was the fate of the Reformation movement, to a large extent. Every new impartation of religious truth seems purer, more vigorous and militant, in the first half century of its activity; then its human organization seems to become gradually more and more worldly and to sacrifice the spirit for the form, until vigorous spiritual life seems nearly to die out of it. Then the Spirit is likely to break out afresh, and this usually results in the formation of a new organization.

Considering the Christ-activity in its largest sweep, it would seem that the impersonal Christ, the true spiritual life, has been virtually dead, even among so-called Christian nations, for many decades, while materialism in belief and practice, human ambition, commercialism and corporate greed, sensuality and worldly lust, discouragement on the part of the comparatively few earnest Christians, and false and schismatic doctrine, have been markedly in the ascendency. It seems to the author that this period of spiritual poverty through which we have been passing is the final apparent death of the impersonal Christ, the spiritual consciousness, in the world of humanity as a whole, and that the Christ-consciousness, at the opening of this twentieth century, is being brought into renewed and vigorous activity in the world, never again to depart, but to unfold and increase uninterruptedly until the Millennium is ushered in.

REVISED TRANSLATION AND SUGGESTIVE PARAPHRASE

SECTION II

THE VISION OF THE SEVEN SEALED LETTERS

Chapter IV. A Vision of the Millennium

Another Revelation in the Realm of Consciousness

Amended Revised Version

1 After these things I saw, and behold, a door opened in heaven, and the first voice which I heard, a voice as of a trumpet speaking with me, one saying, Come up hither and I will shew thee the things which must come to pass hereafter. 2 Straightway I was in the Spirit: and behold, there was a throne set in heaven, and one sitting upon the 3 throne; and he that sat was to look upon like a jasper stone and a sardius: and there was a rainbow round about the throne, like an emerald to look upon.

Suggestive Paraphrase

After this I was permitted to enter the realm of Mind, and I received a powerful mental impulse which urged me to rise to a higher plane of thought, promising that I should behold at once the things which men will experience hereafter.

And when I realized the things of Spirit, I saw Mind enthroned supreme.

And I perceived the glory * and the justice † of God: also I perceived God's mercy,—that is, love ultimating in final peace for men,—symbolized by the rainbow.

* Symbolized by the many-hued jasper or opal.
† Symbolized by the blood-red sardius.

Symbolic Description of the Holy Ghost

4 And round about the throne were four and twenty thrones: and upon the thrones I saw four and twenty elders sitting, arrayed in white garments; and on their heads crowns 5 of gold. And out of the throne proceed lightnings and voices and thunders. And there were seven lamps of fire burning before the throne, which are the seven 6 Spirits of God; and before the throne, as it were a glassy sea like unto crystal: and in the midst of the throne, and round about the throne, four living creatures full of eyes before and be-7 hind. And the first creature was like a lion, and the second creature like a calf, and

God is enthroned in spiritualized and redeemed human consciousness, which, reflecting and enforcing the law of God, constitutes the Holy Spirit, and is symbolized as "the throne" of God. The Holy Spirit is further represented as consisting of all right ideas, symbolized by four and twenty elders, manifesting purity, and crowned with the authority of Principle. The Holy Spirit manifests the swiftness, power and clearness of God's judgments, and makes God manifest to human sense as Spirit, Mind, Soul, Principle, Love, Truth, Life (seven lamps), thus illumining human consciousness and dispelling error. The Holy Spirit is further represented as being changeless and immovable as glass, and transparent as crystal. It is also depicted as omniscient, and as being active in four leading phases; namely, moral cour-

Amended Revised Version

the third creature had a face as of a man, and the fourth creature was like a 8 flying eagle. And the four living creatures, having each one of them six wings, are full of eyes round about and within: and they have no rest day and night, saying, Holy, holy, holy, is the Lord God, the Almighty, which was and which is and which is to come.

9 And when the living creatures shall give glory and honour and thanks to him that sitteth on the throne, to him that liveth for ever and 10 ever, the four and twenty elders shall fall down before him that sitteth on the throne, and shall worship him that liveth for ever and ever, and shall cast their crowns before the throne, 11 saying, Worthy art thou, our Lord and our God, to receive the glory and the honour and the power: for thou didst create all things, and because of thy will they are and were created.

Suggestive Paraphrase

age, self-sacrifice, spiritual intelligence, and spiritual aspiration, which fully equip human consciousness for the service of God. These four activities of the Spirit are described, through symbolic language, as being omnipresent and all-observing, and as continually worshipping the eternal God.

God's Power and Glory Proclaimed

And when these four chief activities of the Holy Spirit give glory and honor and thanks to the ever living God, all the right ideas (four and twenty elders) do the same, because they are included in the four chief manifestations of the Spirit.

Chapter V. The Sealed Book and the Lamb
The Book of Coming Events

1 And I saw in the right hand of him that sat on the throne a book written within and on the back, close sealed 2 with seven seals. And I saw a strong angel proclaiming with a great voice, Who is worthy to open the book, and to loose the seals there-3 of? And no one in the heaven, or on the earth, or under the earth, was able to open the book, or to look thereon.

And I saw that through spiritual discernment alone the problem of human redemption is to be solved, the difficulties attending the solution being the sins of material sense. And there came to my thought a very insistent inquiry,—What mentality is sufficiently intelligent and pure to uncover these sins of sense and loose their hold upon humanity? And there was no human mentality sufficiently free from mortal dross to open up this revelation, or even to see its general scope.

Only the Redeemer Could Open the Book

Amended Revised Version

4 And I wept much, because no one was found worthy to open the book, or to look 5 thereon: and one of the elders saith unto me, Weep not: behold, the Lion that is of the tribe of Judah, the Root of David, hath overcome, to open the book and the seven seals thereof.

Suggestive Paraphrase

And I was much grieved, because it did not seem likely that there would be revealed that which I knew could be revealed, if there were one sufficiently spiritual to discern it. And one of the chief manifestations of Mind made known to me that there was no need for grief, because the Christ-consciousness is sufficient to uncover every falsity of error, and to reveal the things of Spirit.

A Vision of the Lamb of God

6 And I saw in the midst of the throne and of the four living creatures, and in the midst of the elders, a Lamb standing, as though it had been slain, having seven horns, and seven eyes, which are the seven Spirits of God, sent forth into all the 7 earth. And he came, and he taketh it out of the right hand of him that sat on the 8 throne. And when he had taken the book, the four living creatures and the four and twenty elders fell down before the Lamb, having each one a harp, and golden bowls full of incense, which are the prayers 9 of the saints. And they sing a new song, saying, Worthy art thou to take the book, and to open the seals thereof: for thou wast slain, and didst purchase unto God with thy blood 10 men of every tribe, and tongue, and people, and nation, and madest them to be unto our God a kingdom and priests; and they reign upon the earth.

And I saw divine Mind and the Holy Spirit, and all redeemed consciousness expressed as the mediatorial Christ-consciousness, appearing as though it had been sacrificed, having the power and the discernment emanating from the seven primary manifestations of God, and going forth to enlighten all humanity. And this Christ made ready to show the things embraced in the understanding of divine Mind. And as this Christ within showed a readiness to reveal great things heretofore hidden, it seemed as if all those in communion with God humbled themselves and prepared themselves to sing, and to express the holiest thoughts of praise and adoration. And they sang a new song, saying, The Christ-consciousness is worthy to uncover the deep and hidden things, and to redeem to God through his eternal life men out of every kindred, and tongue, and people, and nation; and to make them a kingdom of priests in the service of our God, that they may occupy high spiritual places among men.

His Power and Glory Proclaimed

Amended Revised Version

11 And I saw, and I heard a voice of many angels round about the throne and the living creatures and the elders; and the number of them was ten thousand times ten thousand, and thousands of
12 thousands; saying with a great voice, Worthy is the Lamb that hath been slain to receive the power and riches, and wisdom, and might, and honour, and
13 glory, and blessing. And every created thing which is in heaven, and on the earth, and under the earth, and on the sea, and all things that are in them, heard I saying, Unto him that sitteth on the throne, and unto the Lamb, be the blessing, and the honour, and the glory, and the dominion, unto the ages
14 of the ages. And the four living creatures said, Amen. And the elders fell down and worshipped.

Suggestive Paraphrase

And it seemed as if an innumerable host of spiritual mentalities* were associated with divine Mind, and the Holy Spirit, and the elders; proclaiming mightily, that the mediatorial Christ-consciousness, which had exemplified the spirit of sacrifice, is worthy to express power, and good, and wisdom, and strength, and glory, and blessing. And it seemed as if all living creatures, both in the mental and in the material realm, were redeemed, and were joining in the chorus, ascribing blessing, and honor, and glory, and power, unto God and His Christ, world without end. And the Holy Spirit said Amen. And all the manifestations of Mind humbled themselves in adoration.

---

* Strictly, these may be *right ideas*, instead of "spiritual mentalities." In either case, it is interesting to note that they are represented as having but *one* "voice," rather than *voices*. This is because they are considered collectively, reflecting the one mind, whose utterance is their utterance.

CHAPTER VI. THE OPENING OF THE SEALS

The First Seal. The Militant Christ

1 And I saw when the Lamb opened one of the seven seals, and I heard one of the four living creatures saying as with a voice of
2 thunder, Come. And I saw, and behold, a white horse, and he that sat thereon had a bow; and there was given unto him a crown; and he came forth conquering and to conquer.

And I realized that the Christ-consciousness was opening to me the first of the great revelations, and a manifestation of the Spirit cried to me with a loud voice, Behold. And I saw that the Christ-consciousness, carried by pure thought, and endowed with power, was going forth in the world, conquering and to conquer, until it should have won the victory over all evil.

The Second Seal. Human Will and Ambition

3 And when he opened the second seal, I heard the second living creature saying,
4 Come. And another horse

And a second manifestation of the Spirit called to me, saying, Behold another revelation of things to come. And I saw that the Christ-conscious-

| *Amended Revised Version* | *Suggestive Paraphrase* |

came forth, a red horse: and to him that sat thereon it was given to take peace from the earth, and that they should slay one another: and there was given unto him a great sword.

ness, militant in the world, will be opposed in its work by self-assertiveness or human will which takes peace from the earth, and causes men to kill one another, the emblem of which is the sword.

The Third Seal. Human Selfishness and Greed

5 And when he opened the third seal I heard the third living creature saying, Come. And I saw, and behold, a black horse; and he that sat thereon had a balance in his hand. And I
6 heard as it were a voice in the midst of the four living creatures saying, A measure of wheat for a penny, and three measures of barley for a penny; and the oil and the wine hurt thou not.

And a third manifestation of the Spirit called to me, saying, Behold a further revelation. And I saw that the work of the Christ in the world will be hindered by materialism and selfish stupidity, producing in human consciousness a great famine of "the bread of life," of the demonstrable knowledge of God and of His Christ, though unable to suppress spiritual aspiration and consecration to spiritual ideals, which hold humanity anchored against the tide of materialism until it has run its course and become inert.

The Fourth Seal. Materiality and Sensuality

7 And when he opened the fourth seal, I heard the voice of the fourth living
8 creature saying, Come. And I saw, and behold, a pale horse: and he that sat upon him, his name was Death; and Hades followed with him. And there was given unto them authority over the fourth part of the earth, to kill with sword, and with famine, and with pestilence, and by the wild beasts of the earth.

And a fourth manifestation of the Spirit said to me, Behold yet another revelation of things to come. And I saw that the work of the Christ among men will be hindered by sensuality and worldly lust, which represent and occasion conditions of death and hell. They largely control human consciousness, and induce war, famine, pestilence, and persecution, both mental and physical, thus reaping a wholesale harvest of death.

The Fifth Seal. Revenge and Discouragement

9 And when he opened the fifth seal, I saw underneath the altar the souls of them that had been slain for the word of God, and for the testimony which they held:
10 and they cried with a great voice, saying, How long, O Master, the holy and true,

And when the mediatorial Christ-consciousness had removed the fifth obstacle in the way of perceiving what was to be revealed, I saw the martyrs, who had been slain for their witness of Christ, hiding, as it were, under the protection of God,—so fierce and long-continued was the onslaught of evil: and I seemed to hear

Amended Revised Version

dost thou not judge and avenge our blood on them that dwell on the earth?

11 And there was given them to each one a white robe; and it was said unto them, that they should rest yet for a little time, until their fellow-servants also and their brethren, which should be killed even as they were, should be fulfilled.

Suggestive Paraphrase

them crying, as with a loud voice, How long shall the wicked and the persecutors go unpunished?* And righteousness will be given them in place of these satanic arguments, and they will be told to wait until the evil spirit of persecution in the world has spent itself.

---

*Discouragement and revenge will hinder the work of the Christ, even in the ranks of his professed followers.

The Sixth Seal. False Doctrine

12 And I saw when he opened the sixth seal, and there was a great earthquake; and the sun became black as sackcloth of hair, and the whole moon became
13 as blood; and the stars of the heaven fell unto the earth, as a fig tree casteth her unripe figs, when she is shaken of a great wind.
14 And the heaven was removed as a scroll when it is rolled up; and every mountain and island were moved out of their places.
15 And the kings of the earth, and the princes, and the chief captains, and the rich, and the strong, and every bondman and freeman, hid themselves in the caves and in the rocks of the moun-
16 tains; and they say to the mountains and to the rocks, Fall on us, and hide us from the face of him that sitteth on the throne, and from the
17 wrath* of the Lamb: for the great day of their wrath is come; and who is able to stand?

*This should be rendered *zeal* of the Lamb, which automatically excludes unrepentant mentality from harmony and forces it back upon itself to its own torment and destruction.

And when the sixth illumination came to me, I saw that the greatest hindrance to the progress of Christ among men will be false doctrine and schism in the church. As a result of this, there will be great mental disturbances; and the light of Truth will be completely obscured, and men's sense of religion, which usually reflects God and is mild and merciful, will become contentious and sanguinary; and many of those who had been trying, with some success, to be spiritually minded, will fall back into materiality. And harmony will depart as the writing of a scroll vanishes when it is rolled up; and all established institutions of society will be moved out of their accustomed courses. And all classes of men will be so struck with consternation, from fear of death by war, assassination, or torture, that they will be inclined to hide themselves in the dens and rocks of the mountains; and they will be so crazed with fear over the mighty upheavals and devastating strifes that will come to pass as the result of false doctrine and schism, that they would gladly have the mountains and rocks fall on them, thinking in their frenzy that death may hide them from the terrible results of the self-punishment of human ignorance, false belief, cruelty, tyranny, and general wrong-doing.

Chapter VII. A Forevision of the First Resurrection

A Veiled Vision of the First Resurrection

Amended Revised Version

1 After this I saw four angels standing at the four corners of the earth, holding the four winds of the earth, that no wind should blow on the earth, or on the 2 sea, or upon any tree. And I saw another angel ascend from the sunrising, having the seal of the living God: and he cried with a great voice to the four angels, to whom it was given to hurt 3 the earth and the sea, saying, Hurt not the earth, neither the sea, nor the trees, till we shall have sealed the servants of our God on their foreheads.

Suggestive Paraphrase

And after this I had a vision of a time when, for a season, all the self-destroying forces of evil shall be restrained from injuring any normal human activity, emotion, or institution. And the dawning Christ-consciousness which bears witness to the living God cried out to all the forces of good, saying, Do not allow the forces of evil to hurt any normal human function, feeling, nor institution, until those who serve God shall have attained a demonstrable understanding that life is eternal.*

And those who will be sealed, or resurrected, will be those who have conquered mortal sense and who manifest God.

* See Rev. 20:6 and Romans 8:23.

The 144,000

4 And I heard the number of them which were sealed, a hundred and forty and four thousand, sealed out of every tribe of the children of Israel.
5 Of the tribe of Judah were sealed twelve thousand:
Of the tribe of Reuben twelve thousand:
Of the tribe of Gad twelve thousand:
6 Of the tribe of Asher twelve thousand:
Of the tribe of Naphtali twelve thousand:
Of the tribe of Manasseh twelve thousand:
7 Of the tribe of Simeon twelve thousand:
Of the tribe of Levi twelve thousand:

Note.—The sealing of the servants of God in their foreheads seems to refer to their resurrection from the dead in "the first resurrection" (20:5), which is the special sign of their saint-hood and of their redemption. "Blessed and holy is he that hath part in the first resurrection: on such the second death hath no power, but they shall be priests of God and of Christ, and shall reign with him a thousand years" (20:6). They are "sealed *in their foreheads*"; that is, they are given the *demonstrable understanding* that life is eternal, by being resurrected. As further evidence that their resurrection is their sealing, consider Paul's saying in Romans 8:23: "Even we ourselves groan within ourselves, waiting for the adoption, to wit, the redemption of our body." The "redemption of the body" is evidently the healing of it in case of sickness or the resurrection of it in the case of death. This

Amended Revised Version

Of the tribe of Issachar twelve thousand:
8 Of the tribe of Zabulon twelve thousand:
Of the tribe of Joseph twelve thousand:
Of the tribe of Benjamin were sealed twelve thousand.

Suggestive Paraphrase

sealing or resurrecting takes place while satan is bound; that is, while the four destructive winds are restrained. "Twelve" signifies "manifesting God," and a "thousand" signifies "conquerors." (See Note 2 of Introduction.) Hence, the significance of "twelve thousand" and of 144,000 is readily apparent.

A Vast Throng of Gloriously Triumphant Saints

9 After these things I saw, and behold, a great multitude, which no man could number, out of every nation, and of all tribes and peoples and tongues, standing before the throne and before the Lamb, arrayed in white robes, and palms in
10 their hands; and they cry with a great voice, saying, Salvation unto our God which sitteth on the throne,
11 and unto the Lamb. And all the angels were standing round about the throne, and about the elders and the four living creatures; and they fell before the throne on their faces, and wor-
12 shipped God, saying, Amen: Blessing, and glory, and wisdom, and thanksgiving, and honour, and power, and might, be unto our God for ever and ever. Amen.

After this, I had a vision of the redeemed gentiles rejoicing, and ascribing their salvation unto God and His Christ, enthroned in the power of good.

And I beheld all the conscious ideas or spiritual entities of the mental realm associated with the living creatures and with the elders in the position of power, humbling themselves before creative Mind from which they spring, saying, The eternal and final word is: Let blessing, and glory, and wisdom, and honor, and thanksgiving, and power, and might, be ascribed unto our God, world without end. So let it be.

Full Salvation Through the Lamb

13 And one of the elders answered, saying unto me, These which are arrayed in the white robes, who are they, and whence came
14 they? And I say unto him, My lord, thou knowest. And he said to me, These are they which come out of the great tribulation, and they washed their robes, and

And one of the higher faculties in my mediatorial consciousness raised the question, Who are these redeemed ones and where do they come from? and I said, Why do you ask me; for you know already. And he said to me, These are they which came out of sore trials, and have purified their mentalities by living the life of Christ.

VII : 15-VIII : 1   SECTION II   163

Amended Revised Version

15 made them white in the blood of the Lamb. Therefore are they before the throne of God; and they serve him day and night in his temple: and he that sitteth on the throne shall spread his tabernacle over
16 them. They shall hunger no more, neither thirst any more; neither shall the sun strike upon them, nor any
17 heat; for the Lamb which is in the midst of the throne shall be their shepherd, and shall g u i d e them unto fountains of waters of life: and God shall wipe away every tear from their eyes.

Suggestive Paraphrase

This is the reason that they live in the presence and power of Mind, reflecting Mind continually, and that they are ever at one with Mind. They shall never again experience the sense of lack; neither shall any material manifestation be a source of trouble to them: for the Christ-consciousness, clothed with authority and power, will continually feed them with the knowledge of God, which is the true substance, and shall keep them within the Source of life: and because they realize God, good, they shall never more experience sorrow.

CHAPTER VIII

The Seventh Seal. A Vision of the Millennium

1 And when he opened the seventh seal, there followed a silence in heaven about the space of half an hour.

And the seventh portion of the revelation brought me a vision of the millennial period, during which there will be peace in the mental realm, for a period represented by the latter portion of the duration of the matter-and-time belief.*

---

* See Note 3 of Introduction.

(Continued on Page 237.)

NOTES BY THE READER

NOTES BY THE READER

SECTION III

THE SEVEN TRUMPETS

(Chapter 8:2-11:18)

Under the vision of the seals, in the last Act, we saw the militant Christ ushered upon the field of conflict in human consciousness, meeting there various satanic influences, and finally conquering, as implied in the imagery of the seventh seal. Thus, in one sense, the action of the drama is represented as completed in the vision of the seals; but, as a matter of fact, that vision presents only one phase or aspect of the conflict carried to completion. Under the vision of the trumpets, we shall see the seven chief activities of the Christ-mind, symbolized as seven angels with trumpets, sounding the proclamations of God, which are destructive of evil. These angels are the same seven in whose behalf St. John was commanded to address instructive letters to the human consciousness, symbolized as "seven churches of Asia", as we have already seen.

Error in most of its phases has two aspects. At the commencement of its activity in any line, it is usually pleasant to look upon, and seems pleasant to experience; but, sooner or later, its dissentious and destructive aspect appears, when it is sure to bring great suffering upon those who have been lured into its meshes, finally driving them out of it into truth, and error goes to its own destruction, for lack of witness, when it can no longer find anyone to serve it. In chapters eight and nine, John gives us a prophecy of the punishment which he foresees will be meted out by error to the ungodly who are under its sway,—punishment along certain definite lines, to a fearful, and yet to a limited, extent, "a third part". In the 15th and 16th chapters, he gives us a prophecy of the full measure of punishment or destruction being meted out along exactly the same lines as under the trumpets, and of the final overthrow of error. For this reason, it is extremely useful and enlightening to study the 8th and 9th chapters in connection with the 15th and 16th, as will here be done.

The activities spoken of under the seals operate against the progress of Christianity and of those who are trying to be true Christians. The activities mentioned and described under the first six trumpets (chapters 8 and 9) and under the vials (chapters 15 and 16) operate against evil and evildoers, by forcing evil to continually punish itself and the ungodly who are enmeshed in it.

We are not to understand that the punishment of the ungodly commences *after* the activities which oppose Christianity have spent their force, but that the ungodly are being punished coincidently with the opposition to the godly, all the time from the ascension of Jesus until the Millennium. In other words, the movements forecast under the trumpets are going on at the same time as the movements forecast under the first six seals.

Parallel Visions of the Trumpets and Bowls

CHAPTER VIII

2 And I saw the seven angels which stood before God; and to them were given seven trumpets.

Pentecostal Service

3 And another angel came and stood at the altar, having a golden censer; and there was given unto him much incense, that he should offer it with the prayers of all saints upon the golden altar which was before the throne.

4 And the smoke of the incense, which came with the prayers of the saints, ascended up before God out of the angel's hand.

5 And the angel took the censer, and filled it with fire of the altar, and cast it into the earth: and there were voices, and thunderings, and lightnings, and an earthquake.

6 And the seven angels which had the seven trumpets prepared themselves to sound.

CHAPTER XV

1 And I saw another sign in heaven, great and marvellous, seven angels having the seven last plagues; for in them is filled up the wrath of God.

Pentecostal Service

2 And I saw it as it were a sea of glass mingled with fire; and them that had gotten the victory over the beast, and over his image, and over his mark, and over the number of his name, stand on the sea of glass, having the harps of God. (See 20:4.)

3 And they sing the song of Moses the servant of God, and the song of the Lamb, saying, Great and marvellous are thy works, Lord God Almighty, just and true are thy ways, thou king of saints, Who shall not fear thee, O Lord, and glorify thy name? For thou only art holy: for all nations shall come and worship before thee, for thy judgments are made manifest.

5 And after that I looked, and behold the temple of the tabernacle of the testimony in heaven was opened.

6 And the seven angels came out of the temple, having the seven plagues, clothed in pure and white linen, and having their breasts girded with golden girdles.

7 And one of the four beasts gave unto the seven angels seven golden vials full of the wrath of God, who liveth for ever and ever.

8 And the temple was filled with smoke from the glory of God, and from his power; and no man was able to enter into the temple, till the seven plagues of the seven angels were fulfilled.

After Christ Jesus ascended into heaven, his disciples became Apostles, and took up and carried forward in the world the ministry which he had commenced. They began that ministry with a great prayer and praise meeting, called "the day of Pentecost", at which time they received the Holy Spirit. This succession of events is now dramatized *in form,* though not in actual sequence, by representing *all* the disciples of Christ as Apostles, under the symbolism of *seven* (all) angels, proclaiming and enforcing the message of God and His Christ in the world. The combined spiritual factors in the mentalities of all human beings following and serving the Christ would include and represent the activity and enforcement of the seven chief phases of the Christ-mind, symbolized by the seven angels mentioned above,—namely, *Spiritual Aspiration, Spiritual Reason, Executive Mind, Direct Cognition, Divine Love, Perception of Reality,* and *Perception of Substance.*

The Pentecostal service at which these impersonal Apostles, the angels of the trumpets, receive the energizing of the Holy Spirit is depicted in verses 3-5. Verses 3 and 4 represent the spiritual factor in human consciousness in its activity as the true church, worshiping God, under the leadership of the Holy Spirit. Verse 5 represents this same factor in human consciousness under the leadership of the Holy Spirit, or as itself the Holy Spirit, assuming a militant attitude toward the world. The *"fire of the altar"* surely stands for the inspiration of Truth, acting as a purifying agent. *"Voices and thunderings and lightnings"* also represent the militant activity of the spiritual consciousness. Both this expression and *"fire of the altar"* symbolize the activity of the Holy Spirit. The *"voices"* indicate clear, intelligent utterance; the *"thunderings"* indicate the power and majesty of the utterance; and the *"lightnings"* indicate the swiftness and far-reaching effect of the utterance.

When the activity of the Holy Spirit is *"cast into the earth",* that is, into false material sense, it produces a violent mental upheaval,* often manifest in physical disturbances

---

* "Science and Health," 97:23-25; 401:16-19; 540:5-16.

among men and in the natural world. Whenever a marked impartation of spiritual truth comes to the human consciousness, it always produces such an upheaval, and often results in wars and the overturning of governments and other human institutions.

CHAPTER XV

(Considered out of consecutive order)

Verse 1, Chapter 15. *"The seven last plagues"* is not a fortunate rendering of the original Greek. The word *plêgê* would be much better rendered "blow" or "stroke", as it practically always is in classical Greek. The idea clearly is that the angels of the vials are to give the *finishing strokes* to error. The activity of good does destroy error, but, as indicated before, when strictly speaking, it does not "plague" or "curse" error, though it may force error to plague or curse itself. If this does not seem at this point entirely clear, the reader is referred again to Notes 4, 5 and 6 of the Introduction. In connection with the activities of these angels, we would speak more scientifically in expressing what will happen, were we to say, that evil will continue to advance against truth and good along the seven specified lines, and will be met in its advance by corresponding phases of the truth of good standing as walls of adamant, which will turn evil back upon itself, to the terrible punishment of those enmeshed therein, and to the final destruction of all evil. The seven phases of truth, which, without moving out of their mental places (omnipresence), oppose and turn back to destruction the seven phases of evil, are very properly spoken of as seven angels of God. They represent *the full measure of God's redemptive power,* and so it is said, *"In them is filled up the wrath* (ardor, zeal) *of God";* that is, the power of good to destroy evil.

Verses 2-4 represent, not exactly a Pentecostal meeting in preparation for the conflict, as in the corresponding passage under the trumpets, but a praise meeting, with rejoicing that the conflict is near its end.

The *"sea of glass mingled with fire"* is the same sea of glass as is spoken of in chapter 4, verses 5 and 6. See Notes on those verses in the discussion of Section II. The symbol of fire added to the symbol of the glassy sea simply emphasizes the militant and purifying activity of the spiritual consciousness, the Holy Spirit. The glassy sea alone represents it as in a state of peace and rest. The following comment from *The Self-Interpreting Bible* is also interesting and illuminating:

This sea of glass,—rather crystalline, is a figure drawn, not from a geographical sea, but from a large vessel in the temple called a sea (1 Kings 7:23-39) used by the priests for washing, 2 Chron. 4:6. This sea in the temple was of brass, emblematic of strength—the prophetic sea of crystal is emblematic of purity. It is mingled with fire, as an emblem of purifying judgments. Under the providence of a wise and merciful God, the hour that has most troubled has always most purified his church. Persecution cleanseth the church of hypocrites and luke-warm professors, excites the spirit of prayer, exercises patience, separates from the world, and produces Christ" (Phil. 1:23).

In this second verse, those who have gotten the victory over worldly government, the rule of human desire and will, and have submitted only to God's government, perhaps suffering martyrdom in the process, are represented as standing *by* (not "on" when properly translated) the sea of glass, having the harps of God, and singing the song of Moses and the Lamb. Really, these are mentalities not localized, but pervaded by, or themselves constituting, the glassy sea, the spiritual consciousness. These are they who have profited by the warning given in chapter 14, verses 9-13,—standing against the beast (human misgovernment), even to the death if need be, and receiving their reward as indicated in verse 13.

Verse 5. *"The temple of the tabernacle of the testimony in heaven"* is one of the numerous symbols of the Holy Spirit. The imagery is here drawn from Numbers 1:50. "But thou shalt appoint the Levites over the tabernacle of testimony, and over all the vessels thereof, and over all things that belong to it.". It here symbolizes the mental sphere in which events and movements are hidden from the knowledge of humanity, until humanity has made sufficient progress to "open", or attain to, this sphere. In verse 8 we read: *"The temple was filled with smoke from the glory of God, and from his power"*. This expression symbolizes the fact that consciousness which is highly spiritual is blinding to human sense, until human sense itself has become spiritualized. The last clause of the verse informs us that no human being will be able to fully enter into this temple, the Holy Spirit, till the Christ-angels have delivered their seven last blows destructive of evil, thus purifying and spiritualizing the consciousness of every man.

Verse 6. *"And the seven angels came out of the temple."* Really, the angels of Truth are omnipresent and immovable, and make no advance. The advance is on the part of men, finally attaining to a point where they can discern these angels, become at one with them, and have part in enforcing their power to turn back the various phases of evil to its own torment, finally destroying it completely. These angels are represented in this verse as being dressed as high priests, ministering in God's service.

Chapter IX

The Trumpets Sound and the Bowls Are Poured Out

The First Trumpet and the First Vial

CHAPTER VIII	CHAPTER XVI
7 *The first angel sounded, and there followed hail and fire mingled with blood, and they were cast upon the earth;* and the third part of trees was burnt up, and all green grass was burnt up.*	2 And the first went and poured out his vial (bowl) upon the earth, and there fell a noisome and grievous sore upon the men which had the mark of the beast, and upon them which worship his image.

We have now reached a point where, in order to proceed with clarity of vision, we must make a more definite statement of the significance of symbolism† and of its use in the Apocalypse than we have hitherto done, and this is well expressed in the words of Professor Moulton in the Modern Reader's Bible. He says:

"A modern reader, accustomed to such poetry as Dante's *Paradiso,* must always remember in approaching such a work as this (the Revelation) that Hebrew literature rests upon the symbol rather than the image. . . . Both imagery and symbolism rest upon comparison: some external idea is imported to be compared with a detail in the positive description. But imagery appeals to the imagination, and uses ideas which make pictures; symbolism does not appeal to the pictorial sense at all, but rather to some analytic faculty, or conventional association of ideas. . . . Dante's imaginative forms may be symbolic, but they will never cease to have the characteristic of imagery that they can fit into pictures. Hebrew symbolism is again and again incompatible with the pictorial: it is enough to instance the leading symbol of this vision—the Lamb, which, in the various presentations, could enter into no pictorial imagination.

---

* All modern translations insert after the semicolon: "and the third (part) of the earth was burnt up." Some translations omit the word "part."

† On page 146 of "Life Understood," its author, Mr. Rawson, suggests that the Biblical use of symbols to teach spiritual things is because of the fact that symbols, if rightly understood, do not suggest pictures or outlines. He says: "To form any picture of the material or attempted outline of the spiritual, even in one's clearest realizations, is wrong. Hence the symbolic teaching of things spiritual."

"The most important thing in connection with the symbolism of St. John is a point of literary effect, which further seems in the poem itself to be indicated as extending beyond poetic form into the underlying spiritual interpretation. This is that the symbolism of Revelation is the symbolism of Old Testament prophecy revived; the symbolic ideas being not merely revived, but at the same time varied, massed together, and intensified. Indeed, very few, if any, of St. John's symbols are drawn from any other source. Considered from the literary side this is the device of 'echoing', which distinguishes all 'classical' poetry,—the special line of poetic succession in which each poet makes new creations out of detailed reminiscences of the poetry of the past. But in the present case this is much more than a literary device. *The testimony of Jesus is the spirit of prophecy:* one of the leading thoughts of St. John's work is that the mysteries of the old dispensation find their solution and fulfillment in the new: similarly, the forms of ancient prophecy combine to make the symbolic setting of the supreme revelation."

Verse 7, of chapter 8, quoted above, is an "echo" from Exodus 9:22-25:

"And the Lord said unto Moses, Stretch forth thine hand toward heaven, that there may be hail in all the land of Egypt, upon man, and upon beast, and upon every herb of the field, throughout the land of Egypt. And Moses stretched forth his rod toward heaven: and the Lord sent thunder and hail, and the fire ran along the ground; and the Lord rained hail upon the land of Egypt. So there was hail, and fire mingled with the hail, very grievous, such as there was none like it in all the land of Egypt since it became a nation. And the hail smote throughout all the land of Egypt all that was in the field, both man and beast; and the hail smote every herb of the field, and break every tree of the field."

Let us now place in parallel arrangement the verse which we are to interpret and some selected phrases from the above:

From Revelation	From Exodus
The first angel sounded, and there followed hail and fire mingled with blood, and they were cast upon the earth; and the third part of trees was burnt up, and all green grass was burnt up.	So there was hail, and fire mingled with the hail . . . and the fire ran along the ground; and the hail smote every herb of the field, and break every tree of the field.

Either the long quotation from Exodus, or the short one, could form the basis of a literary "image", since both suggest the picture of a violent tornado, and of nothing but that. The same would be true of our verse from Revelation, were it not for the insertion of the words *"with blood"*. It is perfectly easy to picture a mingling of fire (lightning) and hail, as we often see them in a hail storm; but there is nothing corresponding to the mingling of these with blood in the sky. It is true that a hail storm often produces bloody results; but it will be noticed that our verse represents the blood as mingled with the fire and hail *before* any of them *"were cast upon the earth";* so, in this case, the *"blood"* is a part of the *cause* of the devastation, rather than indicating a *result*. We can only reach a correct understanding of this verse by giving up all attempt to base our interpretation upon what may be suggested to thought by an image or picture, and, on the other hand, by understanding that we have to deal with symbolism, rather than an image, and so must get at the meaning through analysis rather than through the use of imagination.

Let it here be stated, as a fact to which we may need to refer frequently as we proceed in the interpretation of the Book, that the parts or elements of an image have a consistent or reasonable relation to each other, whereas, the parts or elements of a symbol, if it is at all complex, usually have no reasonable or imaginable relation to each other, if taken literally: the relation between them is only to be found when, through analysis, we get back of the parts or elements of the symbol to the meaning of what is symbolized; in which meaning, if our interpretation be correct, there is always perfect unity or reasonableness of relation.

To establish perfect reasonableness of relation in the activities symbolized by the verse now under consideration, without violating a correct understanding of the nature and true activity of God and of all His angels or ideas, we shall have to make a somewhat careful analysis of what is implied by the symbol of the tornado (fire and hail) as well as what is suggested by the symbol of the "blood".

If men are out of doors in a violent hail storm, they are likely to get "hurt", so that their suffering may continue for a considerable period. It will help us to understand, not only the verse under consideration, but many another passage of Scripture, and many an experience of human life, if we consider carefully just the combination of forces and their joint activities, which bring about a hail storm, and which cause suffering to men who are exposed to the storm.

The agencies which render possible a hail storm are the sun, and the earth,—the latter including the elements of air, ground, and water. It is evident that, without the shining of the sun, there would never be a hail storm, as, in that case, there could be no evaporation of water; it is also evident that without the elements of earth upon which to act, the shining of the sun alone would never result in a storm. The light and heat of the sun are constant and practically invariable, and cannot be conceived of as a *source* of a hail storm, though in the conditions of earth they are an indispensable *occasion* of such a storm. In fact, it is only when a given portion of the earth's surface is brought into such relation to the unchanging activity of the sun that the sun shines with considerable directness upon it, thus increasing the earth's reception of the sun's activity, that hail storms are ever produced. In many regions, the more the earth's surface is exposed to the action of the sun, the more likelihood there is of a hail storm,—a paradox so great, that had we not had actual experience to the contrary, we should say that it were impossible that an increase of heat should result in the increased production of ice,—in the form of hail, or in any other form.

In a hail storm, there are three activities that seem terrifying and destructive,—the lightning, the wind, and the hail. The lightning doubtless represents transformed energy from the sun, while the wind and the hail more distinctively represent the material or earth element in the total manifestation of the storm. Except in rare instances, which we do not need to quibble about when we are considering the basis of an illustration, the lightning does not bring physical suffering upon a man exposed to the storm. If it strikes him at all it does not cause him to suffer (except in rare instances), but gives him an instantaneous and (so far as we know) painless passage into the next stage of experience. So the sun-factor in the storm does not cause the man suffering: it is the earth-factors, the hail and the wind, that cause him to suffer.

God, the divine Mind, who is unadulterated harmony and good, who ceaselessly, changelessly, and infinitely radiates love, joy, and peace into the whole realm of conscious experience, cannot possibly be a *source* of suffering, or of punishment, or of anything that occasions discomfort, to a human being, or to anything or anybody whatever: and yet, as the sun is the *occasion* (though never the *source*) of storms upon the earth, so the activity of divine Mind is the *occasion* of disturbances in the human realm which bring great sufferings upon human beings exposed to them.* This happens, and can happen, only because, in the realm of human experience, divine Mind is brought into relation with elements of false, earthly belief, which seem to obstruct the activities of Mind, even as the elements of earth obstruct the course of the sun's rays of light and heat,—the obstruction, in both cases, being the contributing cause of "storms" or disturbances, which are painful and seemingly destructive to human beings.

The annual movement of the earth around the sun, combined with its diurnal revolution on its axis, and the inclination of its axis to the plane of its orbit in its path around the sun,—these three factors result at times in exposing a given region of the earth's surface more directly to the action of the sun (though the sun's action is not in the least modified in the process), resulting in an increase of storms, as already pointed out. Likewise, as mankind, or some considerable portion of it,

---

* "Science and Health," 386:25; 540:11-15.

learns more of God, and more insistently and consciously declares and enforces His law in the world, mortal mind or material sense ("the earth") is thereby more directly exposed to the activity of divine Mind and its ideas (angels); and this results in "storms", upheavals in human experience which prove exceedingly painful to human beings who are exposed to them. Just as it seems paradoxical, and almost impossible of belief, that an increase of heat on the earth could result in an increased production of ice or hail, so it would seem, without careful analysis, impossible that an increased activity of divine Mind, good, in the human realm could result in an increased manifestation of suffering and apparent destruction; yet this is what occurs.* However, as the physical suffering of those exposed to a hail storm results from the earth-factor, rather than from the sun-factor, in the storm, so, likewise, when a strict analysis is made, it is seen that the suffering of human beings in all human experiences which occasion suffering results from the mortal, false, or earthy elements in human consciousness, and never from the activity of the divine factor. As pointed out in the closing paragraph of Note 4 of the Introduction, and as illustrated in the analysis of the activities of the storm which we have just been making, if divine Mind exercises any destructive effect upon anything human, this occurs only at the final stage, when Mind, as Spirit, completely overcomes the manifestation of matter, thus destroying the human sense of body, whereupon the so-called human is completely exchanged for the divine; but this final destructive process, so far as the divine factor is concerned, is painless, and ushers the human being, without suffering, into the unalloyed and everlasting realization of good.† In anything short of this final destruction of the body, the divine factor in human experience always blesses and comforts and improves, rather

---

* "Every sensuous pleasure or pain is self-destroyed through suffering" ("Science and Health," 224:7, 8).

† "Science and Health," 325:2-5.

than injures, even the corporeal man.* Humanity gets its pain and its punishment from the activity of the earth-elements, the false beliefs, which seem to resist the activities of God.

To an unanalytical sense, a hail storm seems like a unified manifestation, although, in fact, as we have seen, widely divergent factors are operative in the storm. So, to unanalytical sense, the "storms" which arise in human experience seem to be unified manifestations, and, consequently, unanalytical sense is likely to attribute them either wholly to God, or wholly to evil (the devil), whereas, the fact is that they are attributable to the action and reaction upon the human sense plane of the impersonal forces of good and evil. A hail storm, through the action of the divergent forces involved in it, purifies the air. Likewise "storms" in human experience purify human consciousness; and, paradoxical as it may seem, while wholly opposed to each other, and never coordinated or combined, the forces of good and of evil, *when acting coincidently*, may be said to cooperate to this end. The element of suffering inherent in evil tends to push men out of evil; and the attractiveness of good tends to "pull" them toward God and eternal life. Up to the final limit, when evil is wholly destroyed, the increased enforcement of the law of God in the realm of human consciousness often results in stirring up evil to increased opposition,† thus bringing out the suffering element more prominently. It often happens that the human consciousness is being purified most rapidly when it suffers most, that it is being brought most rapidly to the final goal where all suffering shall cease at the very time when, as it seems, it is getting farther and farther from that goal.

This line of reasoning, the correctness of which is beyond legitimate dispute, makes it clear that the present (A. D. 1915) conflict in Europe, terrible as it seems, represents a process

---

* "Science and Health," 453:18, 19.
† "Science and Health," 534:24-30; 565:1-4; 569:21-27.

of the purification of human sense. If so, it indicates, not retrogression of the race, but progress, though, in itself, it is not progress. Certain human experiences may be *an indication of the working of good,* though these experiences, of themselves, are not good. Shortly after this war is over, humanity will, doubtless, be found to be occupying higher moral and spiritual levels.

What is termed "weather" results from the joint-action of the sun and the earth-elements. This joint-action results in alternating periods of fair weather and storm, and intermediate conditions. A succession of bright, clear days brings to pass the very conditions which result in a storm. Such days are often spoken of by seamen as "weather-breeders". On the other hand, stormy days bring to pass the very conditions which make for clear weather later. This illustration must not be pressed too far; but it legitimately suggests that, up to a certain stage of the spiritual development of a person or of a people, the action and reaction of impersonal good and impersonal evil in the field of their consciousness is likely to result for them in alternating periods of harmony and discord. So long as their health and prosperity are of the natural order, and have not been established upon the basis of Principle by the conscious recognition and enforcement of the law of God, the very periods when their affairs seem most harmonious are likely to beget conditions which will lead to discord, while, many times, their periods of discord are teaching them lessons and bringing to pass other conditions which will later lead to the establishment of harmony. More or less of these alternating experiences are likely to occur, even after persons or a people have definitely and with full purpose begun to work their way from a natural to a spiritual basis of living.* It is

---

* This accounts for alternating periods of peace and war in advancing human experience; but when humanity has sufficiently advanced, *"they shall beat their swords into plow-shares, and their spears into pruning hooks: nation shall not lift up sword against nation, neither shall they learn war any more."*—Isa. 2:4.

true, even after considerable spiritual progress has been made, that periods of suffering are periods of purification, as above suggested. Fortunate it is, however, that it is a tendency of the mental sunshine to alternate with the mental storm; for if the purifying process were too strenuous and persistent, it might become relatively destructive rather than beneficial. After a time, it ought to be possible to demonstrate painless progress, and this should be the ideal. It is not the intention of the author to suggest that we should look for "storms" in human experience, or hold that there cannot be progress without them; but the purpose is, rather, to show what they may mean, if they do occur, and to make it evident that they need not be regarded wholly in the way in which it is natural to regard them, for they may be blessings in disguise, though not the highest blessings. There must come a stage of spiritual development for every person and people after which periods of discord will no more occur. They are certain to be eliminated after mortal, material sense has been largely banished from consciousness.

To revert again to the passages which we are interpreting, it has been made evident that the "sounding" of the angel in verse 7 represents the activity of divine Mind. To be perfectly clear in thought, we must remember always that divine Mind and its ideas are not more active at some times than at others; so, that, speaking in the absolute, it could not be said that the angel *"commenced"* to sound, in any sense in which it had not been always sounding. But advancing human consciousness comes mentally nearer to divine Mind and its ideas, and so comes into the experience of the "sounding" of the angels, as it had not before. This nearer approach of the human consciousness to the changeless activity of this "angel", the Christ-mind as Spiritual Perception or Soul, results in a mental upheaval which is symbolized in part by a violent tornado with hail. As remarked before, this figure of the fire (lightning) and hail might stand as an image, rather than a symbol, were it not for the fact that *"blood"* is added to the combination of elements before they are *"cast upon the earth"*. A combination of hail, lightning, and blood in the sky is unpicturable, and so must be taken as symbolism rather than as imagery. The "fire" fittingly symbolizes the purifying influence of the Holy Spirit: the *"blood"* may be understood as connoting *"the blood of Jesus Christ, which cleanseth from all sin"*,—in other words, the sanctifying influence of the Christ-life: while the *"hail"* symbolizes the mortal element, the purifying influence of punishment, or suffering for ignorance and wrong-doing. Although the three elements in this symbol are unpicturable if taken literally in a united sense, nevertheless the united activity of the elements which they symbolize,— the activities of the Holy Spirit, of the Christ-life, and of the punitive aspect of error,—is perfectly consistent and thinkable. This brings out clearly the point made by Professor Moulton, that the interpretation of symbolism depends, not on the use of imagination, as does the interpretation of imagery, but on the use of the analytical faculties.

The latter portion of the verse which we are interpreting presents a true image, and its meaning is best made evident by considering it in that way. The set of mental influences set in action by the sounding of the angel are represented as *"cast upon the earth"*, that is, into material sense, just as a hail storm sweeps down from the sky upon the literal earth, with strokes of lightning, wind, and hail. In a violent tornado, when the lightning repeatedly strikes the earth, it manifests the appearance described in Exodus,—*"the fire ran along the ground"*. After the storm has passed, the earth's surface appears devastated. As a matter of fact, about *"a third"* of the trees thereon are destroyed, *"burnt up"*,—either having been struck by lightning, or uprooted by the wind, and all the green herbage is withered and looks as if fire had passed over it. The Greek *chortos chloros* is better translated *"green herbage"*, as by Rotherham, rather than *"green grass"*, as by the Authorized Version. The words *"and a third of the earth was burned up"*, added to the modern translations, symbolize the fact that a third part or considerable portion of the activity of materiality and sensuality in human consciousness is destroyed by the initial activities of this angel.*

If we are to attempt a specific interpretation of *"trees"* and *"green herbage"*, we may well be guided by the fact that, in the literal sense, these are products of the earth, and represent specialized and attractive but more or less transitory manifestations of matter,—the trees being much more enduring manifestations than the herbage. The *"green herbage"* may very properly be taken to symbolize the ordinary details of so-called "happy life" in unspiritualized human experience,— the transitory flood of careless, "happy", or not unattractive thoughts that come and go in unspiritualized consciousness without particular aim or purpose, all of a materialistic order. The *"trees"* probably symbolize well established human doctrines, customs and habits of thought of a sensual and materialistic nature,—more fixed and continuous in consciousness than the kind of thoughts symbolized by "the green herbage". Such customs and habits of thought are often highly prized and respected among men, and yet they may be the very strongholds of error.

To sum up the interpretation of this seventh verse of the eighth chapter, we may say that it gives us to understand that the activity of this first angel of the Christ-mind will make material sense, and sensuality, and their detailed activities in the field of human consciousness, look as if a hail-storm had passed over them; that is, something like a third of their established habits and customs of thought will be destroyed, and the ordinary course of consciousness which they seek to perpetuate will be completely upset and devastated. After a storm

---

*Mr. F. L. Rawson suggests that in an historical interpretation of the Apocalypse, "the reference of 'the third part' is to the three portions into which the Roman empire was split at the time of Constantine, one part having been virtually devastated ('burnt up'). The historical account of the attack on Rome shows that they actually burnt the herbage and trees."

has passed, the herbage and the trees grow up again, the former more quickly than the latter. There is, therefore, nothing in this symbolism to indicate that, at the period of the activity of the angel which is now being spoken of, the daily course of mortal consciousness, though devastated by the storm, will not be in evidence again. Rather, the implication is that materiality and sensuality will continue their activity in human consciousness, but will be *repeatedly* devastated by the activity of the angel, and thus be gradually destroyed in a more lasting sense,—much as repeated hail-storms might in time render a given region of the earth's surface, though naturally fertile, uninhabitable to men. Under the symbolism of the angel with the first *"vial"*, we shall have this same angel represented as finishing the work of the destruction of materiality and sensuality, which is only *"a third part"* accomplished when the angel first appears sounding his *"trumpet"*.

CHAPTER XVI

Rotherham translates verse 2 of chapter 16 as follows:

And the first departed and poured out his bowl unto the earth; and there came to be a baneful and painful ulcer upon the men who had the mark of the beast and them who were doing homage unto his image.

The Greek *phialê*, transliterated into English as "phial", and translated "vial" in the Authorized Version, and "bowl" in most modern translations, really means a *libation saucer,—* a broad, shallow vessel, used at the altar in religious services, where libations of wine are poured out.

The same angel, the same activity of the Christ-mind, which is represented in chapter 8 as sounding the first trumpet, thereby commencing the destruction of material sense in its lowest phases, is here represented as engaging in the activity which will help to finish the task.

Passing by the figurative form of expression, the angel is represented as enforcing against sensuality and materialism *the full measure* of the ardor of God. Strictly speaking, we should not think of this angel as engaging in any special activity at this time, or at any other particular time. He "pours out" his *"phiale"* of the ardor of God only in the sense that the sun always "pours out" light and heat,—uniformly from year to year and from century to century. But advancing humanity comes into such relations to the Christ-mind that it receives this "pouring out" more directly and fully than formerly,—even to the cleansing of it from all error, the final process being very painful before it is finished.

All men who are under the dominion of sensuality and materialism, are, during such experience, bound to be under the dominion of *"the beast"* and *"the false prophet"*. These two symbols represent worldly government and the worldly church (false theology), as will be made fully evident in the Notes on chapter 13. It will also be made evident in the discussion of that chapter that *"the image of the beast",* which men worship, is the anthropomorphic or man-like sense of God and the mortal sense of man, which the false prophet, the worldly church, causes men to set up for worship in their own thought. Hence, the activity of the angel against materiality and sensuality must also be activity against men who have *"the mark of the beast, and . . . worship his image".*

The sensual and materialistic factors in human consciousness are represented as *"ulcerating"* under the joint-action of the angel and material sense, resulting in much suffering, and then going to destruction.

The Second Trumpet and the Second Vial

CHAPTER VIII

8 *And the second angel sounded, and as it were a great mountain burning with fire was cast into the sea: and the third part of the sea became blood.*
9 *And the third part of the creatures which were in the sea, and had life, died; and the third part of the ships were destroyed.*

CHAPTER XVI

3 And the second angel poured out his vial upon the sea; and it became as the blood of a dead man: and every living soul died in the sea.

The second angel may be regarded as identical with the one who is represented as dictating the second of the letters to the churches in Asia; that activity of the Christ-mind which may be described as *Spiritual Reason,* or *Thinking-according-to-Principle.*

"*The sea*", considered in the various connections in which this symbol is used throughout the Apocalypse, would seem to symbolize the sensuous element in human nature,—a region of mental activity which is filled with discord. The fierceness of the activity of the angel against this form of error, and the resulting upheaval, are aptly symbolized by *"a great mountain burning with fire cast into the sea"*. Taken in the literal sense, the boiling of the water, and the disappearance of much of the water in steam, and the killing of the living creatures in the sea, and the making of the water bloody, can readily be imagined,—whence the figurative sense is not difficult to discern. As the result of the activity of the angel, a good commencement is made in destroying the sensuous activity in human consciousness. As indicated before, the activities of the Christ-mind only become operative on the human plane in proportion as men come to understand the Christ-mind and then enforce it. Men who do this may properly be regarded as *carriers* ("ships") of angelic ideas, whereas men in the service of satan may be regarded as *"ships"* of satan. The text declares that in the conflict between the angel and satanic sensuousness, a third part of the human agents will be destroyed.

CHAPTER XVI

Verse 3 of chapter 16 indicates the activity of this same angel finishing his work. As a result, *"the sea"*, sensuousness, becomes *"as the blood of a dead man"*, stagnant, lifeless, without activity: *"And every living soul died in the sea";* that is, there is no more mental activity in the sensuous realm. That phase of mortal mind is destroyed.

The Third Trumpet and the Third Vial

CHAPTER VIII

10 *And the third angel sounded, and there fell a great star from heaven, burning as it were a lamp, and it fell upon the third part of the rivers, and upon the fountains of waters:*

11 *And the name of the star is called Wormwood: and the third part of the waters became wormwood; and many men died of the waters, because they were made bitter.*

CHAPTER XVI

4 And the third angel poured out his vial upon the rivers and fountains of waters; and they became blood.

5 And I heard the angel of the waters say, Thou art righteous, O Lord, which art, wast, and shalt be, because thou hast judged thus.

6 For they haVe shed the blood of saints and prophets, and thou hast given them blood to drink; for they are worthy.

7 And I heard another out of the altar say, Even so, Lord God Almighty, true and righteous are thy judgments.

The third angel is the same as was represented as dictating to John the letter to the church at Pergamos, *Executive Mind, Will, Life.*

To interpret these verses intelligently, we must get a clear definition of what is meant by the word "life". In ordinary human experience, when consciousness has departed from a human body permanently, we say that the person is "dead"; but as long as consciousness is present, we say that he is "alive". Hence, in common human speech, the life is the consciousness. The body of itself "profiteth nothing", and is fit only to be buried. The terms "life" and "consciousness" can be used interchangeably in every phase of practical or philosophical discussion. Whatever supports consciousness supports life. Whatever consciousness is, that life is. True consciousness is true life, and is "eternal life", since all that is true must be eternal. Since God is all truth in origin, and the Christ is all truth in expression, the consciousness of God and His Christ must be consciousness of truth, true consciousness, eternal consciousness, eternal life. *"This is life eternal, that they might know thee the only true God and . . . Christ whom thou hast sent".* False consciousness, consciousness of falsehood, is false life; that is, no life at all. Counterfeit money, though seeming to be money, is not money at all. *"He that hath the Son [the consciousness of the Christ] hath life; and he that hath not the Son of God hath not life",* because he has no consciousness of truth, no true consciousness, and therefore, really, no consciousness or life at all. That which *appears* is only seeming consciousness or life.

For consciousness to continue, it must have something to be conscious of. God, manifest in His ideas, which in the total are the Christ, furnishes all true "food for thought". These ideas are manifestations of Truth and Love; they represent feeling as well as thought. The ideas of Truth and Love, considered as a stream flowing into human consciousness, are aptly symbolized as *"a pure river of water of life"* (Rev. 22:1). Considered as the support of true consciousness, in the sense that water is a support of physical life, they are symbolized as *"living fountains of waters"* (Rev. 7:17).

As true, spiritual consciousness or life must be supported by spiritual ideas and feelings, so even false, mortal consciousness is supported by ideas and feelings of its own order,— namely, ideas resting on a material basis, and feelings that are opposite to divine love in character.

It will be generally admitted that hatred, malice, envy, jealousy and revenge are opposite to divine love. Unmodified human love is equally opposite, though this is not so evident to the majority of people; but it may be made more evident by a bit of consideration. Divine love is impersonal ("no respecter of persons"), and never changes character, cannot be offended, is entirely unselfish. For a full description of it, consult the 13th chapter of First Corinthians. Unmodified human love is always attached to persons, turns to hatred when severely crossed, is often easily offended, and is always more or less selfish. When human love grieves over the misfortune or loss of another, it grieves even more for the effect upon itself than upon the other. The highest type of human love is conceded to be the mother love; yet, a mother, grieving for the death of a child, usually thinks more about how she is going to get along without the child than she does about the fate of the child. If she is a believer in immortality, she will usually concede that the child is in God's care, and that she does not need to be concerned for its welfare; so her love, changed to grief, is, after all, distinctly self-considerate. If the child is seriously ill, the mother's love will beget fear, and thus become, perchance, the chief obstacle to the child's recovery, while divine love will heal the child. In relations between the sexes, human love unmodified by spiritual training gravitates uniformly into sensuality and an endless chain of evil consequences; divine love is absolutely removed from the possibility of such an issue.

As we have seen above, spiritual ideas and spiritual love are symbolized by *"rivers and fountains of waters"*. As is the case with most of the symbols in the Apocalypse, this symbol is also used in a reversed, lower sense, as it is in the verses now under consideration, where it stands for human hatred in its various phases, and unmodified human love.

Among all races of men, human felings are associated with the cardiac region, where they often seem to be located; and the heart is the "fountain" of the "rivers", or streams, of the body,—the arterial system. This fact may have suggested to St. John the use of the phrase *"rivers and fountains of waters"* as a symbol for human emotion.

Like everything human, uncontrolled by the divine, human feelings present in experience a mixture of seeming good and of evil. Except in so far as their action is modified and controlled by divine Mind, even their seeming good is really evil. Hence, when the realm of human emotion is brought more directly under the influence of the Christ-mind,—a state of affairs typified by the sounding of the third angel,—the evil character of mortal love, as well as of mortal hatred, is made more evident and this whole activity of the carnal mind is made to show more plainly its fundamentally discordant nature. To human sense, human love seems like the highest good,—like a *"great star in heaven"*, and it seems to burn with a great light,—though St. John suggests by his symbol that its light is not true, being that of *"a lamp"*, or *"a torch"*, rather than that of the sun. But when the activity of the angel is felt, human emotion loses its apparently "sweet" character, and becomes *"bitter"*, like *"wormwood"*, and in human experience falls out of the apparently high place which it had occupied in the mental realm.

"There fell a great star from heaven, burning as it were a lamp, and it fell upon the third part of the rivers, and upon the fountains of waters". As will be seen from the preceding explanation, human emotion is here represented under two symbols,—first, under that of a star in heaven, that which appears to be a source of light in human experience, and second, under that of rivers and fountains of waters. The whole expression serves to signify that the activity of the angel,—the manifestation of Executive Mind, Life,—causes human emotion to turn upon itself, to its own torment and partial destruction.* The activity of divine Mind always forces every phase of evil to do just this.

Human love, leading to sensuality and resultant evils, has slain untold millions; changed to hatred, fear, and grief, it has fallen upon untold millions more. Considering this fact, it should not be difficult to understand the phrase: *"Many men died of the waters, because they were made bitter."* With the beginning of humanity's experience of the activity of this third angel, human emotion becomes in experience more bitter than it had been by about *"a third part"*.

---

* "Science and Health," 224:7, 8.

CHAPTER XVI

Rotherham translates verses 4-7 of chapter 16 as follows:
"And the third poured out his bowl into the rivers and the fountains of waters; and they became blood. And I heard the messenger of the waters saying—

Righteous art thou Who art and Who wast,
Who art full of loving kindness,—in that these things thou hast adjudged;

Because blood of saints and prophets poured they out, and blood unto them hast thou given to drink: Worthy are they!
And I heard the altar saying—
Yea! Lord God the Almighty:
True and righteous are thy judgments!"

The Greek phrase *ho hosios* in the 5th verse is represented by "and shalt be" in the Authorized Version. The Revised Version, the Twentieth Century New Testament, and Weymouth render it *"the holy one"*. Rotherham renders it *"full of loving kindness"*. "The holy one" seems nearer the ordinary lexicon sense of the phrase. It should also be noted, in the 7th verse, that Rotherham and others represent the altar itself as speaking, rather than "another out of the altar",—which is in accord with the Greek text, and the significance of which will be spoken of presently.

In these verses of the 16th chapter, the third angel, now represented as pouring out the ardor of God from a libation saucer, is shown finishing the task which he began as angel of the trumpet. He is here clearly indicated as the agent of God; for what he accomplishes is represented as God's judgment, and God is accredited as just in this action.

Human emotion, *"the waters"*, instead of becoming *"a third part" "bitter"*, as under the sounding of the trumpet, is now symbolized as water changed wholly to blood,—that is, becoming unnatural in character, and unfit for use,—with the implication that it will, in consequence, perish.

"The angel of the waters" (verse 5) is doubtless the third

angel himself, who, in chapter 2, is seen addressing a letter of instruction to this same phase of the activity of the human consciousness, thus identifying himself as its legitimate ruler, —that is, as the angel of the waters. Since human emotion has meted out destruction to mankind, and has even led to the slaying of *"saints and prophets"*, it is just that destruction ("blood to drink") should be meted out to it. In the end, Executive Mind does destroy it.

The fact that *"the altar"* is represented in verse 7 as speaking, shows that the phrase is used as a symbol, not as a metaphor; for, as a matter of fact, an altar could not speak. The phrase without doubt here symbolizes the spiritualized human consciousness, as the true church, or as representing the Holy Spirit, confirming the justice of God's activity.

The Fourth Trumpet and the Fourth Vial

CHAPTER VIII

12 *And the fourth angel sounded, and the third part of the sun was smitten, and the third part of the moon, and the third part of the stars, so as the third part of them was darkened, and the day shone not for a third part of it, and the night likewise.*

CHAPTER XVI

8 And the fourth angel poured out his vial upon the sun; and power was given unto him to scorch men with fire.

9 And men were scorched with great heat, and blasphemed the name of God, which hath power over these plagues: and they repented not to give him glory.

This Angel is, without doubt, the Christ-mind active as *Direct Cognition, Knowledge-without-Reasoning,* or *Spiritual Intuition, "Mind",*—the angel of the church at Thyatira.

As we have previously indicated, the sun, moon, and stars often symbolize respectively divine Mind, the Christ-mind as reflecting the divine Mind, and the ideas of Mind,—or, in the total, the activity of divine Mind in all its phases. In verse 12, however, they are evidently used in a reversed lower sense, to symbolize material sense in the various phases of its intellectual activity. Specifically, perhaps *"the sun"* symbolizes satan; *"the moon"*, the beast, or human will; and *"the stars"*, various satanic ideas or influences. The mortal, material world, the realm of satan, presents, in experience, a mixture of "good and evil", so that it seems to have a measure of harmony,—a light of its own, which, in its various phases, John represents as coming under the activity of the angel, the result being that a *"third part"* of this false or counterfeit sense of harmony and intelligence is destroyed.

In chapter 16, this same angel, being supplied with the full measure of the ardor of God, is represented as entirely destroying the supposed good or "light" of mortal intellect, driving it to display only, and more violently than ever, its discordant activity,—thus *"scorching"* the men who are still subject to it. They, not perceiving that their discomfort is due to mortal sense, suppose, in their ignorance, that, in some way, God is capriciously withholding good from them and sending evil upon them,—which supposition is in itself a wrong and therefore *"blasphemous"* thought of God, even if these men do not actively and purposely curse God,—the very God whose power would remove *"these plagues"*, if the afflicted men would turn to Him, and away from the beguilements of mortal intellect. The final activity of this angel practically completes the destruction of mortal intellect, since it will not long hold men in its service after it is prevented from deceiving them with a measure of apparent harmony.

The Fifth Trumpet and the Fifth Vial

The text of this trumpet is in chapter 9, verses 1-11. The text of the vial is in verses 10 and 11 of chapter 16. These may be read from the text given with the paraphrase or from a Bible.

The Angel of the fifth trumpet and of the fifth vial is *Divine Love*.

Rotherham translates 9:1 as follows:

"And the fifth messenger sounded; and I saw a star out of heaven fallen unto the earth, and there was given unto him the key of the shaft of the abyss."

The Authorized Version reads:

"And the fifth angel sounded, and I saw a star fall from heaven unto the earth: and to him was given the key of the bottomless pit."

The Greek *phrear* (Genitive, *phreatos*) means literally "a well". The whole phrase, *hê kleis tou phreatos tês abussou*, is translated in the A. V. as *"the key of the bottomless pit"*; in the Revised Version as *"the key of the pit of the abyss"*, in which Ferrar Fenton concurs. Pryse, as *"the key to the crater of the abyss"*; and Weymouth, *"the key of the depths of the bottomless pit"*. Probably the literal foundation for the figure is the mythological conception of a great region below the earth,—supposed to be flat,—with a hole or shaft leading down to it, like the shaft to a mine. This nether region was doubtless thought of as dark and bottomless; so that the thought of "bottomless" is probably legitimately included in the definition of *abussos*. Probably the following would give us the exact literal sense of the Greek: *"The key of the shaft of the bottomless abyss"*.

The star that is fallen from heaven unto the earth is a belief that stands high in the estimation of men, high in their mental realm ("heaven"), but it is really a fallen, apostate belief, and belongs to *"the earth"*. It is the belief that there is life, sensation, pleasure, and intelligence in matter,—a belief which Mrs. Eddy, in Science and Health, has named "animal magnetism". This false belief opens for men *"the bottomless pit"*,—the pit which, because it is bottomless, can hold nothing, and is the origin (?) of evil, which is really nothingness, though asserting a claim, terrible to those who are under its delusion, that it is something. Out of the bottomless pit or abyss ascends a great cloud of "smoke", false belief, which darkens spiritual light ("the sun"), and renders the mental atmosphere dark and stifling. Out of this cloud of false belief spring a perfect swarm of fleshly desires, which have power to inflict suffering on men as terrible as springs from the stings of scorpions.

The attack of these fleshly desires is not directed primarily against the normal activities of human mentality (not against *"the grass of the earth, neither any green thing, neither any tree"*,—see Notes on verse 7), and they are not here considered as directly in the field of conflict, as one and another of them have been considered in the first four trumpets; but the attack is against those who have not "put on the whole armor of God", who have not been so "sealed" by God through their continued and perfect allegiance to Him, that they are invulnerable to fleshly desires. The primary effect of these sinful desires is not to kill men outright, as happens under some of the preceding activities; but the primary effect is to torture men with resulting diseases. In Note 3 of the Introduction, it has been explained that *"five months"*, the portion of the year during which locusts are active, stands for *"locust-time"*; that is, for the entire period of the activity of satanic influences. In other words, as long as men will harbor sinful desires, so long they will be tormented with diseases. Under the torture of these diseases *"shall men seek death, and shall not find it; and shall desire to die, and death shall flee from them"* (verse 6). The symbolism of verses 7-12 may perhaps best be made evident by the following parallel arrangement.

Amended Revised Version

7 And the shapes of the locusts were like unto horses prepared unto battle; and on their heads were as it were crowns like gold, and their faces were as the faces of men.

8 And they had hair as the hair of women, and their teeth were as the teeth of lions.

9 And they had breastplates, as it were breastplates of iron; and the sound of their wings was as the sound of chariots of many horses running to battle.

10 And they had tails like unto scorpions, and there were stings in their tails: and their power was to hurt men five months.

11 And they had a king over them, which is the angel of the bottomless pit, whose name in the Hebrew tongue is Abaddon, but in the Greek tongue hath his name Apollyon.

12 One woe is past; and behold, there come two woes more hereafter.

Suggestive Paraphrase

7 And these sinful desires seem, in human experience, powerful and formidable as war horses; and they seem to offer rewards precious as gold to those who entertain them, and they present an intelligent appearance.

8 And they seem as beautiful as women, but they wound like lions' teeth.

9 And they seem to be strongly protected from being destroyed, and they are continually in evidence in great numbers and create great commotion.

10 And the sting of these sinful desires and pleasures is in their after-effects; and they torment men as long as men will entertain or yield to them.

11 And the source and ruler of these sinful desires is he who has control of the realm of assertive error, which has no foundation, who is called in the Hebrew language Abaddon, and in the Greek language Apollyon.

12 One of the three woes mentioned before (see 8:13) has been revealed; and two are yet to be revealed.

"The idealization of locusts into an army of destruction is the great symbol running through Joel (2:1-11)".—Moulton.

CHAPTER XVI

The text of the fifth vial is given in verses 10, 11 of chapter 16.

"And the fifth Angel poured out his vial upon the seat of the beast, and his kingdom was full of darkness, and they gnawed their tongues for pain, and blasphemed the God of heaven, because of their pains, and their sores, and repented not of their deeds."

Under the fifth vial, the judgment against licentiousness and the licentious is brought to completion. From a study of chapters 12 and 13, we see that *"the seat of the beast"* is *"the dragon", "the devil and satan",* general mortal belief, "animal magnetism". This belief that there is life, pleasure, and intelligence in matter is so crowded to destruction by the activity of this angel exercising the full measure of the ardor of God, and is so aggravated just before destruction, that it terribly afflicts those under its sway, so that they are seen *"gnawing their tongues for pain, and blaspheming the God of heaven because of their pains and their sores".* As is usual with the thoroughly ungodly, they do not see that their own sins are the source of their sufferings, but attribute their sufferings to what they assume to be the caprice of God, and so they curse Him.

The Sixth Trumpet and the Sixth Vial

The text of this trumpet is given in chapter '9' verses 13-21, *quod vide.*

Verses 13, 14 *"And the sixth Angel sounded, and I heard a voice from the four horns of the golden altar, which is before God, saying to the sixth Angel which had the trumpet, Loose the four Angels which are bound in the great river Euphrates."*

This Angel is the angel of the church at Philadelphia, the Christ-mind in its activity as *Perception of Reality, "Truth".* The activity of this angel is against idolatry and idolaters, as shown by verses 20 and 21.

"And the rest of the men, which were not killed by these plagues, yet repented not of the works of their hands, that they should not worship devils, and idols of gold, and silver, and brass, and stone, and wood; which neither can see, nor hear, nor walk. Neither repented they of their murders, nor of their sorceries, nor of their fornication, nor of their thefts."

The *"voice from the golden altar"* is a symbol for the Holy Spirit or some activity thereof. It will require a bit of preparatory statement to make clear what is meant by *"the great river Euphrates".*

The ancient city of Babylon, which was at the heighth of its power about 600 B. C., was the embodiment of worldliness, superstition, tyranny, cruelty, lust, sorcery, materialism, carnality, false doctrine,—all that was apostate from Spirit and Christ. Among the Jews, Babylon was the symbol of all the above evil influences,—all of which have their root in, and follow in the train of, false belief or superstition. The river Euphrates ran through Babylon. It was the avenue of the city's commerce and the source of the city's water supply,—and so was, in a sense, the source or support of the city's material life. Hence, it is used as a symbol of the stream of superstition or false belief in human consciousness.*

---

* Mr. F. L. Rawson writes: "The 'River Euphrates' I take to mean the scientific world"; that is, the learning of natural science, upholding material belief.

In the phrase *"the four angels"*, in verse 14 above, *"four"* is evidently used in the customary collective sense; and *"the four Angels"* here stand for the spiritualized factor in human consciousness,—the consciousness which was formerly in the service of the world, as indicated by the world-sign *"four"*,—a factor which St. John here represents as only potential, indicating that it is held in check or suppressed at or by *"the great river Euphrates"*,—that is, by the stream of human superstition; but the command is, that the Angel shall *"loose"* the human consciousness from this bondage,—with the result that, as we shall soon see, the spiritual factor in human consciousness (the manifestation of the Holy Spirit), being thus "loosed", becomes militant,—becomes the very activity of the Holy Spirit against evil and evil-doers.

As was fully discussed and illustrated in the interpretation of verse 7 of chapter 8 (which see), there is no punishment or suffering or death for even mortal men in divine Mind, or in any of its activities or manifestations, but when the divine Mind and its manifestations act upon mortal mind, causing it to react, there arise mental "storms" which are very afflictive and destructive to human beings who are exposed to them. Thus, in verse 7 of chapter 8, the activity of the first angel is represented as stirring up the destructive influences which are symbolized under the figure of a violent hail storm. In verse 15 of the chapter we are now considering, the *"four Angels"*, which are *"loosed"* by the activity of the sixth angel, are represented as also stirring up destructive activities, which are to *"slay the third part of men"*. Verse 15 is as follows:

"And the four Angels were loosed, and were prepared for an hour, and a day, and a month, and a year, for to slay the third part of men."

The four time periods mentioned would seem to indicate that the *"four Angels"*, the spiritualized factor in human consciousness, are ready for service for *any* length of time, short or long, that may be necessary to accomplish their work.

Verse 16 *"And the number of the army of the horsemen were two hundred thousand thousand: and I heard the number of them."*

The activity of the Christ-mind, or of the Holy Spirit, which in verse 13 is represented by the "sixth Angel", and in verses 14, 15 by "the four Angels", is now represented by the *"army of horsemen"*. This army of *"two hundred thousand thousand"* doubtless symbolizes the activity of the infinite number of divine ideas,—or possibly even the activity of the spiritual factors in the mentalities of the great host of Christ's people on earth in all the centuries,—mentally and actively enforcing the law of God.

Verses 17, 18 *"And thus I saw the horses in the vision, and them that sat on them, having breastplates of fire and jacinth (smoky blue), and brimstone, and the heads of the horses were as the heads of lions, and out of their mouths issued fire, and smoke, and brimstone. By these three was the third part of men killed, by the fire, and by the smoke, and by the brimstone which issued out of their mouths."*

While, as indicated before, there is nothing destructive to men in any of the activities or manifestations of divine Mind as such, yet these activities, acting upon mortal mind and meeting resistance, stir up resultant activities which are very destructive; and here, as in many places, St. John seems to attribute, rather undiscriminatingly, to the divine agencies a destruction of men which, strictly speaking, should be attributed to the satanic element in the "storms" stirred up through the action and reaction of divine and satanic agencies. To mortal sense in its various phases, the activity of divine Mind as the Holy Spirit or as Angels or militant ideas, is as destructive as *"fire"*, as blinding as *"smoke"*, and as stifling and choking as *"brimstone"*. It is by reason of this fact that, in various places in the Apocalypse, the Holy Spirit, or its activity, is symbolized by *"fire, smoke, and brimstone"*. The horses and their riders, in verses 17, 18, are represented by these symbols as destructive to men enmeshed in material sense. As a matter of fact, as the spiritual consciousness becomes active in the world, it does stir up the evil factors in the mentalities of many men who resist it, resulting in disease and death. Then, too, as the spiritual consciousness *begins* to become active among men, it fills them and the so-called Christian nations with missionary zeal, on a rather low plane; and they go forth to convert the so-called heathen. The comparatively few who are receptive to their message are kindly treated, but they conceive it to be their duty to make war with sword and gun on the "heathen" who will not accept their teaching. The history of the last nineteen centuries is filled with records of wars and expeditions of this kind. As a result, the world has been drenched with the blood of the so-called heathen, and of the so-called Christians, in conflicts which have been brought to pass upon the field of human activity by the *small measure* of the Christ-consciousness or Holy Spirit which so-called Christian peoples have received at the beginning of their receptivity of the higher consciousness. When men enter into a *larger measure* of the realization of the Holy Spirit and its activities, they are still militant against evil, but they know that evil is not to be destroyed by killing men, even if they seem to be evil-doers, and, accordingly, more advanced followers of Christ do not try to destroy evil in that way. However, it is safe to say that, in the two ways mentioned, literally *"a third part of men"* have been put to death during the last nineteen centuries, sooner than they otherwise would have died, through the activities stirred up in the world and in the fields of personal consciousness by the advent of the Christ-mind among men.

Verse 19 *"For their power is in their mouth, and in their tails: for their tails were like unto serpents, and had heads, and with them they do hurt."*

The *"power in their mouth"*. (It is instructive to note that, though the horsemen are represented as two hundred thousand thousand, they are here represented as having only one "mouth", which is a way of signifying the fact that their joint activities are the *one* activity of the Holy Spirit). The *"power in their mouth"* may symbolize the *initial* effect of the activity of the Holy Spirit as it becomes a factor in any human situation, while *"the power in their tails"* may symbolize the *after effects* of any activity of the Holy Spirit. It is plain to be seen that where the initial activity, or reception of small measures, of the Christ-mind stirs up religious wars, its first effect is destructive, and it also sets in motion a train of consequences which trail along with destructive effects for years afterward,—even giving rise to feuds and hostilities which are deliberately and purposely kept alive, sometimes for centuries. This may be a reason why these after effects, or *"tails"*, are said to *"have heads"* which *"hurt"*. Because of the initial strife which was destructive, other strifes, which will continue to be destructive, are deliberately planned for, manifesting evil intelligence, symbolized by *"the head"*. In the field of personal consciousness, there is often a similar result. The reception of the Holy Spirit may be attended by a painful mental struggle at the start, during which several or more wicked tendencies in consciousness are slain, and then there continues to be a struggle between good and evil for an indefinite period afterward, during which still other evil activities are slain,—often with painful results in mind and body while the struggle goes on and the elements of the lower nature are being put to death; and yet there is "a more excellent way",—that of "painless progress", for those who can demonstrate it.

Verses 20, 21 *"And the rest of the men which were not killed by these plagues, yet repented not of the works of their hands, that they should not worship devils, and idols of gold, and silver, and brass, and stone, and of wood, which neither can see, nor hear, nor walk: neither repented they of their murders, nor of their sorceries, nor of their fornication, nor of their thefts."*

St. John here indicates that, notwithstanding that the Holy Spirit becomes active enough in the world to stir up the destructive activities above described,—even to the extent of about a third of mankind being slain,—yet for an indefinite period, century after century, the vast majority of the remainder of men will continue on with their superstitions, idolatries, and sins. Only when the sixth Angel finally discards the trumpet and receives the libation saucer filled with the full measure of the ardor of God will his activities become so complete that the wickedness of men will be brought near its end; but, strictly speaking, the change is not in the activity of the angel, but in humanity's near approach to and more direct reception of that activity.

CHAPTER XVI

Verse 12 of chapter 16 reads:
"And the sixth Angel poured out his vial upon the great river Euphrates, and the water thereof was dried up, that the way of the Kings of the East might be prepared."

When Cyrus the Persian besieged Babylon, being unable to capture it by other means, he dug a great trench outside the city's walls, and diverted the Euphrates around the city. Thus he cut off the water supply of the city, and was finally able to march his troops into the city in the old river bed, which he had made dry, leaving an opening in the wall where it had formerly flowed. This historical fact probably furnishes the basis of the above symbolism. As daylight dawns in the East, and seems to proceed from the East, the East is here taken as the symbol of spiritual light, or the Christ-mind; and the *"Kings of the East"* are the followers of the Christ, mentally and actively enforcing the law of God against superstition and false belief (*"the great river Euphrates"*), until *"the water thereof dries up"*; that is, until the stream of false belief in human consciousness is fully overcome and disappears. Thus will mental Babylon be overthrown, as was ancient Babylon, the seat of wickedness.

Between the sixth and seventh trumpets there are introduced two important visions (chapter 10:1 to chapter 11:14), the interpretation of which we shall next consider.

NOTES BY THE READER

Chapter X

John's Vision of the Full Truth

Verse 1 *"And I saw another mighty Angel come down from heaven, clothed with a cloud: and a rainbow was upon his head, and his face was as it were the sun, and his feet as pillars of fire."*

In Science and Health, page 558, Mrs. Eddy has beautifully interpreted this verse. The gist of her interpretation is that: "This angel or message which comes from God, clothed with a cloud, prefigures divine Science. To mortal sense Science seems at first obscure, abstract, and dark [*"the cloud"*]; but a bright promise [*"the rainbow"*] crowns its brow. When understood, it is Truth's prism and praise. When you look it fairly in the face, you can heal by its means and it has for you a light above the sun, for God 'is the light thereof'. Its feet are pillars of fire, foundations of Truth and Love". "Truth and Love" destroy or "burn up" error in human consciousness, and so are symbolized by "fire".

Verse 2 *"And he had in his hand a little book open: and he set his right foot upon the sea, and his left foot on the earth."*

The Angel of verse 1 is undoubtedly the Christ, "Jesus Christ."* The Greek diminutive *biblaridion,* translated "a little book", may be used, as we often use diminutives, as a term of endearment, in the sense of "precious". This view is strengthened by the fact that, in verse 1 of chapter 14, John speaks of the Christ under the symbol of *arnion,* meaning "a little lamb", and so generally throughout the book, instead of employing *amnos,* which means "a lamb". There is no evident reason for his using the diminutive form, except as an expression of endearment. The term "little" may also indicate that the message is comparatively brief, in comparison with its mighty import.

---

* See "Prologue," on page 29 of this book, for interpretation of this term.

It has been suggested by at least one commentator that the *"little book"* refers to the message of the Apocalypse itself, represented, in chapter 5, as "a book sealed with seven seals" in the right hand of the Father; but there should be a definite article before *biblaridion,* if it refers back to *biblion* of the 5th chapter; but no Greek manuscript gives such an article. The *"little book"* doubtless refers specifically to the message of divine Science, the same order of revelation as has now been given to the world in "Science and Health with Key to the Scriptures", as distinguished from, though in part at least included in, the message of the Apocalypse as a whole.

In Science and Health", on page 559, Mrs. Eddy wrote: "This angel had in his hand 'a little book', open. . . . Did this same book contain the revelation of divine Science, the 'right foot' or dominant power of which was was upon the sea,—upon elementary, latent error, the source of all error's visible forms? The angel's left foot was upon the earth; that is, a secondary power was exercised upon visible error and audible sin. The 'still, small voice' of scientific thought reaches over continent and ocean to the globe's remotest bound."

In a more narrow and technical sense, *"the sea"* probably symbolizes the sensuous element in human consciousness, and *"the earth"* symbolizes materiality and sensuality.

Verse 3 *"And (the Angel) cried with a loud voice, as when a Lion roareth: and when he had cried, seven thunders uttered their voices."*

The *"loud voice, as when a Lion roareth"* of the angel symbolizes the majesty and impressiveness of the message, as it is given to John. The Revised Version more correctly renders the Greek by, *"and when he cried, the seven thunders uttered their voices"*, omitting "had" before "cried". In other words, the proclamations of the angel and of the "thunders" were coincident in point of time. Throughout the Scriptures, "thunder" is the conventional symbol for the utterance of God or of the Holy Spirit, as any student can readily satisfy himself by examining a concordance. In the verse which we are now considering, the *"seven thunders"* doubtless represent the utterance of "the seven Spirits, which are before the throne of God", which, considered collectively, are the Holy Spirit; and their utterance ("seven" being the number of completeness) is the message of the full truth, divine Science, "the spirit of Truth, which shall lead you into all truth". The proclamation of the full truth would doubtless, as Mrs. Eddy suggests on page 559 of "Science and Health", "arouse the 'seven thunders' of evil, and stir their latent forces to utter the full diapason of secret tones", driving them to final destruction,—as she further says: "Then is the power of Truth demonstrated,—made manifest in the destruction of error".

Verse 4 *"And when the seven thunders had uttered their voices, I was about to write: and I heard a voice from heaven, saying unto me, Seal up those things which the seven thunders uttered, and write them not."*

This seems to indicate that, when the vision of the full truth came to John, his first impulse was to write what was revealed to him and give it to the world in plain language; but immediately "the spirit of wisdom", *"a voice from heaven"*, commanded him not to reveal *"those things which the seven thunders uttered"*,—not to *"write"*, but to "seal up" the message.

Verses 5-7 *"And the Angel which I saw stand upon the sea, and upon the earth, lifted up his hand to heaven, and sware by him that liveth for ever and ever, who created heaven, and the things that therein are, and the earth, and the things that therein are, and the sea, and the things which are therein, that there should be time no longer. But in the days of the voice of the seventh Angel, when he shall begin to sound, the mystery of God should be finished, as he hath declared to his servants the Prophets."*

The Christ is here represented as affirming most solemnly that the time-sense, the temporal sense, of things shall cease,—with an implication that it is the proclamation of the seventh Angel which will usher in the spiritual, eternal sense, which shall cause the time-sense to disappear. Then St. John goes on to say that when the world shall begin to receive the spiritual message of the seventh Angel,—which is to be understood as the final and complete message, "seven" being the number of completeness,—*"the mystery of God should be finished";* that is, the message sealed up in the Apocalypse will then be unsealed, so that all may plainly understand. In verse 10 of chapter 22, the Angel says to John: "Seal not the sayings of the prophecy of this book: for the time is at hand".

As indicated in the Introduction, and as will be freely acknowledged by all those who understand it, Christian Science is beginning to give to the world a knowledge of all things as being spiritual and eternal, when perceived as they are, thus causing the time-sense of things to be regarded as invalid and untrustworthy; that is, to be believed no more. Accordingly, it is evident that we are now in the midst of the activity of the seventh Angel,—the very period of human development when the Apocalypse itself states that its message shall be plainly revealed.

Some translators render the fundamental thought in verses 6 and 7 as follows: And sware by him that liveth unto the ages of the ages that there shall be *no more delay;* but that, in the days of the proclamation of the seventh Angel, . . . the mystery of God shall be revealed.

This is equivalent to a declaration that the final and complete revelation will not be delayed beyond the days of the beginning of the proclamation of the seventh Angel. There is in this interpretation no direct teaching that the time-sense shall vanish,—though that will be the fact, nevertheless.

Verses 8-10 *"And the voice which I heard from heaven spake unto me again, and said, Go, and take the little book which is open in the hand of the Angel which standeth upon the sea, and upon the earth. And I went unto the Angel, and said unto him, Give me the little book. And he said unto me, Take it, and eat it up, and it shall make thy belly bitter, but it shall be in thy mouth sweet as honey. And I took the little book out of the Angel's hand, and ate it up, and it was in my mouth sweet as honey: and as soon as I had eaten it, my belly was bitter."*

The import of these verses may be taken in a two-fold sense:

First, that the perception of the full truth is delightful to the understanding, but that the working toward it in experience, the "digestion" of it, is "bitter",—as is also the foreview of what the human race will have to go through in attaining the demonstration of the full truth.

Second, that the reception of the full truth into daily living, in the endeavor to work it out, is *"sweet as honey"* to the higher elements in human nature, symbolized by the mouth, but is destructive and "bitter" to the lower elements in human nature, symbolized by the belly,—at least, St. John so found it in experience.

Verse 11 *"And he said unto me, Thou must prophesy again before many peoples, and nations, and tongues, and kings."*

If this translation be correct, this may be taken as a declaration that, after the meaning of the Apocalypse is unsealed so that all may plainly understand its message, John will again become, through this message, a living prophet to a great host of the world's population.

The Greek preposition *epi* (translated *"before"* in the A.V., as above) is translated in the Revised Version "over", with "concerning" in the margin. Rotherham translates it "against", as does also Farrer Fenton. Pryse renders it "in opposition to"; Weymouth, "concerning"; and the Twentieth Century New Testament, "about".

"In opposition to", or "in the face of", is the most characteristic of all these meanings for *epi,* when used with the dative case, as it is in this text. If this is the correct sense, then the meaning is, that John must prophesy again, as he had previously done in his Gospel, against the worldly sense of things, as represented in the thought of "many nations, peoples, tongues and rulers". With the genitive case, *epi* characteristically means "before", or "in the presence of", as in the Authorized Version; but all Greek manuscripts give the dative in this verse following *epi,* instead of the genitive.

NOTES BY THE READER

NOTES BY THE READER

Chapter XI:1-13

A Vision of the Activity of the Holy Spirit

Verses 1, 2 *"And there was given me a reed like unto a rod, and the Angel stood, saying, Rise, and measure the Temple of God, and the Altar, and them that worship therein. But the Court which is without the Temple leave out, and measure it not: for it is given unto the Gentiles, and the Holy City shall they tread under foot forty and two months."*

Having been given the full truth, John was now able to use it as a Principle to separate between truth and falsehood,—somewhat as follows:

If God is sole creator, then all that really is proceeds from Him as Source. It is axiomatic that nothing can come out of a source unlike what is in the source. Hence, nothing has ever proceeded from God which is unlike God; and, if it be true that He is sole creator, sole Source, then whatever appears ungodlike in human experience cannot represent things as they are, but must merely represent a false sense of things. The real universe, the real man, proceeding from God, must be like their Source,—that is, like Spirit, or spiritual; like the eternal God, or eternal; like the perfect God, or perfect; like the infinite God, or infinite. On the other hand, those manifestations in human experience which appear material, temporary, imperfect, and finite, are ungodlike in character, and so must be untrue and unreal,—and should always be denied, and never affirmed. Accordingly, it is evident that the factor in human consciousness which thinks in terms of the spiritual, the eternal, the perfect, and the infinite, is godlike or true consciousness; and this is the true church, and is symbolized in verse 1 as *"the Temple of God, and the Altar, and them that worship therein"*. The *"reed like unto a rod"* is "the Spirit of truth", "the Holy Spirit", used as Principle in the manner above described. It is also evident that the factor in human consciousness which thinks in terms of the material, the temporary, the imperfect, and the finite, is false consciousness, opposing the true church. This false consciousness is symbolized in verse 2 as *"the Court which is without the Temple, . . . given unto the Gentiles."* It cannot be measured in terms of Principle; so St. John is directed to *"leave it out, and measure it not."* The Gentiles, the slaves of false consciousness, will, in human experience, *"tread under foot"*, or keep in subordinate position, the spiritual consciousness, *"the Holy City"*, during the period of the supremacy of satanic activity in the world,—a period symbolized by *"forty and two months"*, equivalent to 3½ years, half of "seven" years, half of *all* years, or half of the time-period, as more fully explained in Note 3 of the Introduction.

Verse 3 *"And I will give power unto my two* witnesses, and they shall prophesy a thousand two hundred and three score days clothed in sackcloth."*

The broadest and most widely applicable interpretation for the *"two witnesses"* of the Christ is to consider them as *truth* and *love*. Their united activity constitutes the activity of the Holy Spirit in human consciousness. Their joint and balanced activity is necessary to the accomplishment of anything worth while in the human realm, as the following brief statement may serve to show:

The Union of Truth and Love

In the divine Mind, truth and love are constantly and indissolubly wedded. All human undertakings which are to count for anything must exemplify this union, for it is "according to the pattern shewed to thee in the mount". "Be ye perfect, even as your Father which is in heaven is perfect."

It is one of the "wiles of the devil" to try to divorce truth and love in the consciousness of men, and to make them believe that truth can be advanced through war and strife, carried on with motives of anger, hatred, revenge, self-interest, or self-

---

* Note the use here of the Spirit-sign "two," and see Note 2 of the Introduction.

justification. Ever and anon, problems of importance must be discussed and settled in our families, in our churches, in our business relations, and in the larger negotiations of politics, law, government, religion, and diplomacy. In these discussions, let us defeat the "one evil" through understanding and bearing in mind that, by no amount of argument, however valid, and by no amount of force of any kind, can we successfully promulgate truth and permanently bring to pass the correct issue, unless, during our efforts, we purposely and habitually exercise the spirit of good-will. In dealing with others, reasoning and good-will are as the wings of a bird. If a bird tries to fly with only one wing, he whirls round and round, to his own confusion, getting nowhere; but using both wings, he makes much progress.

Only as the male principle, truth, and the female principle, love, are wedded in our consciousness can we obey the spiritual command: "Be fruitful (of righteous thoughts and deeds), and multiply (them), and replenish the earth (with them), and subdue it." Truth will go no farther and no faster than love goes as a companion. "What therefore God hath joined together, let no man put asunder."

St. John's statement is that these two witnesses will be active in human consciousness during 1260 apocalyptic days, equivalent to 42 months, and symbolical of the period of the apparent supremacy of satanic activity in the world, during which period these two witnesses will perform their work in an apparently subordinate position, *"clothed in sackcloth",*—that is, they will not have that supreme and unquestioned place in the world to which they are entitled.

Verse 4 *"These are the two olive trees, and the two candlesticks, standing before the God of the earth."*

This symbolism is echoed from Zech. 4:3, 11, 14; and John here likens truth and love to two lighted candlesticks, fed by the oil of two olive trees, standing before the throne of God, and lighting men, so far as they are ready to receive light. The whole verse is a symbol of the Holy Spirit.

Verse 5 *"And if any man will hurt them, fire proceedeth out of their mouth, and devoureth their enemies: and if any man will hurt them, he must in this manner be killed."*

If any man tries to hurt the Holy Spirit (truth and love), he has only error with which to do so, and this error the Holy Spirit destroys when they come in conflict: and if any man persistently attacks the Holy Spirit with a given error or malicious purpose, he is thrown back by the Holy Spirit as from a wall of adamant to have his mortal life destroyed by that same error. Note that, although the "witnesses" are "two", they are spoken of as having only *one* "mouth", indicating their essential unity.

Verse 6 *"These have power to shut heaven, that it rain not in the days of their prophecy: and have power over waters to turn them to blood, and to smite the earth with all plagues, as often as they will."*

Harmony is included within the life of obedience to truth and love, and while these witnesses are held in a subordinate position by men, men are excluded from harmony; and because of this, mankind (see chapter 17:15) will be engaged in bloody wars, and smitten with plagues, as long and as often as men neglect these witnesses. Verse 15 of chapter 17, referred to in the parenthesis above, reads: "The waters which thou sawest, where the whore sitteth, are peoples, and multitudes, and nations, and tongues." So "mankind" is the evident meaning of "waters" in verse 6 above.

Verse 7. This verse seems to the author to be falsely rendered in all of the seven translations which he has examined. They all substantially agree with the Authorized Version in the following rendering:

"And when they shall have finished their testimony, the beast that ascendeth out of the bottomless pit shall make war against them, and shall overcome them, and kill them."

The question of translation is concerning the first clause, the Greek of which is: *Kai hotan telesôsi tên marturian autôn*. The primary or derivative sense of *telesôsi* is unquestionably "shall finish". This is the only argument in favor of the translation above given. On the other hand, the verb *teleô* is very commonly used in the Greek in the sense of "perform", as any student can satisfy himself by consulting Liddell & Scott. Also, *marturian* is quite as correctly translated by "witnessing" as by "testimony". *Hotan* very seldom means "when", but almost invariably "whenever", or "as long as". Accordingly, a translation of the clause, equally correct with the one given in the A. V., is: *"And whenever they shall perform their witnessing"*. This translation is in accord with the general line of John's thought in various passages of the Apocalypse, and is capable of a rational interpretation in connection with its context, as we shall presently see, while the other rendering gives a meaning which cannot be harmonized with its context to bring out a satisfactory exposition. This is the deciding argument in favor of the latter translation, in accordance with which the meaning of the whole verse would be:

And whenever they shall perform their witnessing, the activity of satanic domination, exercising itself through human will and authority, will make war against them, and will overcome them, and will seem to suppress them entirely in the realm of human activity. While the so-called Christian nations have had some degree of the letter of truth in all the centuries since the ascension of Jesus, they have had so little of the spirit of Truth that the Holy Spirit may fairly be said to have been "dead" or "killed" among them.

Verse 8 *"And their dead bodies shall lie in the street of the great city, which spiritually is called Sodom and Egypt, where also our Lord was crucified."*

Here again is a mistranslation, in that the plural "bodies" is given instead of the singular "body", as in the Greek text. This point of rendering is important, since "the two witnesses" clearly stand for a unified entity, the Holy Spirit, which should therefore be thought of as having one "body" (if any at all), and not as having "bodies". The "two" is used in a merely symbolical sense; and does not mean literally "two", just as the "four", in the phrase "four living creatures", does not indicate four separate entities, but is used in a merely collective sense.

The *"dead body"* of the two witnesses may be taken to indicate that worldly and visible church which is practically devoid of the Holy Spirit, unable to perform, to any considerable extent, the works of the Spirit. Mortal sense does not put this worldly church, spiritually dead, out of sight,—does not bury it, as it would the lifeless body of a man,—but keeps it in evidence. *"The great city, which spiritually is called Sodom and Egypt, where also our Lord was crucified"* is a symbolic description of the realm of mortal consciousness, as *"the Holy City"* is symbolical of the realm of spiritual consciousness. It was in the realm of mortal consciousness that the crucifixion of Jesus was conceived and executed.

Verses 9, 10 *"And they of the people, and kindreds, and tongues, and nations, shall see their dead bodies (body) three days and a half, and shall not suffer their dead bodies to be put in graves (the grave). And they that dwell upon the earth shall rejoice over them, and make merry, and shall send gifts one to another, because these two prophets tormented them that dwell on the earth."*

The worldly nations, *"they that dwell upon the earth"* (that is, in material sense) shall look upon the spiritually lifeless worldly church *"three days and a half"* (which, as indicated in Note 3 of the Introduction, symbolizes half of the time-period, or the period of satanic ascendency), and, as previously indicated, will not put it out of sight, but will keep it in evidence as "a laughing stock", making merry because the church is "dead", since, if it were spiritually alive, "the two prophets" (truth and love, the Holy Spirit) would be active in the world, and would torment, and interfere with the plans and pleasures of, those who dwell in material sense.

Verse 11 *"And after three days and a half the Spirit of life from God entered into them: and they stood upon their feet, and great fear fell upon them which saw them."*

At the end of the period of satanic ascendency (symbolized by "three days and a half"), the millennial period of harmony on earth, when satan, discord, will be "bound" (20:2), will be ushered in, as previously indicated, and as fully explained in the Notes on chapter 20. This is the period when the Holy Spirit, which has so long seemed without life in the world, will become the ruling Spirit of this world, as it always is of the absolute realm. The evidence of life and strong activity on the part of truth and love will cause consternation among the dwellers in material sense, the very ones who had been making merry at their apparent lifelessness.

Verse 12 *"And they heard a great voice from heaven, saying unto them, Come up hither. And they ascended up to heaven in a cloud, and their enemies beheld them."*

Truth and love now assume an exalted position, even in the sight of the world, though their real nature and significance is "clouded" (not understood) to their enemies, the worldly minded, who behold them.

Verse 13 *"And the same hour was there a great earthquake; and the tenth part of the city fell, and in the earthquake were slain (names) of men seven thousand: and the remnant were affrighted, and gave glory to the God of heaven."* *

The word "names" appears in the margin of both the Authorized and Revised Versions, and translates the word *onomata* (plural of *onoma*) in the Greek text. There is no possibility of getting a right sense of John's meaning in this

---

* Mr. F. L. Rawson suggests that, in historical interpretation, this verse forecasts "the French Revolution and the number of aristocracy slain, which was just about seven thousand. The remainder, who had been atheistic, immediately after the terrors had abated became religious, and revived religious services."

verse without including the translation of this word, and without also considering the symbolic rather than the literal sense of "seven" and "a thousand".

The Greek *onoma*, like the English "name", means primarily a distinguishing appellative, the written or vocalized word by which a person, place or thing is known; but there comes to be associated with every person's name a sense of his nature or character, and of his authority and power, if he has any. In this way, the Greek *onoma* came to have such meanings as "nature", "character", "authority", "power". Its use in such a sense can readily be discerned in the following verses of Scripture:

"*Many believed in his name (divine nature and authority), when they saw the miracles which he did.*"—John 2:23.

"*I am come in my Father's name (authority), and ye received me not: if another shall come in his own name (authority), him ye will receive.*"—John 5:43.

"*I have manifested thy name (nature and character) unto the men which thou gavest me out of the world.*"—John 17:6.

"*And it shall come to pass, that whosoever shall call on the name (power) of the Lord shall be saved.*"—Acts 2:21.

"*There is none other name (character or nature) under heaven given among men, whereby we must be saved.*"—Acts 4:12.

In the next place, it is necessary to know, as one can learn by consulting Liddell & Scott's Greek Lexicon, that the Greek *onoma* frequently means "*a name and nothing else, opposite to the real person or thing.*" Hence, *onoma* may mean *false or mortal character or nature,* as opposed to real, spiritual nature, and this is what it does mean in the verse under consideration. The "*thousand*" signifies *spiritual conquerors,* and "*seven*" signifies the *complete number.* The meaning of the entire verse is as follows:

At the time that the Holy Spirit attains the ascendency in human consciousness, there will be a great mental upheaval ("earthquake"), and a large number ("a tenth part") of the factors in mortal consciousness ("the city") will be destroyed, and in this period of transition and upheaval the mortal natures or characters of all ("seven") who attain spiritual conquest ("thousand") at this time will be destroyed ("slain"): and those who are not regenerated will nevertheless continue thereafter in fear and trembling, and will recognize God's glory and authority, as the worldly never had during the period of apparent satanic ascendency.

"Three Unclean Spirits Like Frogs"

Following the sixth *trumpet,* St. John introduced an *episode,* which occupies the text of chapter 10, and of chapter 11 as far as the 13th verse, the interpretation of which we have considered.

CHAPTER XVI

Following the sixth *vial,* John introduces an *episode,* chapter 16:13-16, the text of which is as follows:

13 *"And I saw three unclean spirits like frogs come out of the mouth of the dragon, and out of the mouth of the beast, and out of the mouth of the false prophet.*

14 *For they are the spirits of devils working miracles, which go forth unto the Kings of the earth, and of the whole world, to gather them, to the battle of that great day of God Almighty. Behold, I come as a thief.*

15 *Blessed is he that watcheth, and keepeth his garments, lest he walk naked, and they see his shame.*

16 *And he* ["*they,*" according to Revised Version] *gathered them together into a place, called in the Hebrew tongue, Armageddon."*

These unclean, miracle-working spirits may be identified as follows:

That *"out of the mouth of the dragon"* (*the devil*) is healing through hypnotism, mental therapeutics, suggestion, etc.

That *"out of the mouth of the beast"* (*civil misgovernment*) is legalized *materia medica.*

That *"out of the mouth of the false prophet"* (*the worldly church*) is healing through blind faith, shrines, relics, etc.

All these are radically opposed to the true, spiritual healing of Christ; and to the spiritually minded they are as loathsome in appearance as frogs are to the material vision. God says (verse 15), *"Behold, I come as a thief."* This is equivalent to a declaration that no man can tell when any of his evil deeds will accumulate to the point of effectual judgment by truth; in other words, no evil doer can tell when his "day of reckoning" will come. This same thought is very tersely stated in *"The Dhammapada":*

"Even an evil-doer sees happiness so long as his evil deed does not ripen; but when his evil deed ripens, then does the evil-doer see evil. As long as the evil deed done does not bear fruit, the fool thinks it is like honey; but when it ripens, then the fool suffers grief."

Therefore, *"blessed is he that watcheth, and keepeth his garments, lest he walk [spiritually] naked, and they see his shame."*

There is manuscript authority for both the singular and the plural form of the verb in verse 16, the singular form predominating in the manuscripts. If the singular form is what should appear, then its implied subject is God, the sense being that He shall gather together the spiritually watchful to battle against the forces of evil. See verse 14, and also chapter 19, verses 17 and 19. If the plural form of the verb is correct, as recognized by the Revised Version, then its implied subject is "the spirits of devils working miracles", and the sense is a repetition of that of verse 14.

NOTES BY THE READER

NOTES BY THE READER

The Seventh Trumpet and the Seventh Vial

Verses 14-17 (chapter 11). *"The second woe is passed, and behold, the third woe cometh quickly. And the seventh Angel sounded, and there were great voices in heaven, saying, The kingdoms of this world are become the kingdoms of our Lord, and of his Christ, and he shall reign for ever and ever. And the four and twenty Elders which sat before God on their seats, fell upon their faces, and worshipped God, saying, We give thee thanks, O Lord God Almighty, which art, and wast, and art to come; because thou hast taken to thee thy great power, and hast reigned."*

It seems the general policy of St. John, though not invariably so, to dramatize in each Act some special phase of the activity of the Christ-mind in the world, symbolizing the different phases of satanic activity with which it contends, and bringing the whole movement forward to an expression of victory for the Christ-activity at the close of the Act. So, in the instance now before us, the proclamation of the seventh Angel of the trumpeters is a proclamation of triumph and rejoicing,—which, however, is a "woe" to the dwellers in mortal sense.

Verse 18 *"And the nations were angry* [should be translated, *teeming with enthusiasm*], *and thy wrath* [*"ardor"* is the correct sense] *is come, and the time of the dead that they should be judged, and that thou shouldest give reward unto thy servants the Prophets, and to the Saints, and them that fear thy Name, small and great, and shouldest destroy them which destroy the earth."*

When the Greek *ôrgisthasan* is translated according to its derivative meaning, and as the context here plainly requires, it signifies that the nations were in a riot of enthusiasm, filled with love and joy; and *orgê* indicates the divine ardor in mediatorial consciousness. See in this connection Note 4 of the Introduction, where the correct translation of *orgê*, and of other words, from the same root, is fully discussed. The whole of verse 18, when correctly rendered, indicates that the rejoicing in heaven, depicted in verses 15-17, is shared on earth; in fact, verse 18 is a brief presentation of the arrival of the millennial period more fully described at the commencement of chapter 20. In that chapter, it is indicated that a part of the dead are raised at the beginning of the millennial period and the remainder at its close, and that all Christ's faithful people enter into their reward, and that the power of God brings destruction on those activities of satan which had brought discord and destruction upon the earth during the whole period of satanic activity.

Verse 19 of this chapter belongs at the commencement of Act 4.

The Seventh Vial

(Chapter 16:17-21)

Verse 17 *"And the seventh Angel poured out his vial into the air, and there came a great voice out of the Temple of heaven, from the throne, saying, It is done."*

We have little to serve as a basis of judgment as to the proper interpretation of *"air"*, at the end of the first clause; but, by comparison of this verse with the other verses in the chapter which represent the activities of the Angels, we are led to regard *"the air"* as symbolizing something in opposition to the activity of the Angel. The preceding Angels have been represented as attacking phases of human nature, beginning with the lowest and working progressively upward toward those which are considered higher. Accordingly, "the air" may be taken to symbolize those activities of human mentality which the human mind considers spiritual, but which are not so in reality. It may perhaps denote false theology in its phases that seem higher, as "the great river Euphrates", the symbol of superstition, denotes the lower phases of false religion. One commentator says that "air" symbolizes "the invisible influences of evil".

In order to interpret *"It is done"*, we must bear in mind that the whole verse is written prophetically, looking into the distant future. In that distant perspective, it seems as if the activity of the Angel is no sooner commenced than the results thereof are accomplished,—just as all stars in the sky seem equally distant, though some are really much farther away than others. As a matter of fact, there is a great struggle and upheaval intervening between the time when mortal sense begins to feel the destructive effect of this Angel and the time when that destruction is complete; and this conflict and the results thereof are described in verses 18-21, as follows:

"And there were voices and thunders, and lightnings: and there was a great earthquake, such as was not since men were upon the earth, so mighty an earthquake, and so great. And the great City was divided into three parts, and the Cities of the nations fell: and great Babylon came in remembrance before God, to give unto her the cup of the wine of the fierceness of his wrath. And every island fled away, and the mountains were not found. And there fell upon men a great hail out of heaven, every stone about the weight of a talent, and men blasphemed God, because of the plague of the hail: for the plague thereof was exceeding great."

"Voices and thunders and lightnings" symbolize the Holy Spirit.

"A great earthquake" symbolizes the upheaval resulting from the conflict between the Angel and satanic influences.

"The great City" symbolizes mortal consciousness as a whole; and it is here represented as *dismembered, "divided into three parts"*.

"And the cities of the nations (the worldly powers) *fell".*

"And great Babylon (Worldly Lust) *came in remembrance before* (was brought under the full activity of) *God, to give unto her the cup of the wine of the fierceness of his wrath",*—which last phrase is almost wholly a mistranslation, and should be rendered, *to give unto her the draught of the wine of the ardor of his loving zeal,*—an activity which is destructive of evil, but is of a very different order from any mental activity connoted by the words "fierceness" or "wrath". For a full discussion of the proper translation of the Greek words *thumos* and *orgê*, see Note 4 of the Introduction.

"And every island fled away, and the mountains were not found"; that is, all human institutions which had seemed established and enduring will vanish away.

For an interpretation of "the plague of the hail", and for a consideration of how this satanic activity could be occasioned by the activity of an Angel of God, the reader is referred to the interpretation of verse 7, of chapter 8, where the subject is fully discussed.

Then cometh the end of evil. *"It is done"* (verse 17) logically belongs at the end of verse 21.

The interpretation of chapters 15 and 16, in one sense, belongs with the interpretation of the following chapters as far as the end of chapter 20, chapters 15-20 constituting the text of Act V; but it has seemed better to interpret the activity of the Angels of the Vials coincidently with the activity of the Angels of the Trumpets, since, as previously indicated, they are the same Angels,—their activities being more effective at the last than at the first, because mortal consciousness is brought more directly subject to their action.

The Angels of the Trumpets and Vials may be taken as symbolizing the apostolic activity of the Christ-mind. Each group begins its work with a pentecostal service, as did the immediate Apostles of Christ Jesus, and carries it forward until the final triumph over error.

REVISED TRANSLATION AND SUGGESTIVE PARAPHRASE

SECTION III

THE SOUNDING OF THE SEVEN TRUMPETS

Chapter VIII. The Angels of the Trumpets

Pentecostal Service

Amended Revised Version

2 And I saw the seven angels which stand before God; and there were given unto them seven
3 trumpets. And another angel came and stood over the altar, having a golden censer; and there was given unto him much incense, that he should give (add) it unto the prayers of all the saints upon the golden altar which was before the
4 throne. And the smoke of the incense, with the prayers of the saints, went up before God out
5 of the angel's hand. And the angel taketh the censer; and he filled it with the fire of the altar, and cast it upon the earth: and there followed thunders, and voices, and lightnings, and an earthquake.
6 And the seven angels which had the seven trumpets prepared themselves to sound.

Suggestive Paraphrase

And I saw the seven militant manifestations of infinite Mind, prepared to sound a message. And I beheld, as it were, a Pentecostal service at which these impersonal apostles, the angels of the trumpets, received the energizing of the Holy Spirit. And I saw the spiritual factor in human consciousness, in its activity as the true church, worshiping God under the leadership of the Holy Spirit, and, as itself the Holy Spirit, assuming a militant attitude toward the world. And I saw that the Holy Spirit, the inspiration of Truth, will come as a purifying agent into human consciousness, and that there will follow a great contention between the powers of good and evil, and a great upheaval in human consciousness.

And I saw the seven angels (The Christ-mind manifest as Spiritual Aspiration, Spiritual Reason, Executive Mind, Direct Cognition, Divine Love, Perception of Reality and Perception of Substance) ready to perform their offices.

Spiritual Aspiration vs. Materiality and Sensuality

7 And the first sounded, and there followed hail and fire, mingled with blood, and they were cast upon the earth: and the

And as the human consciousness attains in part to the activity of Spiritual Aspiration, there will follow the purifying influences of punishment and of

Amended Revised Version   *Suggestive Paraphrase*

third part of the earth was burnt up, and the third part of the trees was burnt up, and all the green grass was burnt up.

the Holy Spirit, and of the Christ Life, and materiality and sensuality, together with human institutions and the ordinary courses of human thought, will be in part destroyed.

Spiritual Reason vs. Sensuousness and Psychism

8 And the second angel sounded, and as it were a great mountain burning with fire was cast into the sea: And the third part of the sea be-
9 came blood; and there died the third part of the creatures which were in the sea, even they that had life; and the third part of the ships was destroyed.

And as human consciousness attains in part to the activity of Spiritual Reason, the effect upon sensuousness and psychism may be compared to casting a volcano in violent eruption into the sea: and, as a result, the sensuous element in human consciousness will be thrown into violent upheaval, and a large part of its activities will be destroyed; and a large part of the human carriers or messengers of Christ and of Satan will be slain.

Executive Mind vs. Human Emotions

10 And the third angel sounded, and there fell from heaven a great star, burning as a torch, and it fell upon the third part of the rivers, and upon the fountains of
11 the waters; and the name of the star is called Wormwood: and the third part of the waters became wormwood; and many men died of the waters, because they were made bitter.

And as the human consciousness attains in part to the activity of Executive Mind, the falsity and worthlessness of human emotion as compared with divine love will be exposed, and false, sentimental human emotion will be remanded to its own realm of discord; it is really, in the long account, bitter as wormwood; and a large part of human activity will become embittered; and many men will die as the result of the inharmonious activity of human sense.

Spiritual Intuition vs. Worldly Wisdom

12 And the fourth angel sounded, and the third part of the sun was smitten, and the third part of the moon, and the third part of the stars; that the third part of them should be darkened, and the day should not shine for the third part of it, and the night in like manner.

And as the human consciousness attains to the activity of Spiritual Intuition, material sense, as satan, the beast (human will), and various satanic ideas, will be in part destroyed; and the counterfeit or seeming good of material sense will be in part eliminated from human experience.

The Holy Spirit Announces Further Woes for Wickedness

Amended Revised Version

13 And I saw, and I heard *a lone* (an) eagle, flying in mid-heaven, saying with a great voice, Woe, woe, woe, for them that dwell on the earth, by reason of the other voices of the trumpet of the three angels, who are yet to sound.

Suggestive Paraphrase

And the Holy Spirit, as the Spirit of Prophecy, pervading the mental realm, made known to me that mankind will suffer three other phases of woe because of judgments and punishments yet to be revealed.

Chapter IX. The Angels of the Trumpets (Continued)

Divine Love vs. Fleshly Desires

1 And the fifth angel sounded, and I saw a star from heaven fall unto the earth: and there was given to him the key of the *shaft* (pit) of the 2 abyss. And he opened the *shaft* (pit) of the abyss; and there went up a smoke out of the *shaft* (pit), as the smoke of a great furnace; and the sun and the air were darkened by reason of the smoke of the *shaft* 3 (pit). And out of the smoke came forth locusts upon the earth, and power was given them, as the scorpions of the earth have power. 4 And it was said unto them that they should not hurt the grass of the earth, neither any green thing, neither any tree, but only such men as have not the seal of God 5 on their foreheads. And it was given them that they should not kill them but that they should be tormented five months: and their torment was as

And as the human consciousness attains to the activity of divine Love, the belief of life and sensation in flesh will be cast down from the high places of human estimation and will hold sway only in the realm of lower sense, where it will prove a key to unlock the agencies of wickedness and torment. Assertive error as a blinding smoke will proceed from the realm of nothingness, and will obscure the light of true understanding. Out of this false belief there will spring a swarm of fleshly desires, which have power to inflict suffering on men as terrible as that which springs from the stings of scorpions. The attack of these fleshly desires is not directed primarily against the normal activities of human mentality, nor against any flourishing human institutions; but their attack is against those men of every class who have not been so "sealed" by God that they are invulnerable to fleshly desires. The primary effect of these sinful desires is not to kill men outright, but to torture them with resulting diseases during the contin-

Amended Revised Version

the torment of a scorpion, when it striketh a
6 man. And in those days men shall seek death, and shall in no wise find it; and they shall desire to die, and death fleeth
7 from them. And the shapes of the locusts were like unto horses prepared for war; and upon their heads as it were crowns like unto gold, and their faces were as men's
8 faces. And they had hair as the hair of women, and their teeth were as the teeth of
9 lions. And they had breastplates, as it were breastplates of iron; and the sound of their wings was as the sound of chariots, of many horses
10 rushing to war. And they have tails like unto scorpions, and stings; and in their tails is their power to hurt men five
11 months. They have over them as king the angel of the abyss: his name in Hebrew is Abaddon, and in the Greek tongue he hath the name of Apol-
12 yon. The first Woe is past: behold, there come yet two Woes hereafter.

Suggestive Paraphrase

uance of satan-time: and the resulting pain is often as bad as that from the poison of a scorpion. Under the torture of these diseases "shall men seek death, and shall not find it; and shall desire to die, and death shall flee from them." And these sinful desires seem, in human experience, powerful and formidable as war horses; and they seem to offer rewards precious as gold to those who entertain them, and they present an intelligent appearance. And they seem as beautiful as women, but they wound like lion's teeth. And they seem to be strongly protected from being destroyed; and they are continually in evidence in great numbers and create great commotion. And the sting of these sinful desires and pleasures is in their after-effects; and they torment men as long as men will entertain or yield to them. And the source and ruler of these sinful desires is he who has control of the realm of assertive error, which has no foundation. who is called in the Hebrew language Abaddon, and in the Greek language Apollyon. One of the three woes mentioned before (see 8:13) has been revealed; and two are yet to be revealed.

Perception of Reality vs. Idolatry

13 And the sixth angel sounded, and I heard a voice from the horns of the golden altar which
14 is before God, one saying to the sixth angel, which had the trumpet, Loose the four angels which are bound at the great river Euphrates.

And as the human consciousness attains in part the Perception of Reality, the Holy Spirit will give command to the Angel of Trust to loose the spiritual potencies in human consciousness from being held in obscurity and bondage by the stream of superstition; and the spiritual factor in human conscious-

Amended Revised Version

15 And the four angels were loosed, which had been prepared for the hour and day and month and year, that they should kill the third part
16 of men: And the number of the armies of the horsemen was twice ten thousand times ten thousand: I heard the number
17 of them. And thus I saw the horses in the vision, and them that sat on them, having breastplates as of fire and of *smoky blue* (hyacinth) and of brimstone: and the heads of the horses are as the heads of lions; and out of their mouths proceedeth fire and smoke and brimstone.
18 By these three plagues was the third part of men killed, by the fire and the smoke and brimstone, which proceeded out of
19 their mouths. For the power of the horses is in their mouth, and in their tails: for their tails are like unto serpents, and have heads; and with
20 them they do hurt. And the rest of mankind, which were not killed with these plagues, repented not of the works of their hands, that they should not worship devils, and the idols of gold, and of silver, and of brass, and of stone, and of wood; which can neither see, nor hear, nor
21 walk; and they repented not of their murders, nor of their sorceries, nor of their fornication, nor of their thefts.

Suggestive Paraphrase

ness, being thus loosed, will become militant for instant or lengthened service, attacking false belief and causing it to react in mental upheavals which will prove very destructive to mankind. And the number of men acting as the agents of the Christ-mind, according to their understanding, against falsehood and unbelief will be myriads of myriads. And I saw that these militant Christians, intending to serve God, will present to all false beliefs a terrible and destructive aspect. To speak figuratively, it will seem as if they are mounted on horses having breastplates of fire, smoke, and brimstone; and it will seem as if the heads of the horses were heads of lions; and as if fire and smoke and burning sulphur were issuing out of their mouths. By the activities of the men nominally Christian, but using largely satanic methods, a large part of the heathen idolaters will be killed (while only a comparatively few will be converted to Christianity). It will seem to the heathen as if the activities of the Christians were doubly destructive, as of war horses having power not only in the mouths of their lions' heads, but also in tails like unto serpents, having heads, with which they can also sting and hurt. Nevertheless, the most of the heathen who are not killed in the missionary campaigns conducted by the Christians will continue in their idolatry: and will not repent of their deeds.

Chapter X. John's Vision of the Full Truth

A Revelation to John of the Principle and Application of Truth

Amended Revised Version

1 And I saw another strong angel coming down out of heaven, arrayed with a cloud; and the rainbow was upon his head; and his face was as the sun, and his feet as 2 pillars of fire; and he had in his hand a little book open: and he set his right foot upon the sea, and his left upon the 3 earth; and he cried with a great voice, as a lion roareth: and when he cried, the seven thunders 4 uttered their voices. And when the seven thunders uttered their voices, I was about to write: and I heard a voice from heaven saying, Seal up the things which the seven thunders uttered, and write them not.

Suggestive Paraphrase

And I rose to another great vision of the Christ,—a vision which seemed obscure at first; yet it promised much, and showed an aspect bright as the sun, and seemed founded on Truth and Love: and the vision, though important, was not lengthy, but the truth thus revealed has power to suppress both latent, hidden error and the visible and audible forms which it has assumed. And I saw that when this higher vision of truth should be given to the world, the full measure of truth would be revealed, and would stir into redoubled activity all of the forces of evil, as it were in self-defense. And as I was about to write concerning these things in detail, it was revealed to me that this would be unwise at the time, but that I should keep the revelation to myself.

A Prophecy as to When the Revelation Shall Be Made Known to All

5 And the angel which I saw standing upon the sea and upon the earth lifted up his right hand to heaven, 6 and sware by him that liveth *unto the ages of the ages* (for ever and ever), who created the heaven and the things that are therein, and the earth and the things that are therein, and the sea and the things that are therein, that there shall be delay no longer: 7 but in the days of the voice of the seventh angel, when he is about to sound, then is finished the mystery of God, according to the good tidings which he declared to his servants the prophets.

And it was revealed to me by the Christ, on the authority of the everlasting, creative Mind, that there shall be delay no longer than until the seventh or final vision of Truth, the perception of Spirit as the only substance, shall be given to the world, when all the things of God which have been hidden shall be revealed and demonstrated, as has been declared by the prophets of God.

Effect of the Revelation on John

Amended Revised Version

8 And the voice which I heard from heaven, I heard it again speaking with me, and saying, Go, take the book which is open in the hand of the angel that standeth upon the sea and 9 upon the earth. And I went unto the angel, saying unto him that he should give me the little book. And he saith unto me, Take it, and eat it up; and it shall make thy belly bitter, but in thy mouth it shall be sweet as honey. 10 And I took the little book out of the angel's hand, and ate it up; and it was in my mouth sweet as honey: and when I had eaten it, my belly was 11 made bitter. And they say unto me, Thou must prophesy again *in the face of* (over) many peoples and nations and tongues and kings.

Suggestive Paraphrase

And I felt impelled to receive, study and practice the brief but mighty revelation of Truth. And when I had done so, I found that the theoretical understanding of this truth,—my first sense of it,—was very inspiring and agreeable: But I found that the practice of it involved me in bitter struggles. And it was revealed to me that later I must speak forth the truth in the face of the wide circle of humanity.

CHAPTER XI. THE ACTIVITY OF THE HOLY SPIRIT

The Full Truth as Principle, Enabling John to Separate Between Truth and Error in Human Consciousness

1 And there was given me a reed like unto a rod: and one said, Rise, and measure the temple of God, and the altar, and them that worship 2 therein. And the court which is without the temple leave without, and measure it not; for it hath been given unto the nations: and the holy city shall they tread under foot forty and two months.

And this vision gave unto me the Principle of absolute truth: and I felt impelled to use this Principle to make a mental measure or estimate (in order that I might understand aright) of the spiritual consciousness, and of the true method of worship, and of those who worship God correctly. And I saw that the mortal consciousness (outside the spiritual consciousness) cannot be measured by this Principle; for this mortal consciousness is given over to those who do not worship God in truth: and they shall treat the spiritual consciousness with contumely during the apparent ascendency of satan.

The Holy Spirit, Truth and Love, Is to Prophesy During Satantime in a Subordinate Position in the World

3 And I will give unto my two witnesses, and they shall prophesy a thousand two hundred and threescore days, clothed in sackcloth.
4 These are the two olive

And during this period, the Holy Spirit, manifest as Truth and Love, will be active among men, though they will occupy a humble position in the midst of worldliness. As the bearers of the light of God to men, they may be likened to two candlesticks perpetually fed by the

Amended Version

trees and the two candlesticks, standing before the Lord of the earth.

5 And if any man desireth to hurt them, fire proceedeth out of their mouth, and devoureth their enemies: and if any man shall desire to hurt them, in this manner must he be killed.

6 These have the power to shut the heaven, that it rain not during the days of their prophecy: and they have power over the waters to turn them into blood, and to smite the earth with every plague as often as they shall desire.

7 And *whenever they shall perform their witnessing* (when they shall have finished their testimony), the beast that cometh up out of the abyss shall make war with them, and overcome

8 them, and kill them. And their dead *body* (bodies) lies in the street of the great city, which spiritually is called Sodom, and Egypt, where also their Lord was crucified.

9 And from among the peoples and tribes and tongues and nations do men look upon their dead *body* (bodies) three days and a half, and suffer not their dead bodies* to

10 be laid in a tomb. And they that dwell on the earth rejoice over them, and make merry; and they shall send gifts one to another; because these two prophets tormented them that dwell on the earth.

Suggestive Paraphrase

oil of two olive trees. And if any man tries to hurt Truth and Love, he has only error with which to do so, and this error they destroy when it comes in conflict with them: and if any man persistently attacks the Holy Spirit with a given error, he is thrown back to have his mortal life destroyed by that same error. Harmony is included within the life of obedience to Truth and Love, and while these witnesses are held in a subordinate position by men, men are excluded from harmony: and because of this, mankind (See chap. 17:15) will be engaged in bloody wars, and smitten with plagues, as long and as often as men neglect these witnesses. And while they are giving their testimony in a position subordinate to worldliness, enraged evil will use the forces of human government (See interpretation of chap. 13), and will seem to suppress them entirely in the realm of human activity. And the churches and institutions which have embodied Truth and Love in the world will seem to lie dead before the dwellers in sense testimony, whose mental habitation is typified by Sodom and Egypt, in which wicked mental realm the crucifixion of our Lord was conceived and executed. And the dwellers in mortal sense will treat the lifeless human institutions of Truth and Love with contumely during the apparent ascendency of satan. And the wicked will make merry at the apparent suppression of these witnesses and their human embodiments, which had been very troublesome to the wicked.

---

* The dead bodies not buried may signify a condition of lack of religious life among men typified by closed and dilapidated churches.

At the End of Satan-time, the Holy Spirit Gains the Ascendency

Amended Revised Version

11 And after the three days and a h a l f, the breath of life from God entered into them, and they stood upon their feet; and great fear fell upon them which beheld
12 them. And they heard a great voice from heaven saying unto them, Come up hither. And they went into heaven in the cloud; and their enemies beheld
13 them. And t h a t hour there was a great earthquake, and the tenth part of the city fell; and there were killed in the earthquake *names of m e n seven thousand* (seven thousand persons): and the rest were affrighted, and gave glory to the God of heaven.
14 The second Woe is past: behold the third Woe cometh quickly.

Suggestive Paraphrase

And at the end of satan-time, the Spirit of life from God will enter into the human institutions representing these witnesses, and they will begin to flourish again; and great fear will fall upon those who had supposed them dead. And these witnesses will be called to occupy high places, and places of great power. And their enemies, beholding them, will be struck with consternation, though they will be so clouded or obscured to mortal sense that their enemies cannot understand them. And at the same time there will be a great upheaval, and a large part of the power of mortal belief will be overthrown, and in the upheaval the mortal natures of the spiritual conquerors will be destroyed, and those not regenerated will be affrighted and will acknowledge the power of God.

The second of the woes has been revealed, and the revelation of the third cometh quickly.

The Seventh Trumpet, Proclaiming the Millennium

15 And the seventh angel sounded; and there followed great voices in heaven, and they said, The kingdom of the world is become the kingdom of our Lord, and of his Christ: and he shall reign *unto the ages of the ages* (for ever and ever).
16 And the four and twenty elders, which sit before God on their thrones, fell upon their faces, and worshipped
17 God, saying, We give thee thanks, O Lord God, the Almighty, which art and which wast; because thou hast taken thy great power,

And when the human consciousness shall attain unto the perception of Spirit as substance, there will be a mighty energizing of Truth in the spiritualized h u m a n consciousness, declaring, The kingdom of the world is become the kingdom of our Lord, and of His Christ; and he shall reign unto the ages of the ages. And all spiritual consciousness will humble itself before God, saying, We give thee thanks, almighty and everlasting God, because through thy power evil is overcome, and thou alone shalt reign.

Amended Revised Version

18 and didst reign. And the nations were *teeming with enthusiasm* (wroth), and thy *ardor* (wrath) came, and the time of the dead to be judged, and the time to give their reward to thy servants the prophets, and to the saints, and to them that fear thy name, the small and the great; and to destroy them that destroy the earth.

Suggestive Paraphrase

And the nations will be teeming with holy enthusiasm, and the ardor of God's love will be manifest and the dead will be resurrected and cleansed from evil, and God will give reward to all His servants, and will destroy all agencies which render material sense discordant and destructive.

(Continued on Page 307.)

SECTION IV
THE WOMAN, THE DRAGON, AND THE BEASTS
(Chapter 11:19—13:18)

Verse 19, Chapter 11. *"And the Temple of God was opened in heaven, and there was seen in his Temple the Ark of his Testament, and there were lightnings, and voices, and thunderings, and an earthquake, and great hail."*

This is equivalent to saying: And I became spiritually conscious, and in spiritual consciousness I beheld the ultimate safety (the ark) which is made known through the testimony of God; but I also saw the activity of the Holy Spirit, as symbolized by "lightnings, and voices, and thunderings", the activity of satan as figured by "great hail", and the upheaval resulting from the conflict as represented by "an earthquake." Thus does John forecast an additional phase of the struggle between truth and error, good and evil, from which struggle there is ultimate salvation.

CHAPTER XII

The Battle of the Christ-mind and of Satan for the Conquest and Allegiance of the Human Understanding

Verse 1 *"And there appeared a great wonder in heaven; a woman clothed with the sun, and the moon under her feet, and upon her head a crown of twelve stars."*

The first clause of this verse is equivalent to John's saying: I became conscious of another great revelation, symbolized to me as *"a woman clothed with the sun"*, etc.

The "woman" symbolizes the Christ-idea, 'generic man, the spiritual idea of God; she illustrates the coincidence of God and man as the divine Principle and divine idea" (S. & H., 561:22). Although the woman represents the Christ-idea, she represents that idea considered more especially in its feminine phase. "As Elias presented the idea of the fatherhood of God, which Jesus afterward manifested, so the Revelator completed this figure with woman, typifying the spiritual idea of God's motherhood" (S. & H., 562:3-7). The feminine element or representative of Mind is divine Love. From the standpoint of human experience love is the mother of truth. Human beings are ignorant of truth until they learn it. Before they can learn truth, they must desire it; that is, love it, and obey so much of it as they have already become acquainted with. "He that doeth the will of my Father, he shall know of the doctrine, whether it be of God". So, speaking from the human standpoint, St. John represents the Christ-idea as a woman, as a mother, ushering truth into the mental life of humanity, the realm of understanding, "heaven."

This woman is represented as clothed with the sun, moon, and stars; that is, she is clothed with all known forms of light.

In the figure, the light is material, just as the woman is; but a spiritual idea and spiritual light, the light of understanding and of love, are symbolized. Specifically, the sun probably represents God, divine Mind; the moon, the Christ-consciousness, or spiritual creation; while the twelve stars represent all right ideas, specifically the twelve tribes of Israel or the twelve Apostles of the Lamb, or both.

Verse 2 *"And she being with child, cried, travailing in birth and pained to be delivered."*

Those authors who write under inspiration can readily appreciate what is here spoken of. A line of thought develops in consciousness, and then one cannot rest or sleep until it is expressed on paper, or at least in speech.

Verse 3. *"And there appeared another wonder in heaven; and behold a great red dragon, having seven heads and ten horns, and seven crowns upon his head."*

"Heaven" here indicates, as it often does in Revelation, the realm of John's personal consciousness, the realm of his human understanding, wherein the forces of both good and evil are discernible. The phrase: *"There appeared . . . in heaven"* is equivalent to, *I became conscious of.* The dragon could not appear in the consciousness of absolute good or harmony. The dragon is spoken of as *"red"*, the color of blood and of fire, and the emblem of cruelty and murder. The *"seven heads"* of the dragon may represent the seven forms of evil opposed to the seven manifestations or "seven Spirits" of God (1:4): namely, *matter* opposed to *Spirit; mortal mind* opposed to *divine Mind; discord* opposed to *Principle; physical sense* opposed to *Soul; error* opposed to *Truth; death* opposed to *Life;* and *hate* opposed to *Love.* The *"ten horns"* may represent the claim of evil to ten phases of power by which it can break the Ten Commandments. The *"seven crowns"* are emblems of authority. It is interesting to note that here the crowns are seven, and are upon the heads of the dragon, while in the case of the beast of chapter 13, verse 1, the crowns are ten, and are upon the horns. This probably indicates that the authority of the dragon is seemingly more absolute and settled and fundamental than that of the beast. It is well to note that this figure of the dragon is a symbol rather than an image, since it is almost impossible to picture by the imagination how ten horns could be distributed on seven heads, and still have those heads crowned.

Verse 4 *"And his tail drew the third part of the stars of heaven, and did cast them to the earth, and the dragon stood before the woman which was ready to be delivered, for to devour her child as soon as it was born."*

The dragon suggests to us an animal of the crocodile or alligator order. The tail of such animals is a seat of great power and is their chief fighting weapon. So the power of this dragon to seduce men is represented as located in his tail. The dragon is, of course, the whole body of false belief, general mortal mind acting as a unit, *"the devil and satan"*, as John himself declares in verse 9 of this chapter. The *"stars of heaven"* are those who have attained repute for learning and wisdom, and have been regarded as "leading lights" or authorities among men. The symbol may connote both atheistic or materialistic scientists and philosophers, and still others who are professors of Christianity. Though all these may be for a time sincere in their beliefs and teachings, the devil is represented as deceiving and seducing a large part of them, drawing them into the service of their lower natures, and thus *"casting them to the earth"*,—that is, into materiality, sensuality, and wickedness. The devil will continue to do this during the period of apparent satanic ascendency.

Perceiving that the love of Truth, the woman, the spiritual church, would bring the truth into the human consciousness, the dragon is represented as making ready to devour the truth as soon as born into the realm of consciousness, to prevent its growing and becoming spread abroad in the world; but he is prevented from doing this, as we shall see.

Verse 5 *"And she brought forth a man-child, who was to rule all nations with a rod of iron: and her child was caught up unto God, and his throne."*

The love of truth (see 2 Thes. 2:10), the woman clothed with the sun, was a spirit widely prevalent in the mental realm, in the realm of humanity, before the birth of Jesus, and this love of truth became centered or focused in Mary, and enabled her to conceive of the Holy Ghost, and she brought forth a man-child in the person of Jesus of Nazareth, who was the truth incarnate, and who was to reveal that truth which was afterward to rule all nations with a rod of iron (with an inflexible rule of truth and good), even after the human Jesus had passed away.* This man-child, this incarnate Christ, was

---

* Mr. F. L. Rawson has written, on page 138 of "Life Understood," the following: "The pure Virgin birth resulted in purity. Prof. Huxley

not so much the child of Mary as he was of the *"woman"*, of the impersonal love of truth which had prevailed for centuries, which was focused in Mary and of which she was the mere instrument, becoming the agent of this spiritual *"woman"* through her own spirituality and receptiveness. Had there not been vastly more love of truth in the mental realm than Mary could have developed of herself, the miracle of conceiving from the Holy Ghost could not have been accomplished. In like manner, probably no great revelation of truth or good has ever been brought to the world which was not more the child of the "spirit of the time" in which it was born than it was of the human person through whom it attained visible manifestation. It is fortunate that this is the case; for such a child ushered into the world as the result of the labors of a single person, before the mentality of the age was ready to be the real parent of the child and to co-operate in the care of its infancy,—a child thus born, if it were possible, would be born out of time, and would be destroyed. This was nearly the case with the child of the spiritual *"woman"* and of Mary. Herod sought to put him to death before he could give his message to the world; and in this attempt Herod was but the agent of satan, as Mary was the agent of the spiritual idea in giving the child birth. Even after Jesus had grown up and had commenced his ministry, the world-spirit of evil several times tried to put him to death before he had accomplished his ministry.

The Christ was incarnate in Jesus, and he was therefore able to reveal and demonstrate the saving truth to the world, but Jesus did not remain in the world. Having demonstrated the ascension, he was *"caught up unto God and his throne"* (verse 5). The pure spiritual truth, the Christ-truth which

---

has said that 'the Virgin birth presented no difficulty to him, as virgin conception was a fact of nature.' Medical men have found that this is possible. We know now that the expectant thinking of millions over a series of years as to the time of the Messiah must have had a great effect."

he taught, remained militant in the world and among men for a couple of centuries, and then the dragon largely overcame it, so far as the world is concerned, and this truth was seemingly, *i. e.,* historically, *"caught up unto God and to his throne"* for preservation, though ever-present in the hearts of the comparatively small number of true believers, until such time as the dragon should be largely subdued, partly as the result of the activity of so much of the truth as men did retain, and partly as the result of the tendency of evil to destroy itself,— after which the truth would reappear in the visible world of men and become militant again, as it has undoubtedly done in the Christian Science movement.

Verse 6 *"And the woman fled into the wilderness, where she hath a place prepared of God, that they should feed her there a thousand two hundred and three score days."*

Coincidently with the disappearing of pure spiritual truth from the activities of the visible world, the love of pure truth, divine love, the *"woman"*, disappeared, for the most part, from the world of men. Such sense of truth and love as they had was adulterated, after the second or third century, with belief in material powers, love thereof, and with reliance upon material means for healing the sick, etc. When Jesus, near the commencement of his ministry, was not active in the visible world, preaching and healing, but was absent from the stage of active affairs for a period of forty days, he was spoken of as being " in the wilderness." There is no probability that he was in an unpopulated place during this period, but he was simply "withdrawn from the world", withdrawn from material sense into spiritual sense. Likewise this *"woman"*, this spirit of divine love, is represented as being "withdrawn from the world", and so *"in the wilderness"* from the standpoint of the world's activity, for *"a thousand two hundred and threescore days."* As before mentioned in these Notes, this is the period or length of time repeatedly spoken of by St. John as the period during which the dragon, or evil, is to have marked and undoubted ascendency in the mental realm and in the world, so far as men are concerned.*

Verses 7-12 *"And there was war in heaven: Michael and his angels fought against the dragon; and the dragon fought, and his angels, and prevailed not; neither was their place found any more in heaven. And the great dragon was cast out, that old serpent, called the Devil, and Satan, which deceiveth the whole world: he was cast into the earth, and his angels were cast out with him. And I heard a loud voice saying in heaven, Now is come salvation, and strength, and the Kingdom of our God and the power of his Christ: for the accuser of our brethren is cast down, which accused them before our God day and night. And they overcame him by the blood of the Lamb, and by the word of their testimony; and they loved not their lives unto the death. Therefore, rejoice, ye heavens, and ye that dwell in them. Woe to the inhabitants of the earth and of the sea! for the devil is come down unto you, having great wrath, because he knoweth that he hath but a short time."*

During the time that the man-child is *"caught up unto God and to his throne"* for protection, and while the woman is *"in the wilderness"* for protection, there is war in the realm of human understanding, where the search for truth and reality goes on. The dragon tries to devour the man-child, the new understanding of truth born into human consciousness, but

---

* It is interesting to note that one Bible commentator has described this period as a period of 1,260 "years" lasting "from A. D. 606, when the Pope of Rome was, by Phocus the Emperor, constituted the universal Bishop of the Christian church, to A. D. 1866" (The Self Interpreting Bible.) This commentator does not call attention to the fact, and probably did not know, that 1866 was the date when Mrs. Eddy discovered Christian Science, that reappearance of pure spiritual truth in the world, which undoubtedly presages the early fall of the dragon and of all those human institutions, organizations, and forms of government which derive their power largely from the dragon. Coincidently with the reappearing of the pure spiritual truth among men, the "woman," the love of pure truth, divine love, comes out of the wilderness, out of the "place prepared of God" for her temporary protection, and becomes active again on the stage of human affairs.

Michael, the militant Christ, and the faithful in heaven take up spiritual arms against the dragon, being resisted by the dragon and those agencies favorable to him. The result is that the dragon and his angels lose their hold upon human understanding; that is, the human mind gradually comes to know that the satanic presentations of matter and evil as realities of being are not true. The *falsity,* and consequent nothingness, of satan and the satanic ideas is recognized, at last, by humanity. In proportion as this happens, the devil can work among men only so far as he can tempt them through their lower natures, against their understanding. Thus is the dragon *"cast into the earth",* as the only field for his activity. His power to tempt men against their understanding,—that is, when they know that they are being deceived, is immeasurably less than his power to tempt them while they believe his deceiving presentations in consciousness to be truth. By the conquest of the human understanding (heaven), satan is shorn of most of his seeming power, and his complete destruction is a question of but *"a short time".* The Holy Spirit is heard as *"a loud voice in heaven"* celebrating the victory, and exhorting the spiritually minded to rejoice, and pronouncing *"woe"* to the dwellers in material sense. Satan can no longer work, or maintain a hold, in the higher activities of human consciousness, but can only work among the lower propensities of men, where it is represented that he will be doubly active for *"a short time"* because of rage at being cast out of the higher realm of activity. Consequently, the men whose thought is upon lower levels come in for an unusual share of satanic temptation and discord.

The name Michael (verse 7) means in Hebrew, *Who is like unto God?* On page 566 of Science and Health, we read: "Michael's characteristic is spiritual strength. He leads the hosts of heaven against the power of sin, satan, and fights the holy wars. Gabriel has the more quiet task of imparting a sense of the ever presence of ministering Love." Michael may be thus regarded as the militant Christ.

Verse 10 *"Which accused them before our God day and night."*

Satan, false sense, is constantly declaring that man is more or less sinful, more or less imperfect, temporal, finite, and material,—none of which accusations are true; for man is the image, the continuous expression of his perfect Creator, and is therefore perfect. To prove this, is to overcome satan, and to work out our salvation; it is to "put on Christ."

In verses 1-6 of this chapter, St. John represents the conflict between truth and error as discerned in the realm of human understanding where the knowledge of truth and reality is sought. In verses 7-12, he represents satan, the belief in matter and evil as realities, as losing in the contest for a hold upon the understanding of men. Christ, the revelation of Spirit, of good, as the only reality, is completely victorious, and, theoretically, the unreality, the nothingness of satan, and of all his agencies and activities, is seen. In verses 13-17, the activity of satan in the lower realms of human nature, and the relations of such activity to the higher mental forces at work, is symbolically described. The movements indicated in these three groups of verses (1-6, 7-12, 13-17) are not to be considered as succeeding each other, but as coincident,—that is, they are all going on at the same time, and cover the period represented by a "thousand two hundred and threescore days" (verse 6) and "a time, and times, and half a time" (verse 14), the whole period of apparent satanic activity in the world.

Verse 13 *"And when the dragon saw that he was cast unto the earth, he persecuted the woman which brought forth the man-child."*

The lower activities in human nature, and those men predominantly subservient to them, are now turned in conflict against the higher activities, against the love of truth, symbolized by the *"woman"*, and against those men serving the Christ-mind.

Verse 14 *"And to the woman were given two wings of a great eagle, that she might flee into the wilderness into her place, where she is nourished for a time, and times, and half a time, from the face of the serpent."*

"A great Eagle" symbolizes the Holy Spirit, the two wings of which in human consciousness are the realization of truth and love. By this realization, the spiritual factor in human consciousness is lifted above or removed apart from the ragings of material sense, and is nourished with "bread from heaven" until the apparent reign and activity of satan are finished.

Verses 15, 16 *"And the serpent cast out of his mouth water as a flood after the woman; that he might cause her to be carried away of the flood. And the earth helped the woman, and the earth opened her mouth, and swallowed up the flood which the dragon cast out of his mouth."*

In verse 15, chapter 17, St. John tells us what he means, sometimes at least, by "water", or "waters",—namely, "peoples, and multitudes, and nations, and tongues." The *"serpent"* is defined as "satan." The *"woman"* here symbolizes the true church (compare verse 1 of the 2nd Epistle of John). Hence, when we are prophetically told that *"the serpent cast out of his mouth water as a flood after the woman, that he might cause her to be carried away of the flood,"* we may understand that satan will try to overwhelm the true spiritual church among men by stirring up against it the wicked activities of a vast number of ungodly men. But in verse 16 we are given to understand that satan characteristically overreaches himself. Some of these ungodly men will fight among themselves, and many of them will be thus slain. Furthermore, 'the satanic activity of the lower nature begets disease and suffering, thus weakening the apparent power of those who are opposed to righteousness, and even driving them to turn to the Christ-mind for relief. Again, rabid resistance to truth has always overreached itself and begotten that protest in general thought which is being expressed today in the criticisms by non-religious writers of professed Christians who are hurling their shafts at those whom they deem unorthodox. Thus the attack of assertive evil upon the godly is largely neutralized. These are ways in which *"the earth"*, symbolizing the lower elements in human nature and crude "common sense", may be said to prove a virtual help to *"the woman"* in resisting the attack of satan, since thus *"the earth opens her mouth and swallows up the flood which the dragon casts out of his mouth."*

On page 570 of "Science and Health" Mrs. Eddy suggests another way in which "the earth helps the woman", in the following note:

"The march of mind and of honest investigation will bring the hour, when the people will chain, with fetters of some sort, the growing occultism of this period. The present apathy as to the tendency of certain active yet unseen mental agencies will finally be shocked into another extreme mortal mood,— into human indignation; for one extreme follows another."

In the same line of thought, Mr. J. S. Hughes writes as follows: "Worldly people who in any way help to destroy ignorance or to destroy degrading superstition or otherwise do good, while they may not choose the better part for themselves, may upon a lower plane help this world into better conditions, and so hasten the reign of the rightful king and prince of the earth."

Mr. F. L. Rawson presents a very lucid interpretation of these verses by suggesting that the natural scientists of the present day, through teaching the unreality and destructibility of matter and the harm done by hypnotic practices, are helping the spiritual church, by showing the people that its doctrines, in the denial of matter, etc., are true, thus showing the falsity of the flood of materialistic teachings and the falsity of mental practice using the carnal mind.

Though materialistic in his order of thought, Robert G. Ingersoll, in his work of destroying superstition and clearing away blind and undiscriminating reverence for the Bible and the church, may be regarded as an example of the earth helping the woman. He did much to prepare the way for the spiritualization of human thought, the establishment of the true church.

In the highest sense, the true church is made up of the unorganized body of true believers, some of which can be found in every organized church, and some of which belong to no organized church or denomination. The characteristic of these true believers has always been their absolute loyalty in thought, and in conduct so far as possible, to God, Spirit, as the only power. They have refused to "live after the flesh", and to substitute matter in any form, or mortal mind in any form, or civil or ecclesiastical government in any form, for God as the object of their allegiance and obedience. It was this pure spiritual consciousness which brought the man-child, Christ Jesus, and his revelation to the world, and it was this pure spiritual consciousness, incarnate in the unorganized church above spoken of, which gave pure Christianity a start in the world, and which kept in the world such remnant of pure Christianity as there was during the centuries known as "the dark ages"; and it was this spiritual consciousness, incarnate as above mentioned, against which satan, in his diabolical work on earth, commenced to make war in the first centuries of the Christian era. Satan practically drove this true church, this woman, off the stage of active affairs during the first few centuries; but to the true church was given the Holy Spirit with its two wings, truth and love, by which it succeeded in escaping the deadly attack of satan, and in withdrawing from the stage of active affairs *"into the wilderness"*, where it was taken care of and nourished, through its loyalty to truth and love, during the ascendency of *"the dragon"*, spoken of in this chapter, and of *"the beast"* described in the next chapter.

Verse 17   *"And the dragon was wroth with the woman, and went to make war with the remnant of her seed, which keep the commandments of God, and have the testimony of Jesus Christ."*

The phrase *"the remnant of her seed"* shows that the true church, during the period of satanic ascendency, is small in numbers and unorganized. This verse as a whole serves as a sort of final brief introduction to the chapters which immediately follow.

All modern authorities are agreed that what is given as the first clause of the first verse of chapter 13 ("And I stood upon the sand of the sea") should be attached to verse 17 of chapter 12, and should be translated: "and he stood upon the sand of the sea". That is, satan is represented as standing at the dividing line between "the sea" and "the earth", or the land,—meaning that he takes a position in the midst of all the lower activities of human nature, "whose host of desires, passions, and longings is indeed as the sand of the sea."

CHAPTER XIII

The Two Beasts, the False Claimants of Authority in State and Church, and the Sin of Worshiping Human Organizations, Civil or Ecclesiastical

Judging from his own experience, the author believes that the average reader of the Apocalypse is not prepared, without some special study and consideration of human government in church and state, to see and appreciate the teaching that is symbolized by the two "wild beasts" of chapter 13.

At any stage of human progress thus far reached, human government, both civil and ecclesiastical, has been and is a necessity. Absence from it, thus far, would mean, not the realization of divine government which is the ideal and only absolutely right and perfect government, but would mean the anarchy of satan. However, human government, at its best, is far from being entitled to be regarded as synonymous with divine or perfect government. At its best, it is a mere makeshift, an expedient, a concession to human immaturity. At its worst it is the summation of all that is corrupt, materialistic, lust-producing, tyrannical, and misleading in doctrine and practice.*

Different human governments and organizations, especially the ecclesiastical, are apt to start at as high a level as the conditions of society in which they spring up permit, but history bears witness, that, almost invariably, if not quite so, they have shown strong tendencies to gravitate toward the lowest level that the conditions of society in which they existed permitted. Many of them have stopped short of going the whole distance, but the tendency has always been downward, rather than upward, for all such organizations, as they have grown in

---

* In this connection the author would recommend the reading of Judge Lindsay's book, entitled "The Beast." showing conditions of human government which existed in Denver, Colo., and which still exist there, and in every other large city, to a great extent, bearing out all that is said above about human government at its worst.

years. Accordingly, it is folly, and always has been, for people to regard the voice of any human organization to which they may have belonged as necessarily synonymous with the voice of God upon points of doctrine and conduct. The government or organization is often, and in many cases usually, right in its teachings and demands; nevertheless, it is always the religious duty of each and every person under any form of human government to avoid regarding the government or organization without reservations. If he looks upon it with unbounded confidence, he places, so far as he is concerned, that which is human, and in part of the earth earthy, in the place of God. This is to be guilty of idolatry and blasphemy. Human governments and organizations are necessarily established by human beings, and administered by human beings, and human beings are not yet divine; and, manifestly, a fountain cannot rise higher than its source. Hence, human governments and organizations, unless at their very start, are apt to impede rather than assist the mental, moral, and spiritual growth of the better class of people under them, and are apt to fall short of placing as high ideals as they should before the people. Some of the special points of danger to individuals from human governments and organizations may be succinctly stated:

1. Human governments and organizations are apt to be regarded by many of the people under them with unreserved love and confidence; and those in authority are apt to do all they can to foster this spirit among the people. For instance, the distinct claim of the Roman Catholic church for the Pope as head of the church is, that he is "in the place of God." This is to fail to discriminate between the human and the divine, and, as before pointed out, it tends to encourage idolatry.

2. Human governments and organizations often lose the affection and confidence of those under them, and come to be regarded with fear by many; and they tend to foster this spirit of fear on the part of those who do not agree with them. In so far as the organization occasions itself to be feared at

times when members have no sense of having been disobedient to God, it is a hindrance and a menace to the spiritual growth of those under it.

3. Human governments and organizations almost invariably are a check upon the mental and spiritual progress of the more advanced of those under them. Especially is this true of ecclesiastical organizations. They tend to crystallize the advancement of spiritual knowledge and liberty of conscience at a certain level, and to virtually say to those under them: "Beware of daring to think and to express any thoughts beyond what the organization has pronounced canonical and authentic; and especially, beware of daring to express any ideas in opposition to those considered orthodox by the organization. If you presume to do these things, you will be regarded with disfavor, and you may be expelled for heresy."

4. Wherever there are human governments or organizations, there must always be those in official places. These must usually have much to do with appointing those who are to fill lower official places. They can scarcely be expected to appoint or use their influence for those with whom they are not acquainted, or those whose ideas do not largely agree with their own. This inevitably begets a tendency on the part of many members of the organization to cultivate the acquaintance, and in various ways to gain the favor of those in authority. This is very apt to grow into a system of unworthy and degrading "politics" within the organization, be it of church or of state.

5. Those in authority are given power to punish and to discipline, the intention being that such power shall be used only upon those who deserve punishment and discipline in the sight of God. But innumerable times, in the history of both states and churches, the power of those in authority has been used to thwart, hinder, cast into disfavor, ruin, and even kill, men and women who have been personal enemies of those in authority, or have refused to favor their schemes for advancement, or have ventured to disagree with those in authority

about matters of doctrine or practice, notwithstanding that those so perscuted have been clean in the sight of God.

Said Jesus: "Beware of men: for they will deliver you up to the councils, and they will scourge you in their synagogues" (Matt. 10:17). "They shall put you out of the synagogues: yea, the time cometh, that whosoever killeth you will think that he doeth God service. And these things will they do unto you, because they have not known the Father, nor me" (John 16:2).

6. Ecclesiastical organizations have often refused the right to receive or to administer the spiritual offices of Christianity, such as baptism, communion, preaching, healing the sick, teaching, etc., except to those officially recognized by the organization. This interference is often just; but many times in history it has been unjust, to the point of an unbearable tyranny, which has repressed that liberty of thought and action which is the inalienable heritage of the children of God.

7. Ecclesiastical organizations often unwittingly are a stumbling block to progress through a disposition on the part of some of their members to be satisfied with bearing the name of a Christian organization, having a feeling that this makes them respectable and even righteous, while omitting to be as zealous as they should be to attain the essence of Christianity in thought and practice, independently of its name and form.

There is no religion so spiritual that the people adhering to it do not need to be on their guard against being entangled in error through its human organization.

THE TWO BEASTS

The broadest interpretation of chapter 13 would seem to be this,—that the first beast, described in verses 1-8, symbolizes *worldly government,* rising up out of disorganized states of human society, and largely taking its incentive for organization and activity from the carnal propensities of human nature. As "seven" is a number of completeness, the "seven heads and ten horns" of the beast probably symbolize *all* worldly empires and kingdoms. The second beast, described in the remainder of the chapter, seems to typify the worldly church in its various branches. The two beasts stand for what may be termed *human domination* in all its forms, both political and ecclesiastical.

In verses 7-18 of chapter 17, St. John partially interprets chapter 13. When he says (verse 10 of chapter 17), concerning the seven heads of the beast, *"five are fallen, and one is, and one is yet to come",* he may mean to indicate that the reign of worldly government has largely, or five-sevenths, passed away.

When he says, in verse 3 of chapter 13, *"I saw one of his heads as it were wounded to death; and his deadly wound was healed; and all the world wondered after the beast";* he undoubtedly means to indicate that he sees the Roman empire, as one of the chief manifestations of worldly government, destroyed; and perhaps he felt that the pure teaching of spiritual Christianity in a century or two following his own time would nearly destroy worldly government once for all; but he sees that there is still too much evil and materiality in human nature for this to be so soon accomplished, and so worldly government will be rehabilitated under other forms concerning which he prophesies in the seventeenth chapter.

Although the primary and broadest significance of the word "seven" in this chapter is denoted by the word *all,* and so all forms of worldly government are prophesied against, nevertheless a very interesting and instructive historical interpretation can be given in terms of the number "seven" taken literally, and this interpretation merits rather extended comments, most of which, however, apply equally well, if considered in connection with *all* the kingdoms and empires representing worldly government in all ages.

It is impossible to make an intelligent interpretation of the earlier portion of this chapter without considering the partial interpretation of it which St. John himself gives in verses 7-18 of the 7th chapter, and without considering the 7th chapter of Daniel, upon which this prophecy of the beast is founded. Therefore, it will be exceedingly helpful to place what Daniel has to say and what St. John has to say on the subject side by side for the purposes of comparison. Interpretative notes will be incorporated with the text, enclosed in parentheses, which will suggest how Daniel's prophecy was actually fulfilled,* and also what seems to have been St. John's meaning.

DANIEL, CHAPTER VII	REVELATION, CHAPTER XIII
Amended Revised Version	*Suggestive Paraphrase*
2 Daniel spake and said, I saw in my vision by night, and behold, the four winds of the heaven strove upon the great sea.	1 And I saw a beast (The Roman Empire) rise up out of the sea, having seven heads and ten horns, and upon his horns ten crowns, and upon his heads the name of blasphemy.
3 And four great beasts came up from the sea, diverse one from another.	
4 The first was like a lion, and had eagle's wings: I beheld till the wings thereof were plucked, and it was lifted up from the earth, and made stand upon the feet as a man, and a man's heart was given to it. (The Babylonian Empire.)	2 And the beast which I saw was like unto a leopard (The Macedonian Empire), and his feet were as the feet of a bear (The Medo-Persian Empire), and his mouth as the mouth of a lion (The Babylonian Empire), and the dragon gave him his power, and his seat, and great authority.
5 And behold another beast, a second like to a bear, and it raised up itself on one	

---

* The writer does not feel sure that Daniel could foresee the future as to exact names, places and dates; but he foresaw human tendencies at work, concerning the future results of which he prophesied in general terms. The inserted notes suggest the specific way in which the general forecast was actually fulfilled.

XIII SECTION IV

Amended Revised Version

side, and it had three ribs in the mouth of it between the teeth of it: and they said thus unto it, Arise, devour much flesh. (The Medo-Persian Empire.)

6 After this I beheld, and lo another, like a leopard, which had upon the back of it four wings of a fowl; and the beast had also four heads; and dominion was given to it. (The Macedonian Empire.)

7 After this I saw in the night visions, and behold a fourth beast, dreadful and terrible, and strong exceedingly; and it had great iron teeth: it devoured and brake in pieces, and stamped the residue with the feet of it: and it was diverse from all the beasts that were before it; and it had ten horns. (The Roman Empire.)

8 I considered the horns, and, behold, there came up among them another little horn (The worldly church), before whom there were three of the first horns plucked up by the roots: and, behold, in this horn were eyes like the eyes of man, and a mouth speaking great things.

11 And I beheld then because of the voice of the great words which the horn (The worldly church) spake: I beheld even till the beast (the Roman Empire) was slain, and his body destroyed, and given to the burning flame.

12 As concerning the rest of the beasts (the three empires), they had their dominion taken away: yet their lives were prolonged for a season and time.

Suggestive Paraphrase

3 And I saw one of his heads as it were wounded to death; and his deadly wound was healed: and all the world wondered after the beast.

4 And they worshipped the dragon (mortal mind, the devil) which gave power unto the beast: and they worshipped the beast, saying, Who is like unto the beast? Who is able to make war with him?

5 And there was given unto him a mouth speaking great things and blasphemies; and power was given unto him (to worldly government, the Roman Empire and its successors) to continue forty and two months (that is, during the time of satanic ascendency).

6 And he opened his mouth in blasphemy against God, to blaspheme his name, and his tabernacle, and them that dwell in heaven.

7 And it was given unto him to make war with the saints, and to overcome them: and power was given him over all kindreds, and tongues, and nations.

8 And all that dwell upon the earth shall worship him, whose names are not written in the book of life of the Lamb slain from the foundation of the world.

REVELATION, CHAPTER XVII

Amended Revised Version

17 These great beasts, which are four, are four kings, which shall arise out of the earth.

18 But the saints of the Most High shall take the kingdom, and possess the kingdom forever, even forever and ever.

19 Then I would know the truth of the fourth beast which was diverse from all the others, exceedingly dreadful, whose teeth were of iron, and his nails of brass; which devoured, brake in pieces, and stamped the residue with his feet.

20 And of the ten horns that were in his head, and of the other which came up, and before whom three fell; even of that horn that had eyes, and a mouth that spake very great things, whose look was more stout than his fellows.

Suggestive Paraphrase

7 And the angel said unto me, Wherefore didst thou marvel? I will tell thee the mystery of the woman (Worldly Lust, typified by Babylon)* and of the beast (Worldly Government, manifest in John's day as the Roman Empire) that carrieth her, which hath the seven heads and ten horns.

8 The beast that thou sawest was and is not; and shall ascend out of the bottomless pit, and go into perdition: and they that dwell on the earth shall wonder, whose names are not written in the book of life from the foundation of the world, when they behold the beast that was, and is not, and yet is.

9 And here is the mind which hath wisdom. The seven heads are seven mountains, on which the woman sitteth (Seven or *all* manifestations of worldly government).

10 And there were seven kings: five are fallen (the Egyptian, Assyrian, Babylonian, Medo-Persian, Macedonian Empires), and one is (the Roman), and the other is not yet come (the Early German or "Holy Roman" Empire); and when he cometh, he must continue a short space.

---

* Notes on "Babylon." The ancient city of Babylon, which was at the height of its power about 600 B. C., was the embodiment of worldliness, superstition, tyranny, cruelty, sorcery, materialism, carnality, false doctrine,—the embodiment of all that was apostate to Spirit and Christ. Among the Jews, Babylon was the symbol of all the above evil influences. Hence, John, born a Jew and writing to Christians most of whom had been born Jews, speaks of Babylon as "the great whore" (17:1), and uses it as the personification of Worldly Lust, upheld by seven (all) great empires of this world (17:9, 10), and calls Lust, personified as Babylon, "that great city, which reigneth over the kings of the earth" (17:18).

It is this mental Babylon, Worldly Lust, which John declares, "is fallen, is fallen" (14:8; 18:2), and concerning which he exhorts: "Come out of her, my people, that ye be not partakers of her sins, and that ye receive not of her plagues" (18:4). He sees the mental Babylon as fallen, that is, apostate from Truth and good, in his own time, and continuing in that condition for centuries, but he does not prophesy its destruction until near the end of the world. All people who are under the dominion of the influences above enumerated are under the dominion of mental Babylon, and are tributary to it, whether they are classed by men or by themselves as Catholic or Protestant, Jew or Christian Scientist. Those who are not under the dominion of these mental influences are not tributary to mental Babylon, even though they bear the name of any church or no church.

Amended Revised Version

21 I beheld, and the same horn (the worldly church) made war with the saints, and prevailed against them;

22 Until the Ancient of days came, and judgment was given to the saints of the most High; and the time came that the saints possessed the kingdom.

23 Thus he said, The fourth beast shall be the fourth kingdom upon earth, which shall be diverse from all kingdoms, and shall devour the whole earth, and shall tread it down, and break it in pieces (The Roman Empire.)

24 And the ten horns out of this kingdom are ten kings (nations built out of the fragments of the Roman Empire) that shall arise: and another shall rise after them (the worldly church taking form as the early Papal dominion, which came to virtually control the affairs of the nations of western Europe, or about three-tenths of the former Roman Empire); and he shall be diverse from the first, and he shall subdue three kings.

25 And he shall speak great words against the most High, and shall wear out the saints of the most High, and think to change times*· and laws: and they shall be given into his hand until a time and times and the dividing of time. (The period of time here spoken of is the same as the "time, times,

Suggestive Paraphrase

11 And the beast that was, and is not, even he is the eighth, and is of the seven, and goeth into perdition.

12 And the ten horns which thou sawest are ten kings (Nations which later were to rise out of the ruins of the Roman Empire), which have received no kingdom yet; but receive power as kings one hour with the beast.

13 These have one mind, and shall give their power and strength unto the beast.

14 These shall make war with the Lamb, and the Lamb shall overcome them; for he is Lord of lords, and King of kings: and they that are with him are called, and chosen, and faithful.

15 And he saith unto me, The waters which thou sawest, where the whore sitteth, are peoples, and multitudes, and nations, and tongues.

---

* Pope Gregory XIII changed the calendar, and the Roman Church, during its ascendency, changed many laws.

Amended Revised Version	*Suggestive Paraphrase*
and half a time," spoken of in Revelation, and denotes the whole period of apparent satanic supremacy in the world).	16 And the ten horns which thou sawest upon the beast, these shall hate the whore (Lust), and shall make her desolate and naked, and shall eat her flesh, and burn her with fire.
26 But the judgment shall sit, and they shall take away his dominion, to consume and to destroy unto the end.	
27 And the kingdom and dominion and the greatness of the kingdom under the whole heaven shall be given to the people of the saints of the most High, whose kingdom is an everlasting kingdom, and all dominions shall serve and obey him.	17 For God hath put in their hearts to fulfil his will, and to agree, and give their kingdom unto the beast until the words of God shall be fulfilled.
28 Hitherto is the end of the matter. As for me, Daniel, my cogitations much troubled me, and my countenance changed in me: but I kept the matter in my heart.	18 And the woman which thou sawest is that great city, which reigneth over the kings of the earth.

It will now be useful to comment upon these verses from Revelation, verse by verse, commencing with the thirteenth chapter of Revelation.

Verse 1 *"And I stood upon the sand of the sea, and (I) saw a beast rise up out of the sea, having seven heads and ten horns, and upon his horns ten crowns, and upon his heads the name of blasphemy."* (literally, *names of profanation*).

As already noted, the first clause of this verse belongs with the preceding chapter. The beast mentioned in this verse, and following, seems to symbolize civil government, although it is civil government largely identified in St. John's thought with the Roman Empire, since, in his day, the Roman Empire embodied within itself all the civil government of the known world, or of the world with which St. John was acquainted. Why civil government, as represented by the Roman Empire and later forms of government, was inimical to the progress of men toward true Christianity has been spoken of already, and will be spoken of, especially in the comment upon the last few verses of this 13th chapter. This beast is represented as rising up *"out of the sea"*, while the second beast spoken of in verse 11 of this chapter is represented as *"coming up out of the earth."* The *"sea"* seems here to symbolize unorganized and uncivilized humanity, while the *"earth"* seems to symbolize organized, civilized society. Civil government, the Roman Empire, and the various previous empires out of which the Roman Empire was formed, are represented as springing up out of disorganized conditions of humanity, producing a comparative condition of order. The *"seven heads"* of this beast, civil government, may be considered as the five great empires which had passed away, the Roman Empire which was in existence in John's time, and another empire which St. John foresaw would follow, his vision being fulfilled in the early German empire, which styled itself "the Holy Roman Empire", and which held under its sway practically all of the nations of western Europe for a short time about the 11th century A. D. (See Chapter 17:10). This empire succeeded to the power and many of the customs and practices of the heathen Roman Empire of St. John's day. The five *"heads"*, or empires which had fallen, were the Egyptian, Assyrian, Babylonian, Medo-Persian, and Macedonian empires. These empires had all, in their time, been exceedingly materialistic and wicked in their character, and had been, more or less, persecutors of spiritual religion as held among the Jews of Old Testament times. The *"ten horns"* symbolize nations which were to spring up out of the fragments of the Roman Empire, after it went to pieces. Whether the nations that did spring up were exactly "ten", does not especially matter. These nations or *"kings"* had *"received no kingdom as yet"* in St. John's time, but, somewhat later, were to receive the power of civil government, especially that derived from the fallen Roman Empire, unto themselves for a time. (See chapter 17:12.) The *"ten crowns"* were symbols of the authority of these nations, when they should spring up. All of the seven empires, or "heads", claimed that the primary allegiance of their subjects was due to them; and, in fact, all of them claimed, more or less, to stand in the place of God, or of the higher unseen powers, and claimed that their laws and edicts were the voice of supreme good. For instance, if a citizen of Russia or Germany, in this year of 1915, were to say, "My sense of my duty to God forbids my enlisting in the army, or taking part in war", the state, through its officers, would virtually say to him, "Never mind about your sense of your duty to God. Obey the commands of the officers of your country, else you will go to prison or to death." In assuming such an attitude, as all nations do or may at times, the state, by trying to place itself in supreme authority, assumes that power which belongs to God only. Thus, it virtually puts itself in the place of God, and so is irreverent toward God. This is why St. John says that *"the name of blasphemy"* (Greek, *names of profanation*) was upon all these heads. As a matter of fact, many of their laws and edicts were very far from being founded upon supreme good, as has been the case with all civil governments in the world thus far. The laws, edicts, and policies of all governments have been founded upon the supposition that matter is real and is substance, that evil is as real as good, that material possessions are more to be guarded by government than spiritual riches. Governments resting upon such a false foundation could never fail to be an obstacle to the spiritual growth of their citizens toward that which is highest.

Verse 2 *"And the beast which I saw was like unto a leopard, and his feet were as the feet of a bear, and his mouth as the mouth of a lion: and the dragon gave him power, and his seat, and great authority."*

The first portion of this verse will be absolutely plain, if the reader will first read verses 4-7 of the 7th chapter of Daniel. The Roman Empire was the immediate successor of the Babylonian, Medo-Persian, and Macedonian Empires, and gathered up into itself all the worldly power and wealth, and all the lusts, sorceries, idolatries, superstitions, cruelties, and tyrannies of the three empires from which it sprang, making abundant additions of its own. One acquainted with history knows that the Roman Empire was well symbolized by "the leopard, with his sudden, cruel spring; the bear, with his slow, relentless brutishness; and the lion, with his all-conquering power" (Prof. Wm. Milligan). The *"dragon"*, satan, the devil, gave to this Roman Empire, and usually gives to civil government, *"his power, and his seat, and great authority"*. This is not saying that civil government is not necessary to human progress thus far, and it is not saying that it does not represent good as well as evil; it is simply saying, that the Roman Empire represented "the prince of this world" instead of Christ far more than it should, even considering the condition of the people over whom it ruled, and it is saying that all other civil governments, thus far, have fallen short of their duty in the same manner.

In this second verse St. John tells us that human governments, on occasion, exhibit all the fierce cruelty of a leopard, the untiring, relentless cunning of a bear, and the pitiless voracity of a lion. When aroused, they care not how much suffering they occasion through war, but will spring at each other like leopards, sometimes with scarcely a moment's notice. Through their subtle, and often lying diplomacy, they will pursue some selfish object for decade after decade, and century after century, always working relentlessly for the same end—material conquest—no matter what temporary checks they may receive, often pursuing their objects with such cunning that their purposes are not detected for a time. Russia's continued plotting to gain possession of the Dardanelles is an example; Germany's policy, pursued for years, to gain mastery of the world's trade, and England's consistent policy to prevent this, are other examples. Nothing so aptly symbolizes the devouring of property and human life at the instigation of human governments, especially in war time, as the lion's mouth.

Verse 3 *"And I saw one of his heads as it were wounded to death; and his deadly wound was healed; and all the world wondered after the beast."*

In St. John's time, the one prominent "head" assumed by civil government was the Roman Empire, which, like other human governments, asserted the claim, through its emperors, to supreme authority. In fact, some of its emperors demanded that they be worshipped as God. Through the teaching and demonstrations of Christ Jesus and his followers, the supremacy of worldly authority came near being overthrown, in favor of such a generally recognized sense of the supremacy of the government of Spirit that people came near gaining liberty to render allegiance to God alone in matters of conduct. Thus, this "head" of worldly government, the Roman Empire, was seen "as it were wounded to death" through being nearly destroyed by the demonstration of spiritual power; but the Christian church made the mistake of taking the Emperor Constantine and his court into it, without their being really converted. They joined the church for political reasons, because it was becoming popular; and, because of their worldly prominence, the church placed many unspiritual men in positions of ecclesiastical influence and authority. In this and other ways, the church lost its hold upon spiritual power, and the material and worldly sense of things again gained supremacy. Thus "the deadly wound" of worldly authority and power "was healed." Since that time, "all the world" has been "wondering" after the "beast"; that is, marveling at the magnificence and seeming power of human government, as represented in the various nationalities.

Jesus knew the falsity of this magnificence and seeming power of the material world, as did John, who gave the following warning: "Love not the world, neither the things that are in the world. If any man love the world, the love of the Father is not in him. For all that is in the world, the lust of the flesh, and the lust of the eyes, and the pride of life, is not of the Father, but is of the world." (I John 2:15, 16.)

Verse 4 *"And they worshipped the dragon which gave power unto the beast: and they worshipped the beast, saying, Who is like unto the beast? who is able to make war with him?"*

And men would continue to worship the dragon, the devil, with his claims of materiality, fleshly pleasure, worldly magnificence, etc., in the desire for which on the part of men is rooted both the power of satan and of worldly government over them. Citizens of every nation are wont to exclaim, "What nation is like our nation? Who is able to make war with our nation?" Whether, as a matter of fact, the given nation is particularly strong or not from a worldly standpoint, does not matter. The mass of its citizens think of it as all-powerful. This is part of what they call "patriotism."

You can hear the Russian, or the German, or the Frenchman, or the Englishman, or (in the early autumn of 1914) even the citizen of little Belgium, exclaiming, "What country is like unto my country? Who is able to make war with it?" Thus do they each think of a human government as supreme in power, and so they virtually worship it. They virtually take part in the sentiment, "My country! May she be right; but, right or wrong, my country!" This is to render supreme mental allegiance to that which is not God, and this is to *"worship the beast."*

Verse 5 *"And there was given unto him a mouth speaking great things and blasphemies; and power was given unto him to continue forty and two months."*

And there was given unto the various forms of civil government a mouth speaking great things, making extravagant claims, and exalting its own power to such an extent that it virtually or openly claimed to stand in the place of God, thus uttering *"blasphemies"*. And St. John prophesies that power will be given to the beast, after its deadly wound is healed, to seduce and tyrannize over men for forty and two apocalyptic months, which, as before pointed out, is synonymous with three and one-half apocalyptic years ("time, times, and half a time," chap. 12:14), or 1260 apocalyptic days (chapter 11:13). This is the length of time which St. John repeatedly speaks of as the period during which he foresees that evil will manifest marked preponderance over good in the world.

We are elsewhere (Rev. 20:1-3) prophetically informed that, during the latter portion of the time sense, satan, the spirit of discord and worldliness, will be bound and cast into "the bottomless pit" (the realm of nothingness; for that which is bottomless will hold nothing), and the millennium, the period of perfect harmony and of a high degree of spirituality, will appear. Thus, at the last, God will be recognized as the only ruler in the world, even before the material sense of earth, and the sense of time with it, is finally destroyed. We are yet in the period where satan and "the beast" are in dominant authority in human affairs. Any observing citizen can readily see that, in any nation or city, when an issue is squarely drawn between peace and war, between greedy commercialism and a spirit of fairness, between vice and purity, between temperance and the saloon forces, the government of the nation or city, through its officials, is very prone to take the side of evil.

Verse 6 *"And he opened his mouth in blasphemy against God, to blaspheme his name, and his tabernacle, and them that dwell in heaven."*

As already pointed out, practically all civil governments blaspheme God in practice, even though they may claim to be serving Him and to be ruling by His authority, and they blaspheme His tabernacle because they do not in practice recognize God's spiritual covenant with His people as being inviolable, and as having the right of way over any demands which they are inclined to make. Civil governments are also accustomed to regard as "impossible" citizens those who are most loyal to the demands of spiritual living, and who refuse to have part in war, and to countenance laws which bulwark lust, intemperance, etc. In most of these respects, the most enlightened modern governments are, of course, less flagrantly sinful than was the Roman Empire and the earlier governments.

Verse 7 *"And it was given unto him to make war with the saints, and to overcome them: and power was given him over all kingdoms, and tongues, and nations."*

Nearly all civil governments have persecuted, at times, their most spiritual citizens in one way or another; and the Roman Empire and some of the earlier governments which sprang from it made it impossible for its most spiritual citizens to live.

It has never been the case in any nation in the world, thus far, that any of its citizens could live in strict obedience to the nature of God, for any considerable length of time, and maintain their human lives and liberties. Invariably, the state has forced its citizens into war, or into paying taxes for the support of war and other ungodlike undertakings, and into being parties to the enforcement of ungodlike laws. Those who have refused to do these things, on any and every occasion, the state has cast into prison or killed. Thus has it *"made war with the saints,"* and outwardly *"overcome them,"* and has had power over all humanity, as a whole.

Verse 8 *"And all that dwell upon the earth shall worship him, whose names are not written in the book of life of the Lamb slain from the foundation of the world."*

In all centuries since the time of Jesus, the most spiritual, *"whose names are written in the Lamb's book of life"*, have persisted in rendering allegiance to God rather than to the civil power, when there was any conflict between the demands of the two, sacrificing their lives if need be. All others have acknowledged by their conduct, if not by their thought, that the civil power was supreme. *"The Lamb"* is, of course, the Christ-mind, and as human consciousness has been, for the most part, "dead to the truth" since the foundation of the mortal world, from the world's standpoint the truth or Christ-mind is dead, or "slain". Mortal sense is always attempting to kill the truth, and, thus far, has mostly succeeded in keeping it out of human consciousness.

Verse 9 *"If any man have an ear, let him hear."*

If any man has the capacity to understand this teaching, let him govern himself accordingly.

Verse 10 *"He that leadeth into captivity shall go into captivity; he that killeth with the sword must be killed with the sword. Here is the patience and faith of the saints."*

He that would put another in bondage thereby shows his implicit belief that there is some other power or law than God's law of liberty. Thus he mentally entangles himself in the belief of bondage, and by that very fact he is in bondage mentally, and, sooner or later, this inner belief is almost sure to externalize itself. He that kills with the sword enmeshes himself in a mental atmosphere of cruelty and death and in outward associations that are on that level; consequently, he places himself in a position, mentally and outwardly, for becoming subject to the very evil that he metes out to another. No human can inflict evil of any kind upon another without mentally selling himself to that same evil; consequently, of a necessity he himself falls into the pit which he digs for another. Knowing this, St. John says that the saints, while suffering outward persecution at the hands of evil-doers, can have patience and confidence, with the full assurance that all evil doing will automatically punish and destroy itself, while "It can never destroy one iota of good" ("Science and Health," p. 186) ; for all good is of God, and so is eternal.

NOTES BY THE READER

CHAPTER XVII

Verse 7 *"And the angel said unto me, Wherefore didst thou marvel? I will tell thee the mystery of this woman, and of the beast that carrieth her, which hath the seven heads and ten horns."*

The *"woman"* spoken of in this verse is symbolical of Worldly Lust, typified by Babylon, and regarded as the incarnation of lust and false doctrine. The *"beast"* spoken of is the same beast as the one described in chapter 13. As there pointed out, this beast is the civil government; but the civil governments which sprang up out of the ruins of the Roman Empire, so far as those governments were included in Christendom, were, in the early centuries of the Middle Ages, so dominated by the Papacy that it was difficult to determine where civil government left off and where ecclesiastical government began. So nearly were church and state one in these early times, that many commentators have thought that the first beast should be regarded as referring to the Papacy, when the beast came to life after "its deadly wound was healed"; but, strictly speaking, this is not the case. In verse 10 of this chapter, St. John is careful to tell us that the "king" or "head" which "is not yet come" "must continue *a short space."* Accordingly, when the beast comes to life under the seventh head, St. John does not represent its coming to life as the Papacy; for if he did, his prediction was not fulfilled, since the Papacy has endured more than "a short space". The beast came to life as a civil power, as it had been before it received the "deadly wound". It came to life as the early German or "Holy Roman" Empire, which was a civil power, embodying for "a short space" (about the 11th century A. D.) practically all the nations of Christendom; but it was a civil power closely related to the Papacy, as above indicated, as were the nations preceding it and those immediately following it.

Verse 8 *"The beast that thou sawest was, and is not; and shall ascend out of the bottomless pit, and go into perdition: and they that dwell on the earth shall wonder, whose names were not written in the book of life from the foundation of the world, when they behold the beast that was, and is not, and yet is."*

St. John writes this verse as from the point of view of one who is living in the time when the Roman Empire has gone to pieces, and so speaks of it as the *"beast that was, and is not"*. St. John lived a little earlier than this, but he projects himself forward in thought to this time. When he says that the beast *"shall ascend out of the bottomless pit, and go into perdition"*, he means to assert that human organization on its material side comes from nothing and goes to nothing,— whence one could readily infer that, in the meantime, it really is nothing. In the last half of this verse, St. John virtually tells us that those having the material sense of things *"shall wonder"* at the apparent magnitude, splendor, and strength of human government, but those *"whose names were written in the book of life from the foundation of the world"* (that is, those who have attained the spiritual mind) will not wonder or be astonished at the apparent power or magnificence of the Roman Empire, or any other human government, because they see its nothingness, and see that the government of God is the only true and permanent government.

Verses 9, 10 *"And here is the mind which hath wisdom. The seven heads are seven mountains, on which the woman sitteth. And there are seven kings: five are fallen, and one is, and the other is not yet come; and when he cometh, he must continue a short space."*

In these two verses the *"seven heads"* are made to do duty for a double symbolism. The Twentieth Century New Testament translates these two verses as follows: "The seven heads are seven mountains upon which the woman is seated. They are also seven kings, of whom five have fallen and one remains, while one is not yet come. When he comes, he must stay for a little while." The seven mountains represent seven or *all* phases of worldly government, which is always dominated by, and, in turn, upholds Worldly Lust. The five *"kings"* or *"heads"* of civil government that had fallen in St. John's time were the Egyptian, Assyrian, Babylonian, Medo-Persian, and Macedonian empires. The *"king"* that *"is"* in his time is the Roman Empire. The prophecy, concerning the *"king"* that *"is not yet come"*, was fulfilled in the early German or "Holy Roman" Empire, as already pointed out.

Verse 11 *"And the beast that was, and is not, even he is the eighth, and is of the seven, and goeth into perdition."*

St. John does not foretell in detail how the problem of civil government will work out beyond the time when the overthrown Roman Empire shall be rehabilitated as ten kingdoms (see next verse), a portion of which, he forsees, will be gathered together for a little time into a kingdom, as happened in the "Holy Roman" Empire; but he evidently foresees that civil government will continue beyond the period of which he more definitely speaks, and he foresees that, as long as civil government lasts, it will be fundamentally human and materialistic, rather than divine, in its character. So he tells us in this verse that the *"beast"*, civil government, will continue for a time in some form after the seven *"kings"* that he tells us of have passed away, and that this continuing civil government will derive its power as the successor of the seven great governments which had preceded it, but that this continuing civil government, after whatever forms it may finally assume, will ultimately *"go into perdition"*, destruction, nothingness.

Verse 12 *"And the ten horns which thou sawest are ten kings, which have received no kingdom as yet; but receive power as kings one hour with the beast."*

The "ten kings" here spoken of, without doubt, refer to nations that would spring up out of the fallen Roman Empire. Whether the number that did spring up was exactly ten or not, does not especially matter. These kingdoms *"received power as kings one hour with the beast";* that is, they exercised civil authority for a short time, the civil authority which they derived as the immediate successors of the Roman Empire. So, during this time, they were in general sympathy with the spirit of Roman imperialism. However, after a short time, some of them were swallowed up in the "Holy Roman" Empire above spoken of, and others east and south of the Mediterranean Sea gradually changed their forms and boundaries.

Some commentators have believed that the scarlet colored beast was intended by John to symbolize a definite forevision which he had of the Roman Catholic church, and that the woman seated on the beast was intended to typify the Catholic hierarchy at Rome, and that he meant "seven mountains" to refer to the seven hills of Rome. They also say that the sentence, *"These have one mind, and shall give their power and strength unto the beast,"* was intended to mean that the kingdoms which would spring up after the fall of the Roman Empire would be tributary for a time to the Catholic church; but when, later, *"these shall hate the whore"* (verse 16), they will turn away from Catholicism and the Papacy. The commentators maintain that this part of the prophecy was partially fulfilled at the Reformation, and that it has been partly fulfilled in more recent times in the partial defection of Italy, France, Portugal, etc., from the Papal rule,—a defection which is likely to become practically complete.

The author does not believe that John foresaw quite so definite a program as this, though this program is in line with the general movements which John forecasts, as indicated previously.

Because of the uniformity of human nature, history keeps repeating itself along somewhat the same general lines; and, accordingly, a general description of the relations of human activities to Worldly Lust and worldly government, and of the outcome of such relations, would be sure to include, and resemble in description, any particular movement along these lines in human history,—so much so that any given historical movement, viewed in the retrospect, might fulfill the general prophecy in such minute details as to deceive many into believing that that particular movement was prophetically referred to by definite forevision.

Verse 13 *"These have one mind, and shall give their power and strength unto the beast."*

This verse asserts that the ten kingdoms *"have one mind"*, that is, the "carnal mind", *"and shall give their power and strength unto the beast";* that is, as long as they exist, they shall be exponents of civil power or government, with its evil and materialistic tendencies.

Verse 14 *"These shall make war with the Lamb, and the Lamb shall overcome them: for he is Lord of lords and King of kings; and they that are with him are called, and chosen, and faithful."*

All civil governments, on their human and material side, are opposed to spiritual truth, and war with it, but shall ultimately be overcome and destroyed.

Verse 15 *"And he saith unto me, The waters which thou sawest, where the whore sitteth, are peoples, and multitudes, and nations, and tongues."*

This verse refers back to the earlier portion of the 17th chapter, and is self-interpretative.

Verses 16, 17 *"And the ten horns which thou sawest upon the beast, these shall hate the whore, and shall make her desolate and naked, and shall eat her flesh, and shall burn her with fire. For God hath put into their hearts to fulfil his will, and to agree, and give their kingdom unto the beast, until the words of God shall be fulfilled."*

The significance of these verses probably is, that the kingdoms which will spring up after the fall of the Roman Empire, and for that matter all the kingdoms of the world, will ultimately be so converted to the Christ, that they will turn against Worldly Lust, and will thus leave it without followers and without substance, and they will so mentally enforce truth against it as to cause it to utterly disappear. For in the order of their development, they will first serve worldly government, but when the purpose of God is fully revealed to them, they will *"fulfill His will"* by hating Worldly Lust and destroying it.

The interpretation of the seventh chapter of Daniel will be evident, if read as given, with notes interspersed, on pages 270-272 of this book.

NOTES BY THE READER

The Second Beast

(Chapter 13:11-18)

Verse 11 *"And I beheld another beast coming up out of the earth; and he had two horns like a Lamb, and he spake as a dragon."*

This beast symbolizes ecclesiastical organization or government, which may well be spoken of in this connection as the Worldly Church. The first beast mentioned in this chapter is described as rising "out of the sea"; that is, out of disorganized states of society, as previously explained: and this second beast is represented as *"coming up out of the earth";* that is, out of an organized state of society, as before explained. Ecclesiasticism almost invariably, if not quite so, springs up in a state of society where civil government (the first beast) is already pretty firmly established. Ecclesiasticisms, at their start at least, and largely throughout their continuance, derive their power of organization and their ability to enforce many of their own laws largely from the civil governments of the countries in which they exist. The first Pope of Rome was proclaimed universal bishop of the Christian church by the Emperor of Rome; this occurred in A. D. 606, when Phocas was Emperor. And the civil rulers of western Europe continued to support the Papacy, until, in time, it became more powerful, even in civil affairs, than they were; and, for a time, much of the civil policy of the nations of Christendom was dictated by the Pope. This was especially true from the 12th to the 14th centuries, and has been true with some of the governments down to very recent times. All of the Protestant ecclesiasticisms of Europe and America are organized under charters from the civil governments of the several countries in which they exist and work; and their power to enforce their decrees and discipline among their members along many lines depends upon the fact that the civil authorities will support them in so doing. So ecclesiasticism is largely a creature of civil government, of the first beast, and so, the second beast, *"exerciseth all the power of the first beast before him"* (verse 12).

"The Lamb" is especially the symbol of Christ throughout the Apocalypse. This second beast is represented as having *"two horns like a lamb"*. The horn, in the Apocalypse, is always the symbol of power. Accordingly, the declaration that the Worldly Church has two horns like a lamb is equivalent to saying that it claims to exercise the power of Christ in two phases; and that is exactly what it does, although its claim is usually largely false. The Worldly Church formulates a creed, and then declares that this creed has the authority of Christ, and is backed by his power. As a matter of fact, no creed has the authority of Christ, except in so far as it represents eternal truth. Secondly, the Worldly Church claims to do the healing work of Christ; and yet, since the first few centuries, the methods of healing authorized and propagated by the Worldly Church (with the exception of the Christian Science organization) have not been the methods of Christ, but of antichrist. The Christ-method of healing is to rely upon the activity of the divine Mind, Spirit; while the churches have, since the third century, authorized and propagated methods of healing which depend upon matter, and, within the last few years especially, many of them, through their clergy, have directly used and fostered methods of healing which depend upon the use of hypnotism, and other recognized manifestations of "the carnal mind", which St. Paul described as "enmity against God". For centuries, various so-called Christian churches have sent medical doctors and others schooled in material medicine into their missionary fields; and it is a matter patent to all beholders, how both the Catholic and Protestant churches have worked hand in hand, for centuries, with this material system. They have founded almost unnumbered hospitals, in which the sick are treated wholly by material means, notwithstanding Christ taught that Spirit alone is to be depended upon for healing, and for all other help in time of need. The disposition of various churches to propagate

healing methods known as "psycho-therapy" and "suggestive therapeutics" is well known. Thus, through their creeds on the one hand, and through their healing methods on the other, the various churches of Christendom have claimed to represent both the word and the works of Christ (that is, they have *claimed* to have the two horns of the Lamb) ; and in both cases their claim has been largely false, and so, largely, they have stood, not for Christ, but for antichrist. That is one of the reasons why ecclesiasticism is spoken of as a beast.

It is interesting to note that the word in the original Greek which is translated *"beast"* in both the first and eleventh verses of this chapter is the word *"tharion"*, which, in the Greek, always means *"wild beast"*, as distinguished from a domestic beast. Civil and ecclesiastical governments are represented as untamable. They may be held in subjection in a measure, and may even be made to do useful work; but they must always be watched, and they can never be converted wholly to God's service. The millennium, the kingdom of God on earth, will never fully come until all need of human government has been outgrown; that is, not until humanity has advanced to that point where it can do better without human organization than it can with such organization. This time is probably considerably in the future as yet, but note that the destruction of "the beast and the false prophet" is foretold in 19:20, *before* the millennium is foretold in 20:1-4.

Whenever a new discovery of religious truth has been made and spread among men, that truth soon built up an ecclesiasticism, which was useful for guarding and disseminating that phase of truth; but when a still further advance was made in the discovery of truth, this same worldly organization has invariably opposed the propagation of the newer discovery. This fact Jesus referred to, when he told us not to put new wine (new inspiration or discovery of truth) into old skins (old ecclesiastical organizations), because the old skins cannot hold the new wine without breaking, when it ferments (becomes active) ; but he told us to put new wine (new discoveries of truth) into new skins (statements and organizations). So, we see that ecclesiastical organization has ever been first a help and then a hindrance to the propagation of truth in all its phases among men.

This beast is represented in verse 11 as speaking *"as a dragon"*; that is, his voice is really the voice of satan (see chapter 12:9).

Verse 12 *"And he exerciseth all the power of the first beast before him, and causeth the earth and them which dwell therein to worship the first beast, whose deadly wound was healed."*

The first clause of this verse has been interpreted in the comment on verse 11. Let it here be briefly stated that a dominant ecclesiasticism has usually derived its authority in matters of government largely from the civil authority, and is usually strongly backed by the civil authority in whatever it tries to do. In return, a dominant ecclesiasticism always co-operates with the civil government of the country in which it is instituted. The church teaches the people "patriotism". It will usually exercise its influence to induce the people to stand by the civil authorities, whether they be right or wrong, in either internal or external affairs. When a civil government is about to take a wrong course, the ecclesiasticisms within that country seldom take the part of a prophet, standing firmly, even in their mental attitude, against the civil government. A few clergymen, here and there, or other ecclesiastics, may take such a stand; but there is scarcely a case in history where the entire body of an ecclesiastical organization has stood firmly and unitedly against a wrong course of the civil government.

More than this, reforms in government and in morals are never originated, or in their early stages propagated, by previously established ecclesiastical organizations. Promoters of such reforms have always had to work outside the churches, against both civil and ecclesiastical opposition, until they have made their reforms considerably popular; then the churches have taken them up. In our own country, neither the abolition of slavery, nor the abolition of alcoholic intemperance, nor the equal suffrage movement received any encouragement at the start from the churches as such. Both civil government and ecclesiastical government are conservative; they tend to stand for the established order, be it good or bad; and almost invariably they work together, and try to inspire the people with confidence in both. This is why St. John declares in this 12th verse that the second beast (ecclesiasticism) *"causeth the earth (organized society) and them which dwell therein to worship the beast (civil government), whose deadly wound was healed."* The healing of the "deadly wound" is commented upon under verse 3 of this chapter.

Verses 13, 14 *"And he doeth great wonders, so that he maketh fire come down from heaven on the earth in the sight of men, and deceiveth them that dwell on the earth by means of those miracles which he had power to do in the sight of the beast."*

Deut. 13:1-3 *"If there arise among you a prophet, or a dreamer of dreams, and giveth thee a sign or a wonder, and the sign or the wonder come to pass, whereof he spake unto thee, saying, Let us go after other gods, which thou hast not known, and let us serve them; thou shalt not hearken unto the words of that prophet, or that dreamer of dreams: for the Lord your God proveth you, to know whether ye love the Lord your God with all your heart and with all your soul."*

2 Thess. 2:9 *"Even him, whose coming is after the work of Satan, with all power and signs and lying wonders."*

St. John himself once asked our Lord to allow him to make *fire come down from heaven* on those who would not receive them. Our Lord replied: "Ye know not what manner of spirit ye are of". In these words Jesus rebuked the presumptuous disposition on the part of ecclesiastics and other men to judge and act for God. Ecclesiastics are prone to make this attempt, and in so doing they disobey the injunction: "Dearly beloved, avenge not yourselves, but rather give place unto wrath (divine love, the divine nature)*: for it is written, Ven-

---

* See Note 5, of the Introduction.

geance (judgment) is mine; I will repay (make even), saith the Lord." Despite such Scriptural teaching as this, some churches have openly claimed to be the official dispensers of wrath from God. This is especially true of the Papacy, but many other religious organizations have not been wanting in like practices. Probably the false claim of ecclesiastics that they have the right and the ability to curse people in the name and by the authority of God is what is referred to by the words, *"He maketh fire come down from heaven on the earth in the sight of men."* The authority and power of the church often has been so wielded against both individuals and groups of men as to utterly derange their affairs, and even bring them to death; so that it appeared that the church was able to make good its claim; and many times it has succeeded in inducing the great majority to so believe,—all those, in fact, who did not have discernment enough to see that it was the power of the devil, and not the power of God, which was being wielded. Did space permit, it would be instructive to recount from history some of the terribly destructive works and judgments wrought by ecclesiasticisms in the sight of men, claiming that they were administering God's consuming fire.

By the use of hypnotism, and other agencies of the carnal mind, ecclesiastics have been able to do many "wonderful" things in the line of curing sickness, claiming to act by the power of Christ, and perhaps believing that they were so doing, although it was not the divine Mind that they were using.

By means of the remarkable hold which religious hierarchies have been able to gain over their members, and by means of their seeming wonderful success in enforcing their judgments, and by means of such false miracles as are above mentioned, all done in the sight of the civil authorities, and often partly by their aid, these hierarchies (the second beast) have *"deceived them that dwell on the earth"* (verse 4) a great many times; and so have made men believe that their power was divine, and have caused men to reverence them accordingly. And so, when these ecclesiasticisms have said *"to them that dwell on the earth, that they should make an image to the beast, which had the wound by a sword, and did live"* (that is, the civil government), men have been very prone to obey the ecclesiastics.

The question arises, What does it mean to *"make an image to the beast?"* This quoted phrase does not give the meaning of the original Greek in idiomatic English. It should be, *make a likeness to the beast;* that is, *make an image of the beast.* (The Greek is, "poiêsai eikona tǫ̃ thêriǫ̃." Students of Greek will recall that after words signifying *likeness* the Greek idiom is to use a noun or pronoun in the dative case, where the English idiom is to use the preposition "of", followed by the objective.)

"The beast which had a wound by the sword, and did live", as already signified, symbolizes the authority and power which is administered by civil government, but which human sense supposes to emanate from God and to be sanctioned by Him. Here, for instance, is the foundation of the idea of "the divine right of kings." Among many peoples the emperor or the state stands explicitly or by implication for the supreme power, or virtually for God. In other words, many peoples have formed their idea of God from their observance of the ways of human government, especially in the case of nations where church and state have been united, as was the case with most nations until a comparatively recent time. In the earlier centuries, the nations of Christendom were no exception to this rule. This disposition on the part of people to regard God as the apotheosis of the state has been distinctly fostered and encouraged by the state itself in its capacity as the administrator of religion, or by ecclesiastical organizations virtually at one with the state, though having an organization more or less separate. Thus has the Worldly Church caused *"them that dwell on the earth"*, the worldly-minded, to form in imagination a "beast-like", an enlarged man-like, or anthropomorphic sense of God. And the Worldly Church has had power to cause the worldly-minded to look upon this false sense of God

as real, to regard it as alive, and as having power *"both to speak, and to cause that as many as would not worship the image of the beast* (the anthropomorphic God, supposed to be changeable and subject to human passions) *should be killed".* Unnumbered thousands, if not millions, of people have been put to death because they would not accept the idea of God, and of His ways with men, which was considered orthodox by the human government under which they were living.

Verses 16, 17 *"And he causeth all, both small and great, rich and poor, free and bond, to receive a mark in their right hand, or in their foreheads: and that no man might buy or sell, save he that had the mark, or the name of the beast, or the number of his name."**

Civil governments, in all ages, have been prone to grant special commercial privileges to their own citizens, or to those who would swear loyalty to them, and have been prone to cut off commercial privileges from those who were not citizens, and especially from those who were known not to regard the established civil government with favor. Ecclesiastics have often used their power and influence to support civil governments in this position; and especially did the Roman hierarchy of the Dark Ages and Middle Ages thus cooperate with the civil authorities of western Europe. *"To receive a mark in the right hand"*, is to be loyal in one's *deeds* to a given government, however one may feel inwardly; while to receive a mark *"in the forehead"*, is to be loyal in *thought,* as well as in deed. *"To have the mark of the beast",* is to wear a uniform, or some badge, prescribed by a given government. *"To have the name of the beast"*, is to be a citizen of a given government. To have *"the number of his name"* is to be working under a numbered license issued by the civil authorities, or to wear some prescribed number, or other distinctive mark.

---

* Mr. Rawson suggests that the "mark in the right hand" is the hard, horny character of the hand of the unspiritual, and that the "mark in the forehead" is the hard metallic look in the eyes of the worldly minded.

One of the first marks of decadence of early Christianity was the setting up of the claim that none except the priests should heal the sick.

Verse 18 *"Here is wisdom. Let him that hath understanding count the number of the beast: for it is the number of a man; and his number is six hundred threescore and six."*

I have seen at least five different explanations of this number 666. The most probable seems to be that given in the comment on verse 16 of chapter 1,* namely, that this number represents the numerical value of the letters of the Greek *hê phrên*, meaning "the lower mind", or "mortal mind". Another plausible one is the following: St. John was a Jew, and he was writing to Jewish Christians, who had been brought up as Jews. Among the Jews, *seven* was the number of completeness, and *six*, being short of *seven*, was a symbol of incompleteness. Hence, among the Jews, the number *six* was a number of evil omen, as the number *thirteen* is among people of Christendom, though for a different reason. Hence, the number 666 suggested to the Jewish mind the thought of an evil omen to a triple degree. In this chapter, St. John has already pointed out that civil government, especially the heathen Roman Empire and its civil successors, is a very corrupt institution and a great hindrance to liberty and spiritual growth. Civil government is human in its character, and so is typified by *"a man"*, especially as, in St. John's time, a man, the Roman Emperor, was at the head of all civil government, and practically stood for it. Hence, St. John concludes his arraignment of corrupt and tyrannical human government by applying to it as an ephitet the most evil omen that he could think of, the number 666.

The Jews used the letters of the Hebrew alphabet as signs for numbers, each letter having a definite numerical value. The title of Nero as Emperor of Rome, being written in

---

* See page 52.

Hebrew, and the value of the several Hebrew letters in the title being added together, the sum is 666. The Greeks used the letters of their alphabet to express numbers in the same manner that the Jews did. One of the Greek adjectives, meaning *Roman,* was the adjective *Latinos,* sometimes spelled *Lateinos:* If the numerical value of the Greek letters in the latter spelling be added together, the sum is 666. This latter explanation might be especially plausible, were it not for the fact that the adjective *Latinos* was little used in St. John's time, and the spelling *Lateinos* is comparatively rare. In the New Testament, the adjective *Rômaikos* (as nearly as the English alphabet will serve to transliterate the Greek) is uniformly used for Roman. St. John evidently saw and prophesied much farther ahead than the reign of Nero; so it is improbable that he would use the number 666 as applying to Nero alone. Other explanations that I have seen are even more improbable than the two last mentioned. So, either the explanation that 666 is the numerical value of the Greek *hê phrên,* meaning "the lower mind", or that it is merely the sign of an evil omen, is more likely the correct one, either of these having that universal application which the nature of the prophecy in its farreaching extent calls for.

THE VIOLATION OF LIBERTY

A Sin of the Beasts

It has been noted above that civil governments are inclined to restrict commercial privileges more or less to their own citizens. Ecclesiasticisms are even more inclined than are civil governments to restrict certain spiritual and certain semi-commercial privileges connected with their work to their own members, and especially to members in favor with the officials in control of their affairs. It may be doubted whether civil governments are ever ethically justified in imposing such commercial restrictions. At any rate, it may be safely asserted that they are often imposed when there is no ethical justification. Such restrictions tend strongly to interdict the brotherhood of man, and to prevent the development throughout the human race of that spirit of universal and impersonal love which will do away with tyranny, selfishness, bigotry, strife, and many other evils. Ecclesiasticisms are doubtless justified in prescribing rules and regulations as to who shall represent them in speaking, writing and teaching; but they are not justified in persecuting those outside their membership who do not agree with them; and when it comes to placing restrictions as to who shall receive the sacraments, etc., they are assuming authority which Christ probably never delegated to a human organization. All such restrictions tend to prevent the consummation of human brotherhood, and the exemplification of the words of St. Paul, who declares that God "hath made of one blood all nations of men for to dwell on all the face of the earth." In churches, certain restrictions are necessary, but the *tendency* should be to avoid them, and to regard them with suspicion, rather than to multiply them or more rigidly enforce them. Restrictions are human, not divine. There are no divisions, and no limitations, in truth.

The following contrast of ecclesiasticism (the second beast) with true religion will be found illuminating:

ECCLESIASTICISM VERSUS RELIGION

The tendency with all human movements organized in the name of religion, especially if closely organized, is to substitute ecclesiasticism for religion. The two may be justly contrasted as follows:

Ecclesiasticism cuts men off for non-conformity in doctrine and practice. *Religion* leaves the ninety and nine who are safe within the fold and goes forth to seek and save that which is lost, and seeks *until it finds*.

Ecclesiasticism is a judge, casting men out and down for breaking laws, whether human or divine. *Religion* forgiveth unto seventy times seven and has more joy over one sinner that repenteth than over ninety and nine just persons that need no repentance.

Ecclesiasticism views with suspicion for an indefinite period, and keeps in the far corners of its province, those who have transgressed its regulations, even though they are willing to forego that transgression. *Religion* seeth the returning prodigal afar off and killeth for him the fatted calf and putteth the best robe on him and giveth him the honor of a son.

Ecclesiasticism is on the watch, and peers around to see if it can discover evidence of non-conformity. *Religion* "thinketh no evil, rejoiceth not in iniquity, but rejoiceth in the truth."

Ecclesiasticism casts men out for provocation small or great. *Religion* is a fisher of men. Having gotten hold of them, it keeps hold of them, even though, time and again, it is obliged to give them plenty of line and let them run away with the bait, each time reeling them in again, until, at last, they are safely landed within the Kingdom.

Ecclesiasticism represses and hedges about. *Religion* declares that "where the spirit of the Lord is, there is liberty," and cries, "Stand fast in the liberty wherewith Christ hath made you free."

Ecclesiasticism makes conformity to the church law a matter of even greater importance than conformity to the moral law. It "pays tithe of mint, anise and cumin, and neglects the weightier matters of mercy, judgment and faith." *Religion* is not a stickler about laws, but says: "Thy sins are forgiven thee; go and sin no more."

Ecclesiasticism makes regulations, repressing and limiting spiritual activities. *Religion* commands: "Preach, saying, The Kingdom of heaven is at hand. Heal the sick, cleanse the lepers, raise the dead, cast out devils; *freely* ye have received, *freely* give;" and to him who neglects to obey this command because he is "afraid" of ecclesiastical condemnation or for any other reason, and so "hides his talent in the earth," religion saith: "Take the talent from him, and give it unto him that hath ten talents; for to every one that hath shall be given, and from him that hath not shall be taken away even that which he hath."

Ecclesiasticism would rule its adherents with man-made regulations "after the traditions of men and not after Christ;" but *religion* saith to the ecclesiastics: "Woe unto you, scribes and Pharisees, hypocrites! for ye shut up the Kingdom of heaven against men; for ye neither go in yourselves, neither suffer ye them that are entering to go in."

Ecclesiasticism is often sincere, and its sincerity can be respected, but it is full of misguided zeal. *Religion* wrote the thirteenth chapter of First Corinthians, commencing: "Though I speak with the tongues of men and of angels, and have not *love,* I am become as sounding brass, or a tinkling cymbal. . . . *Love* suffereth long, and is kind . . . beareth all things, endureth all things. *Love never faileth.*"

Saul, "breathing out threatenings and slaughter," as he started for Damascus to arrest the Christians, was an *ecclesiastic;* Paul, taking Christianity out of the narrow trammels of Judaism, with its rules, forms, customs, and ceremonies, and giving it freely to the world, was a man of *religion.* Christ had set him free from ecclesiasticism.

It is the attempt at repressing the religious activities and utterances of men that gives ecclesiasticism its hold, filling organizations, which are intended to serve religion, with suspicion, heresy hunting, hatred, unjust condemnation, misunderstandings, and strife, ever and anon violating the law of Christian love and manifesting instead the activities of satan. *Constructive work* fulfills the purpose of a religious organization; attempts at repression pervert its activities and their effects. *Nothing but love is the fulfilling of the law.*

The problem of human misgovernment in church and state is directly traceable to misgovernment in the mentalities of human individuals. Were it not for varying degrees of ignorance on the part of all members of the human race, and were not the higher natures of the vast majority of humans suppressed by their lower natures, civil and ecclesiastical misgovernment would be impossible. The first beast (the false sense of reality and value), and the second beast (superstition, or a misplaced sense of the source of power and authority), do their work, first of all, on the field of each human mentality. The root of the activity of these beasts in personal consciousness is "the dragon", general mortal belief, "the devil and satan."

Each person needs to be even more watchful to subdue these beasts within than to keep free from domination by their magnified activities in the world without. In fact, he who has become free from their inward domination cannot and will not be dominated by them outwardly. He will sooner suffer physical death, if necessary. *At any cost,* he will keep his name written in the Lamb's book of life, and so will have his part in the first resurrection.

NOTES BY THE READER

REVISED TRANSLATION AND SUGGESTIVE PARAPHRASE

SECTION IV

THE WOMAN, THE DRAGON AND THE BEASTS

Chapter XI

A Further Revelation from the Spirit of Prophecy

Amended Revised Version

19 And there was opened the temple of God that is in heaven; and there was seen in his temple the ark of his covenant; and there followed lightnings, and voices, and thunders, and an earthquake, and great hail.

Suggestive Paraphrase

And from higher consciousness there was given me another vision of the impending and continuing struggle between good and evil, in which I foresaw the activity of the Holy Spirit and of the seeming power of evil, and the great upheaval in the human realm resulting from the conflict.

Chapter XII. Warfare of the Spiritual Church With Satan

The Spiritual Church

1 And a great sign was seen in heaven; a woman arrayed with the sun, and the moon under her feet, and upon 2 her head a crown of twelve stars; and she was with child: and she crieth out, travailing in birth, and in pain to be delivered.

And a wonderful vision appeared to me,—humanity's love for Truth, reflecting the divine Mind, and upheld by the Christ-consciousness, and made brilliant with all spiritual ideas; and I saw humanity's love of Truth ready to bring the divine idea into the realm of human experience.

Satan, the Devil, Impersonal Evil

3 And there was seen another sign in heaven; and behold, a great red dragon, having seven heads and ten horns, and upon his heads 4 seven diadems. And his tail draweth the third part of the stars of heaven, and did cast them to the earth: and the dragon stood before the woman which was about to be delivered, that when she was delivered, he might devour her child.

And there appeared another astounding vision,—that of humanity's love of evil,—mortal mind, presenting seven phases (opposing the seven Spirits of God), crowned with the asserted authority of evil, and also claiming power to break the ten commandments. And the influence of this mortal monster of false belief will keep drawing into backsliding many of those struggling toward Truth: and I saw this mortal monster ready to attack and destroy, if possible, the love-of-Truth's child, as soon as it appeared among men.

Humanity's Love of Truth Brings the Christ to Human Sense

Amended Revised Version

5 And she was delivered of a son, a man child, who is to rule all the nations with a rod of iron: and her child was caught up unto God, and unto his throne.
6 And the woman fled into the wilderness, where she hath a place prepared of God, that there they may nourish her a thousand two hundred and threescore days.

Suggestive Paraphrase

And humanity's love of Truth brought into human consciousness the Christ, who was and is to rule all nations with an inflexible law: and the infantile appearing of the Christ was protected by Mind with its power. And humanity's love of Truth, the true church, will dwell in spiritual consciousness, apart from the world, resting confidently in God, and fed by his angels or ideas, during the apparent ascendency of satan.

Human Understanding is Purified from False Belief, the Lower Nature Remaining in Evidence

7 And there was war in heaven; Michael and his angels going forth to war with the dragon; and the dragon warred and his
8 angels; and they prevailed not, neither was their place found any more in heaven.
9 And the great dragon was cast down, the old serpent, he that is called the Devil and Satan, the deceiver of the whole world; he was cast down to the earth, and his angels were cast down, with him.

And I saw that there will be strife in the mental realm: the militant Christ and His militant ideas fighting against militant evil and its ideas; but militant evil will not prevail, and its claim to reality and power will be rejected from human understanding. Satan, general false belief, which deceives the whole world of humanity, and all evil thoughts, will thenceforth tempt men only through their lower natures, against their understanding of what is real and desirable.

Rejoicing Among the Spiritually Minded Over the Victory

10 And I heard a great voice in heaven, saying, Now is come the salvation, and the power, and the kingdom of our God, and the authority of his Christ: for the accuser of our brethren is cast down, which accuseth them before our God day and night. And they over-
11 came him *through* (because of) the blood of the Lamb, and *through* (because of)

And I foresaw the time of victory and I seemed to hear the Holy Spirit rejoicing, saying, Now is come into realization salvation, and strength, and the kingdom of our God, and the power of his Christ: for the accuser and deceiver of our brethren is cast down, which, in the very face of Truth, was misrepresenting them continually. And they overcame assertive evil by living the life of Christ, and by the message to which they bore testimony; and in their

Amended Revised Version	*Suggestive Paraphrase*
the word of their testimony; and they loved not their life even unto death. 12 Therefore rejoice, O heavens, and ye that dwell in them. Woe for the earth and for the sea: because the devil is gone down unto you, having great wrath, knowing that he hath but a short time.	love of true life they did not shrink from mortal death. Therefore rejoice, ye whose lives are established in spiritual consciousness. But woe to men whose lives are still grounded in material sense, for enraged evil is stirred up among them, greatly aggravated, because it seems to know that it will soon be destroyed utterly.

The Lower Elements in Human Nature Make War Against the Higher

13 And when the dragon saw that he was cast down to the earth, he persecuted the woman which brought 14 forth the man child. And there was given to the woman the two wings of the great eagle, that she might fly into the wilderness unto her place where she is nourished for a time, and times, and half a time, and from the face of the 15 serpent, And the serpent cast out of his mouth after the woman water* as a river, that he might cause her to be carried away by 16 the stream. And the earth helped the woman, and the earth opened up her mouth, and swallowed up the river which the dragon cast out 17 of his mouth. And the dragon waxed wroth with the woman, and went away to make war with the rest of her seed, which keep the commandments of God, and 18 hold the testimony of Jesus; and he stood upon the sand of the sea.	And when assertive evil is cast wholly into the lower nature, it will do all it can to overthrow humanity's love of Truth which brought the Christ into human consciousness. But to the love of Truth, the spiritual factor in human consciousness, will be given the truth and love of the Holy Spirit, by which it may dwell in the spiritual realm, apart from the world, and be preserved during the continuance of satan-time from the attack of assertive evil. And assertive evil will try to overwhelm the truth-loving portion of humanity with a horde of ungodly men under its influence. But this horde of ungodly men will fight among themselves and many of them will be thus slain, and many others will be civilized and converted to at least nominal Christianity, and so the attack of assertive evil upon the godly will be largely neutralized. And assertive evil will still be enraged against the love of Truth, and will continue to make war against those who love Truth, which keep the commandments of God, and cling to the teachings of Christ Jesus. And assertive evil will continue to take its stand in the midst of all the lower activities of human nature.

* On "water," see chap. 17:15.

CHAPTER XIII. THE STRUGGLE WITH HUMAN DOMINATION

The Ten-horned Beast. Worldly Government

Amended Revised Version

1 And I saw a beast coming up out of the sea, having ten horns and seven heads, and on his horns ten diadems, and upon his heads
2 names of blasphemy. And the beast which I saw was like unto a leopard, and his feet were as the feet of a bear, and his mouth as the mouth of a lion: and the dragon gave him his power, and his throne, and great
3 authority. And I saw one of his heads as though it had been smitten unto death; and his death-stroke was healed; and the whole earth wondered after the beast;
4 and they worshipped the dragon, because he gave his authority unto the beast; and they worshipped the beast, saying, Who is like unto the beast? and who is
5 able to war with him? and there was given to him a mouth speaking great things and blasphemies; and there was given to him authority to continue forty and two
6 months. And he opened his mouth for blasphemies against God, to blaspheme his name, and his tabernacle, even them that dwell
7 in the heaven, And it was given unto him to make war with the saints, and to overcome them: and there was

Suggestive Paraphrase

And I saw so-called civilization, civil government, so corrupt that it might better be called civil misgovernment,—springing up from barbarous and disorganized states of human society (which are even worse). And I saw worldly government as seven (all) great ungodly empires, and later as ten (all) ungodly kingdoms, —the seven empires making a blasphemous assertion that they had power, whereas God alone has power. And I saw worldly government having the cruelty of a leopard, and the relentless cunning of a bear, and the savage power of a lion: and clothed with the power and position and authority of the dragon, "that old serpent, called the Devil and Satan."* And I saw that one of the ungodly empires will be destroyed; but worldly government will be rehabilitated; and all the world will follow after it, wondering. And men will bow down in submission to mortal belief which gives power to worldly government: and they will submit to this misgovernment, saying, What authority is so great as the authority of human government? Who is able to stand against it? And worldly authority makes great boasts, and makes a blasphemous claim of power, either asserting that it is the only power, or claiming that its wicked and worldly deeds are authorized by God; and it will exercise its asserted power during the apparent ascendency of satan. And worldly government will often mock at the power of God, and will curse His name, and His church, and those who live in spiritual consciousness. And it will harass and kill those men who live godly lives; and it will

---

* See Chap. 12:9.

Amended Revised Version

given to him authority over every tribe and people and
8 tongue and nation. And all that dwell on the earth shall worship him, every one whose name hath not been written in the book of life of the Lamb that hath been slain from the foundation of
9 the world. If any man hath
10 an ear, let him hear. If any man *leadeth into captivity* (is for) captivity, into captivity he goeth: if any man shall kill with the sword, with the sword must he be killed. Here is the patience and the faith of the saints.

Suggestive Paraphrase

seem to have power over all kindreds and tongues and nations. And all inhabitants of the earth shall bow down in willing or unwilling submission to worldly government, save only those who are wholly loyal to the life inculcated by the Christ, whose human representatives evil has always sought to crucify since the beginning of mortal sense. If any man has sufficient understanding to see the point of this message, let him not fail to govern his thought and live accordingly. He that would lead another into captivity to evil shall himself go into captivity to evil; and he that would kill through any form of evil shall himself die a moral, if not a physical, death, through that same form of evil. Knowing this, the godly can be patient.

The Two-horned Beast. The Worldly Church

11 And I saw another beast coming up out of the earth; and he had two horns like unto a lamb, and he spake
12 as a dragon. And he exerciseth all the authority of the first beast in his sight. And he maketh the earth and them that dwell therein to worship the first beast, whose death-stroke was
13 healed. And he doeth great signs, that he should even make fire to come down out of heaven upon the earth in
14 the sight of men. And he deceiveth them that dwell on the earth by reason of the signs which it was given him to do in the sight of the beast; saying to them that dwell on the earth, that they should make an image *of* (to) the beast, who hath the stroke of the sword, and
15 lived. And it was given unto him to give breath to

And I saw that ecclesiastical misgovernment, a worldly and ungodly church, will spring up in so-called civilized nations; and this worldly church (in its different branches) will claim to have both the word and the works of Christ, though its voice is really the voice of the dragon (mortal sense). And the worldly church will be upheld by all the power of worldly government, and will cause those who dwell in mortal sense to bow in submission to worldly government, after its rehabilitation: and this worldly church will do things that will seem as marvelous as though fire came down from heaven in the sight of men, and will deceive the dwellers in material sense by means of the seeming wonders which it will accomplish in the presence of worldly government; and the worldly church (in its various branches) will cause the dwellers in material sense to form a false sense of God based upon their sense of worldly government, which was once nearly over-

Amended Revised Version

it, even to the image of the beast, that the image of the beast should both speak, and cause that as many as s h o u l d not worship the image of the beast should
16 be killed. And he causeth all, the small and the great, and the rich and the poor, and the free and the bond, that there be given them a mark on their right hand, or
17 upon their forehead; and that no man should be able to buy or to sell, save he that hath the mark, even the name of the beast or the number of his name.
18 Here is wisdom. He that hath understanding, let him count the number of the beast; for it is the number of a man: and his number is six hundred and sixty and six.

Suggestive Paraphrase

thrown, but was rehabilitated. And the worldly church will have power to endow with seeming life this false sense of God, so that it shall make strong claims for allegiance, and shall cause that as many as will not worship this anthropomorphic idea of God shall be killed. And the worldly church will cause all men, small and great, rich and poor, free and bond, either to render outward submission and service, or inward allegiance, to worldly government (though a true, spiritual church would often do otherwise); so that it will come to pass that no man can carry on business, except he have a license from worldly government (no matter how corrupt and ungodly it is). Now here is the test of wisdom. Let him that has discernment note the character of worldly government: for it has the same character as mortal man by whom it is instituted: and that character is well indicated by the number 666, which is a number signifying apostasy from Christ.

(Continued on Page 327.)

NOTES BY THE READER

SECTION V
VISION OF CHRIST JUDGING THE WORLD
(Chapter XIV)

The vision opens with a view and a description of those who endure the test of temptation in the struggle between good and evil, and who survive the judgment described in the latter part of the chapter.

Verses 1-5 *"And I looked, and lo, a Lamb stood on the mount Sion, and with him an hundred forty and four thousand, having his Father's name written in their foreheads. And I heard a voice from heaven, as the voice of many waters, and as the voice of a great thunder: and I heard the voice of harpers harping with their harps: and they sung as it were a new song, before the throne, and before the four beasts, and the elders: and no man could learn that song but the hundred and forty and four thousand, which were redeemed from the earth. These are they which were not defiled with women; for they are virgins. These are they which follow the Lamb whithersoever he goeth. These were redeemed from among men, being the first fruits unto God and to the Lamb. And in their mouth was found no guile: for they are without fault before the throne of God."*

This description is very similar to the description of the redeemed in chapter 7, and probably indicates the same company. The song which the redeemed are heard singing (verse 3) is of such a spiritual nature that none except those spiritually redeemed are able to understand or learn it.

"These were redeemed from among men, being the first-fruits unto God and to the Lamb" (verse 4). They are probably identical with those raised from the dead in the first resurrection (20:4-6). This may be the reason that they are spoken of as *"first-fruits."*

Verses 6, 7 *"And I saw another angel fly in the midst of heaven, having the everlasting gospel to preach unto them that dwell on the earth, and to every nation, and kindred, and tongue, and people, saying with a loud voice, Fear God, and give glory to him; for the hour of his judgment is come: and worship him that made heaven, and earth, and the sea, and the fountains of waters."*

In these verses, we are given a vision of an angel or messenger flying in the mental realm, having the everlasting Gospel to preach unto all mankind. This angel is doubtless intended by John to represent the Christ-idea acting as Spiritual Aspiration, his preaching commencing with the ministry of Jesus of Nazareth, and continuing until the end of matter and time. During all this time, this angel is proclaiming,

"Fear God, and give glory to him; for the hour of his judgment is come: and worship him that made heaven, and earth, and the sea, and the fountains of waters."

The spiritual heaven, and the spiritual earth, and the spiritual sea, and the spiritual fountains of waters or sources of life, all of which are ideas of Mind, not forms of matter, without shapes, unpicturable, but knowable, are, of course, referred to. The judgment spoken of is not a grand final judgment, as many have inferred, but, like the judgment spoken of in the concluding verses of the 25th chapter of Matthew, and like the judgment described in verses 14-20 of this chapter (14), it is a continuing judgment of individuals and of the world, in which the ungodly are continually being punished, and in which error is continually being separated from truth, and the error destroyed. There is not an hour in the life of an individual, nor in the life of humanity as a whole, in which it is not true that *"the hour of God's judgment is come"*, or is at hand. *"Now is the judgment of this world; now is the prince of this world cast out."* John 12:31.

In verses 8-11, there are announced two points or lines of conduct with regard to which men are to be judged; namely, as to whether or not they have part with or keep free from the wickedness of mental Babylon, and as to whether or not they *"worship the beast and his image, and receive his mark in their foreheads, or in their hands."*

Verse 8 *"And there followed another angel, saying, Babylon is fallen, is fallen, that great city, because she made all nations drink of the wine of the wrath of her fornication."*

This angel is the Christ-mind as Spiritual Reason, Principle.

The ancient city of Babylon, which was at the height of its power about 600 B. C., was the embodiment of worldliness, superstition, tyranny, lust, sorcery, materialism, carnality, false doctrine,—the embodiment of all that was apostate to Spirit and Christ. Among the Jews, Babylon was the symbol of all the above evil influences. Hence, John, born a Jew, and writing to Christians most of whom had been born Jews, speaks of Babylon as *"the great whore"* (17:1). Rome, seated on seven hills (17:9), *"that great city, which reigneth over the kings of the earth"* (17:18), was the Babylon of John's day, and he foresaw that Rome would be the Babylon of the world for an indefinite period after his time. However, it is not primarily the material city of Rome that he prophesies against, but against mental Rome, against those evil influences mentioned above, which, from John's day to ours, have centered at Rome, whether heathen or Papal. It is this mental Babylon, this mental Rome, which John declares, *"is fallen, is fallen"* (14:8, 18:2), and concerning which he exhorts: *"Come out of her, my people, that ye be not partakers of her sins, and that ye receive not of her plagues"* (18:4). He sees the Roman Babylon as fallen, that is, apostate from Truth and good, in his own time, and continuing in that condition for centuries, but he does not prophesy the destruction of this mental Babylon until near the end of the world. Let it here be reiterated, that this Roman Babylon is to be regarded as primarily mental, rather than as a material city. All people who are under the dominion of the set of mental influences above enumerated are under the dominion of the mental Roman Babylon, and are tributary to it, whether they are classed by men or by themselves as Catholic or Protestant, Jew or Christian Scientist. Those not under the dominion of these mental influences are not tributary to mental Babylon.

Babylon may also be regarded as *"fallen"* from the mentalities of those saints of God who have worked their way free from its trammels.

Verses 9-11 "And the third angel followed them, saying, with a loud voice, if any man worship the beast and his image, and receiveth his mark in his forehead, or in his hand, the same shall drink of the wine of the wrath of God, which is poured out without mixture into the cup of his indignation; and he shall be tormented with fire and brimstone in the presence of the holy angels, and in the presence of the Lamb: and the smoke of their torment ascendeth up for ever and ever: and they have no rest day or night, who worship the beast and his image, and whosoever receiveth the mark of his name."

The third angel is the impersonal Christ as Executive Mind, Divine Will.

The first half of verse 10 should be translated:

He himself shall drink of the wine of the ardor (thumos) of God, which is prepared unmixed in the cup of his frenzy to save (orgê).

There seems to be no single English word that gives the correct sense of *orgê* in this connection; but the phrase *frenzy to save* adequately represents the force and degree, in mediatorial consciousness, of the divine passion for good, which overcomes evil. The significance and meaning of the words *thumos* and *orgê* is fully discussed in Note 4 of the Introduction.

"And he shall be tormented with fire and brimstone, in the presence of the holy Angels, and in the presence of the Lamb."

The sun, without in the least degree changing its normal activity, melts snow and ice, when they are exposed to its rays with sufficient directness. If the snow and ice were sentient, the melting process would probably seem painful to them, and it could be said that they were tormented in the presence of the sun and of its rays,—and this without thinking that the sun was cruel, or subject to anger or indignation, or that it purposely inflicted any suffering on the snow and ice. Likewise, God is ever radiating divine love, through the Christ and through His angels (divine ideas) into the whole realm of consciousness, and never changes His activity in the least. If falsehood and evil are exposed to the activity of Love with sufficient directness, they are disintegrated and destroyed more or less gradually, and suffering attends the process, because ignorant and evil mentality has the claim of being sentient; so it can be said that an evil mentality *"shall be tormented . . . in the presence of the holy Angels, and in the presence of the Lamb"*,—and this without thinking that either God, or the Christ, or the divine ideas, which are angels of God, are cruel, vindictive, indignant, or that they purposely or consciously inflict any suffering on evil mentality or evil-doers. However, when mortal sense is exposed to the activity of divine Love, it is gradually burned and tormented, as though by fire, and smothered and choked, as though by brimstone.

Weymouth, in his "New Testament in Modern Speech", translates the first clause of verse 11, *"And the smoke of their torment goes up until the Ages of the Ages";* and in a footnote he comments as follows: "*Torment.* This noun also occurs in 9:5 and in 18:7, 10, 15. A noun, unlike a verb, (or time-word, as the Germans call it), does not indicate time. So, 'the smoke of their torment' may mean that of pain endured once for all, and then at an end. There is nothing in this verse that necessarily implies an eternity of suffering. In a similar way, the word 'punishment' or 'correction' in Matt. 25:46 gives in itself no indication of time. Compare Gen. 19:28 and Jude 7."*

The error of "beast-worship" has been fully discussed in

---

* By the late R. F. Weymouth, M. A. D. Sect., Fellow of University College, London. His interesting translation of the New Testament is published by the Pilgrim Press (Congregational), Boston.

the Notes on chapter 13. It may be well to remark here, that to "worship the beast" is to love and be devoted to any human personality or organization, whether civil or ecclesiastical, in the same degree, or in the same unreserved way, that one loves God. To receive the mark of the beast, is to obey a personal, civil or ecclesiastical mandate instead of obeying God, when one believes that God calls him to do one thing, and a human sense calls him to do another. To obey what was believed to be the call of God, defying the opposing human mandate, has often meant confiscation of property, imprisonment, and even death. John foresaw that this would be the case, and so he wrote in verses 12 and 13:

> "Here is the patience of the saints: here are they that keep the commandments of God, and the faith of Jesus. And I heard a voice from heaven, saying unto me, Write, Blessed are the dead which die in the Lord from henceforth: yea, saith the Spirit, that they may rest from their labors; and their works do follow them."

John thus declares that it is really better to die serving God, than to live at the price of serving the beast. An example, in modern times, of those who have not been "beast-worshipers" are the Quakers, who, in accordance with what they conceived to be obedience to God, refused to go to war at the behest of civil government, even though fined or imprisoned for their refusal.

"The 'dead' are the *living dead,* who 'die in the Lord' only when they attain liberation from the sepulchre of the carnal body, ceasing then from their toil, but retaining the fruition of their good works."* However, it is not intended to suggest that anyone attains liberation from the carnal sense of body simply by physical death, but only by that absolute perception of and service to Spirit which overcomes the sense of matter, resulting in dying to the carnal sense, but being "alive unto God."

---

* "The Apocalypse Unsealed."

Verses 14-20 *"And I looked, and behold a white cloud, and upon the cloud one sat like unto the Son of man, having on his head a golden crown, and in his hand a sharp sickle. And another angel came out of the temple, crying with a loud voice to him that sat on the cloud, Thrust in thy sickle, and reap: for the time is come for thee to reap; for the harvest of the earth is ripe. And he that sat on the cloud thrust in his sickle on the earth; and the earth was reaped. And another angel came out of the temple which is in heaven, he also having a sharp sickle And another angel came out from the altar, which had power over fire; and cried with a loud cry to him that had the sharp sickle, saying, Thrust in thy sharp sickle, and gather the clusters of the vine of the earth; for her grapes are fully ripe. And the angel thrust in his sickle into the earth, and gathered the vine of the earth, and cast it into the great winepress of the wrath of God. And the winepress was trodden without the city, and blood came out of the winepress, even unto the horse bridles, by the space of a thousand and six hundred furlongs."*

In these verses, we have a vision of the Christ-mind judging the world, essentially parallel to the vision in Matthew 25:31-46. The different angels here spoken of are to be regarded as still other activities or phases of the Christ-mind, the Holy Spirit. The angel of verses 14 and 16 seems to symbolize Spiritual Intuition; that of verse 15, Divine Love; that of verses 17 and 19, Perception of Reality, Truth; that of verse 18, Perception of Substance, Spirit. The four angels of this passage, with the three mentioned in the earlier portion of the chapter, will be recognized as identical with the Angels of the Seven Churches, the Angels of the Trumpets, and the Angels of the Vials.

As already remarked, the judgment spoken of in verses 14-20 constantly goes on to the end of the world. The Christ consciousness separates the good from the evil, and gathers the wheat (the good) into his garner, but the chaff (the evil, error) he burns with destroying fire (Matthew 3:12). Men are punished as long as they continue in ungodliness, and even their worldly lives (physical lives in this belief) are destroyed during the judging process, so that blood is flowing as described in verse 20; but the mentalities of even the most wicked live on in a world to come, until finally they are redeemed from error and sin, and "put on Christ." *"God will have all men to be saved, and to come into the knowledge of the truth." "As in Adam all die (are dead in trespasses and sins), so in Christ shall all be made alive."*

The phrase "wrath of God" at the close of verse 20 should be *ardor* of God, the Greek noun being *thumos*.

"The horses" of verse 20 are probably the same symbols as are employed in chapter 6, the white horse, the red horse, the black horse, and the dun horse. This 14th chapter represents the impersonal Christ idea, "the white horse and his rider", as gaining the victory over those mental activities and influences which are symbolized in the 6th chapter by "the red horse and his rider", "the black horse and his rider", "the dun horse and his rider", and are symbolized in the 14th chapter as "the harvest of the earth" and "the vine of the earth". The severity of the conflict is symbolized by blood flowing, so deep that it reaches to the bridles of the horses. The last phrase of verse 20 is correctly translated in the Revised Version, *"as far as a thousand and six hundred furlongs."* This phrase is probably indicative of the influence of Greek philosophy upon John's thought, the character of which, however, is not impaired thereby. In the Apocalypse, "the sun" is used as the symbol of divine Mind, Spirit. Hence, to John's thought, the Greek adjective *hêliakos,* meaning *pertaining to the sun, solar,* would be equivalent in meaning to the word *spiritual.* The early Christian disciples had a concept of what they termed "the spiritual body", evidently meaning thereby *the body of right ideas,* synonymous with the spiritual man, who is, as "Science and Health" expresses it (p. 475), "the compound idea of God, including all right ideas." St. Paul declares: "There is a spiritual body" (1 Cor. 15:44), and it is likely that he derived this form of expression from his familiarity with Greek literature,—a fact clearly indicated in the circumstance of his quoting from one of the Greek poets in his famous speech to the Athenians on Mars Hill (Acts

17:28); but Paul uses the Greek *sôma pneumatikon* for "spiritual body", though *sôma hêliakon* was equally common among the Greek philosophers. John does not use this expression, but probably had it in mind when he wrote the Greek equivalent of *"as far as a thousand and six hundred furlongs",* since the numerical value of the Greek letters *to sôma hêliakon* is 1600, which would thus become the numerical symbol of the consciousness of the spiritual man. There seems no other way of accounting for the use of the specific number 1600 in this connection; and the evidence that this is the correct interpretation will be found to be still more convincing if the reader will refer to verse 16, chapter 21, where it is stated that 12000 stadia (furlongs) is the measure of the spiritual city, the spiritual consciousness. Now the Jews reckoned 7½ stadia to the mile (though the Romans reckoned 8). Dividing 12000 by 7½ we get exactly 1600, the symbol for the spiritual consciousness as above. In verse 17 of chapter 21, John states that 144 cubits is the measure or symbol of the angelic or spiritual man, but this need not be regarded as inconsistent with the above exposition, since it is characteristic of the Apocalypse to employ numerous symbols for the same idea. We have noted, for instance, no less than five numerical symbols for satan-time. The number 144 probably came to be used as a symbol for the spiritual consciousness in the following manner. The sun and its rays constitute all material light. Among the Greeks, the sun was symbolized by the letter *alpha,* the numerical value of which is 1, and the rays of the sun were spoken of as *hê doxa,* the numerical value of which is 143. Therefore 144 is the numerical value for the sun and its rays, and is therefore the symbolical number for Mind and its ideas, that is, for the total of the spiritual consciousness, which is the angelic man.*

The literal idea which we are to take from verse 20 is probably as follows:

---

* With acknowledgments to Mr. Pryse for important suggestions.

And the separation between truth and error takes place outside of the cognizance of pure spiritual consciousness, where nothing but harmony is known, although that consciousness is the agent of the casting out and destruction of error; and during the process, the whole realm of human consciousness is suffused with suffering, as far as, but not entering into, the spiritual factor in consciousness.

The spiritual factor in consciousness rules, controls, and circumscribes the lower activities of human nature, even before it destroys them. Hence, this spiritual factor is here spoken of as a *"bridle"*, or *"bridles"*, for the red, black, and dun *"horses"*, which symbolize these lower activities. Hence, both the phrase *"unto the bridles of the horses"*, and the phrase *"as far as a thousand and six hundred furlongs"*, indicate that the suffering attending the separation of error from truth is to be kept outside of spiritual consciousness, thus reiterating the first clause of the verse, *"and the wine-press was trodden without the city."*

NOTES BY THE READER

REVISED TRANSLATION AND SUGGESTIVE PARAPHRASE

SECTION V

THE HARVEST ANGELS

Chapter XIV

The Rejoicing of the Faithful

Amended Revised Version

1 And I saw, and behold, the Lamb standing on the mount Zion, and with him a hundred and forty and four thousand, having his name and the name of his Father, written on their foreheads. 2 And I heard a voice from heaven, as the voice of many waters, and as the voice of a great thunder: and the voice which I heard was as the voice of harpers harping with their harps: 3 and they sing as it were a new song before the throne, and before the four living creatures and the elders: and no man could learn the song save the hundred and forty and four thousand, even they that had been purchased out of the earth. 4 These are they which were not defiled with women; for they are virgins. These are they which follow the Lamb whithersoever he goeth. These were purchased from among men, to be the firstfruits unto God and unto the Lamb. 5 And in their mouth was found no lie: they are without blemish.

Suggestive Paraphrase

And I saw the Christ exalted, and with him the complete number of the redeemed, having God in their understanding. And there was great rejoicing: and the redeemed sang a new song of gladness in the presence of God, and of the Christ, and of the elders: and this song of rejoicing was of a spiritual nature, so that none could understand its meaning or learn it, save those who had been converted from material to spiritual sense. These are they who had never yielded to the defiling impulses of the flesh, and who follow where Truth leads. These were redeemed from among men, being the first who came unto God and to the Christ. And they cover no deceit or evil: for they are without fault by the test of Principle.

The Christ as Spiritual Aspiration

Amended Revised Version

6 And I saw another angel flying in mid-heaven, having the eternal gospel to proclaim unto them that dwell on the earth, and unto every nation and tribe 7 and tongue and people; and he saith with a great voice, Fear God, and give him glory; for the hour of his judgment is come: and worship him that made the heaven and the earth and sea and fountains of waters.

Suggestive Paraphrase

And I saw the Christ-mind as Spiritual Aspiration, extending itself in the mental realm, making known the everlasting facts of good to humanity, to every nation, and kindred, and tongue, and people, proclaiming insistently, Reverence God, and give glory to Him; for the time for discrimination and separation between truth and error is now and always at hand; and worship Mind, which thought into being and sustains His ideas, all the manifestations of Life.

The Christ as Spiritual Reason

8 And another, a second angel, followed, saying, Fallen, fallen is Babylon the great, which hath made all the nations to drink of the wine of the *ardor* (wrath) of her fornication.

And the Christ-mind as Spiritual Reason revealed that material and worldly belief, the great mental habitation of men, is fallen and apostate from truth, having brought all nations of mankind under the maddening mesmerism of its wickedness.

The Christ as Executive Mind

9 And another angel, a third, followed them, saying with a great voice, If any man worshippeth the beast and his image, and receiveth a mark on his forehead, or 10 upon his hand, he also shall drink of the wine of the *ardor* (wrath) of God, which is prepared unmixed in the cup of his *frenzy* (anger), and he shall be *tested* (tormented) with fire and brimstone in the presence of the holy angels, and 11 in the presence of the Lamb: and the smoke of their *testing* (torment) goeth up *unto the ages of ages* (for ever and ever); and they have no rest day and night, they that worship the beast and

And the Christ as Divine Will, Executive Mind, revealed clearly, that if any man reverences worldly misgovernment and the anthropomorphic sense of God, and becomes subject thereto either inwardly or outwardly (contrary to the service of God), that man shall drink of the wine of the ardor of God, which is prepared unmixed in the cup of his loving zeal to save men from evil, and he shall be disciplined by the Holy Spirit in the presence of all right ideas and of the Christ himself. And the discipline of such never ceases as long as they sin:— those who reverence worldly misgovernment and the man-made sense of God, and bow down to human authority, when it conflicts with the

Amended Revised Version

his image, and whoso receiveth the mark of his 12 name. Here is the patience of the saints, they that keep the commandments of God, 13 and the faith of Jesus. And I heard a voice from heaven saying, Write, Blessed are the dead which die in the Lord from henceforth: yea, saith the Spirit, that they may rest from their labours; for their works follow with them.

Suggestive Paraphrase

decrees of God. To heed the lesson of this vision will require much endurance on the part of Christ's people, who would keep the commandments of God, and continue in the truth taught by Jesus. And I was commanded to make known that those are really fortunate who suffer physical death while loyally obeying Christ; for the Spirit testifies, that such will experience mental rest and peace; and their good deeds will continue to accrue to their credit.

The Christ as Spiritual Intuition

14 And I saw, and behold, a white cloud; and on the cloud I saw one sitting like unto a son of man, having on his head a golden crown, and in his hand a sharp sickle.

And I beheld Spiritual Intuition, a manifestation of Christ, appearing in glory, clothed with authority, and exercising discernment.

The Christ as Divine Love

15 And another angel came out from the temple, crying with a great voice to him that sat on the cloud, Send forth thy sickle, and reap: for the hour to reap is come; for the harvest of 16 the earth is over-ripe. And he that sat on the cloud cast his sickle upon the earth; and the earth was reaped.

And I saw divine Love manifested by the Christ-mind, and giving insistent direction to Spiritual Intuition to separate between truth and error in the human consciousness; for the time for such separation is ever at hand; and there is need for the execution of judgment among men. And Spiritual Intuition will continue to execute this command.

The Christ as Perception of Reality

17 And another angel came out from the temple which is in heaven, he also having a sharp sickle.

And there appeared another active manifestation of Christ, destructive of evil, namely, Perception of Reality.

The Christ as Perception of Substance

18 And another angel came out from the altar, he that hath power over fire; and he called with a great voice to him that had the sharp sickle, saying, Send forth

And there appeared another manifestation of the Christ-mind; and it directed Perception of Reality, that it shall bring into judgment the works of men which are ripe for

Amended Revised Version

thy sharp sickle, and gather the clusters of the vine of the earth; for her grapes
19 are fully ripe. And the angel cast his sickle into the earth, and gathered the vintage of the earth, and cast it into the winepress, the great winepress, of the *ardor*
20 (wrath) of God. And the winepress was trodden without the city, and there came out blood from the winepress, even unto the bridles of the horses, as far as a thousand and six hundred furlongs.

Suggestive Paraphrase

judgment. And Perception of Reality will do so, and will bring men and their works to the test under the impulsion of divine Love. And evil will be kept excluded from the spiritual consciousness, and will be destroyed in its own realm, with much bloodshed and suffering on the part of men who are enmeshed in it ("but they themselves shall be saved—saved out of evil—yet so as by fire." See 1 Cor. 3:15.)

(Continued on Page 349.)

NOTES BY THE READER

SECTION VI

THE VISION OF THE LAST DAYS

(Chapter XV-XX)

This vision occupies chapters 15 to 19. Movements in the mental realm which are prophesied under the visions of the preceding chapters of the Book are those which commence at or soon after the birth of Jesus and continue until near the end of the reign of discord or satan. They are distinctly dominant during a period which St. John speaks of variously as "time, times, and half a time", "forty and two months", and "twelve hundred sixty days", which are all equivalent, reckoning thirty days to the month. As already indicated in Note 3 of the Introduction, there are reasons for believing that these expressions were not intended to refer to a definite period of time, but to what may be spoken of as "world-time", or "satan-time", the period of the ascendency of evil and falsehood in their various manifestations. Near the end of this "world-time", the movements described as *"the seven last plagues"*, and other movements having to do with the destruction of evil, commence, and continue until all evil and, at the last, the sense of matter and time disappear; so that these last chapters may properly be called "THE VISION OF THE LAST DAYS", as already indicated.

In chapter 15:2-4, is given what may be regarded as a praise service among the redeemed, because the conflicts which are to result in the complete destruction of evil and evil-doers are near their end. In verses 5-8 following, is given a vision of the seven angels, the seven active manifestations of Truth, which are to remand seven phases of assertive error to punishment and final destruction, as described in chapter 16.

There is foretold the destruction of sensuality and materialism (verse 2); and of sensuousness and psychism (verse 3); and of human emotions (4-7); and of false doctrine (8-9); and of animal magnetism (10, 11); and of idolatry and superstition (verse 12); and of general mortal belief (verses 17-21).

In verses 13, 14, is given, as an episode, a vision of three unclean miracle-working spirits, loathsome to a spiritually minded person as frogs are to the material sense of many people. These probably indicate un-Christlike methods of healing,—hypnotism, mental therapeutics, suggestion; materia medica; healing through blind faith, shrines, relics, etc.

The interpretation of chapters 15 and 16 is given fully in connection with the interpretation of chapters 8 and 9.

CHAPTER XV

Verses 1-8 The interpretation of these verses is to be found on pages 171-173, and on pages 349, 350 of the *Suggestive Paraphrase,* following.

CHAPTER XVI

Verse 2 The interpretation of this verse is to be found on pages 186, 187, and on page 350 of the *Suggestive Paraphrase.*

Verse 3 The interpretation of this verse is to be found on pages 190, and on page 350, *Suggestive Paraphrase.*

Verses 4-7 The interpretation of these verses is to be found on pages 194-196, and on page 351, *Suggestive Paraphrase.*

Verses 8-9 The interpretation of these verses is to be found on pages 197, 198, and on page 351, *Suggestive Paraphrase.*

Verses 10-11 The interpretation of these verses is to be found on pages 201, 202, and on page 351, *Suggestive Paraphrase.*

Verse 12 The interpretation of this verse is to be found on page 208, and on page 352, *Suggestive Paraphrase.*

Verses 13-16 The interpretation of these verses is to be found on pages 227, 228, and on page 352, *Suggestive Paraphrase.*

Verses 17-21 The interpretation of these verses is to be found on pages 233-235, and on pages 352, 353, *Suggestive Paraphrase.*

CHAPTER XVII

Verses 7-17 The interpretation of these verses is to be found on pages 283-288, and on pages 354, 355, *Suggestive Paraphrase.*

In chapters 17 and 18, wicked mental Babylon, the personification of Worldly Lust, is described. Men are warned to come out of her and to keep free from her. She is as wicked as a fallen woman, and is a fallen city. The ultimate destruction of Worldly Lust is foretold.

To any one who understands, as John undoubtedly did, that all God's creation, the only real creation, is spiritual and good, and that all that appears as material and evil is totally unreal,—to anyone having such an understanding, the very appearance of matter and evil in all their forms is a mystery. The mystery is, how such falsehoods and unrealities could have sprung into appearance at any time in the past, or how they can continue in appearance now, since good is omnipresent and all powerful. To John's sense, Babylon was the symbol of practically all materiality and evil; and it may be for the reason above described that John speaks of Babylon as a "mystery", as he does in verse 5.

On chapter 18, Mr. Pryse makes the following very clear and interesting comment:

"In the rejoicing and lamentation over the prospective fall of Babylon (an event which, for the mass of mankind, lies in the extremely remote future) the four castes take part. The highest caste, or distinctive class, is given as three-fold, composed of devotees, apostles and seers; but they utter no rejoicings, the Divinities acting as their spokesmen. The profane, comprising the rulers or dominant warlike class, the merchants or trading class, and the sailors, the toiling masses on the sea of life, indulge in lamentations over the downfall of the great city. For the present, and for ages to come, in Christian and pagan lands alike, Astarte remains enthroned on the scarlet Dragon, "who is the Devil and Satan", and in this twentieth century her cup is more overflowing with abominations, and the traffic in the bodies and souls of men and of women goes on even more briskly and heartlessly, than in the days when Ioannes penned his mystic scroll. The destruction of the Apocalypse Babylon will come only when humanity shall have learned to loathe the lusts of the flesh and to love the glories of the Spirit."

In 19:1-10, are prophesied the triumphant song of the redeemed and the marriage of the Lamb,—the union with Christ of the human mentalities which had been striving to gain that union. In 19:11-21, we have a vision of Christ and his followers riding forth to victory. It is interesting and important to note that at this time *"the beast was taken, and with him the false prophet"*, and *"these both were cast alive into a lake of fire burning with brimstone"* (verse 20); that is, at this time worldly government and the worldly church,—every form of human organization,—will be destroyed. This will come to pass because mankind has finally grown sufficiently spiritual and good so that men will neither need to instruct each other or restrain each other, for every man will know and obey God sufficiently to understand right conduct, and not to trespass upon his neighbor's rights, without being restrained by fear of human punishment. *"And they shall teach no more every man his neighbor, and every man his brother, saying, Know the Lord: for they shall all know me, from the least of them unto the greatest of them, saith the Lord"* (Jer. 31:34). St. John indicates that this condition, where every man is self-governed, because he has demonstrated the divine government, must be attained by humanity before satan (discord) can be bound, and the millennium can be ushered in, as described in the first four verses of chapter 20.

Verse 10 *"And I fell at his feet to worship him. And he said unto me, See thou do it not: I am thy fellow servant, and of thy brethren that have the testimony of Jesus: worship God: for the testimony of Jesus is the spirit of prophecy."*

John would do honor to the angel who reveals these things to him; but the angel forbids it, saying that God alone is to be worshipped, *"for the testimony of Jesus is the spirit of prophecy."* This spirit of prophecy is not a personal possession, and does not entitle the one who exercises it to be worshipped. As St. Paul says: *"We have this treasure in earthen vessels, that the excellency of the power may be of God, and not of us"* (2 Cor. 4:7). The spirit of prophecy, like every other manifestation of good, emanates from the divine Mind, and that Mind, God, is alone to be worshipped. The tendency to worship persons or institutions because they are channels for good is blasphemy and idolatry.

If the student will consult a Greek lexicon for the meaning of *proskuneô,* he will see that John was not only forbidden to worship the angel or messenger in our sense of the word "worship", but he was forbidden to prostrate himself, to make a profound bow, to reverence, or even do honor to the angel. He was commanded to do these things to God alone.

Verses 17, 18 *"And I saw an Angel* [Greek, *a lone angel*] *standing in the sun, and he cried with a loud voice, saying to all the fowls that fly in the midst of heaven, Come and gather yourselves together unto the supper of the great God; that ye may eat the flesh of kings, and the flesh of captains, and the flesh of mighty men, and the flesh of horses, and of them that sit on them, and the flesh of all men both free and bond, both small and great."*

The *"lone angel"* is the militant Christ as Michael, who drove the dragon out of "heaven", as related in chapter 12. *"The fowls that fly in the midst of heaven"* are spiritual ideas, all right ideas, which are summoned and commanded to destroy falsehood,—to consume the *"flesh"*, the seeming substance and reality, of all phases of mortal mentality, whether exalted or humble in appearance,—to consume all the self-assertive forces that claim power to oppose the Christ.

Eschatology

The events forecast in chapter 20 have been spoken of by theologians under the title "Eschatology", which means *the science, or the account of, the last things.* There is no reason why all the movements described from the beginning of chapter 15 should not be included under this title, and some do so include them. To a more detailed interpretation of the final events in the overcoming of error, as outlined for us in chapter 20, we now turn.

The Order of Progress

The order of the working out of the human problem,—that is, the order in which the different phases of evil, falsehood, will be overcome,—through the application of the scientific knowledge of Truth, would seem to be as follows: First, sin, disease, accident and poverty will be overcome. This work has already commenced. There will remain to be destroyed the false concepts named death, matter, and limitation. These false concepts are so deeply seated in general mortal belief that, as yet, it is possible to make little apparent headway in overcoming them with the limited realization of Truth which we, at present, have; but when the whole race shall have come into the understanding of the Christ-Science sufficiently to have eliminated sin, disease, poverty and accidents, the racial and individual realization of Truth will be very much clearer and more powerful, while the power of general mortal belief will be correspondingly lessened.

Sin, disease, poverty and accidents having been eliminated, there will be nothing to lead up to "death" in human experience; hence, in the last days they will not die any more,* but

---

* Students quite frequently raise the question, If the time comes when people do not die any more, will not the earth become overpopulated? It will not, because in proportion as the race becomes spiritually-minded enough to successfully resist sin, disease, and death, in that proportion it will be spiritually-minded enough not to be tempted by the lusts of the flesh in begetting children, and the desire for children after the flesh will pass from human consciousness. Thus, as the race comes into the knowledge and demonstration of Christian Science, the birth-rate will decrease in exact proportion as the death-rate decreases. St. Paul wrote: "They which are the children of the flesh, these are not the children of God" (Rom. 9:8). According to an ancient manuscript known as *"The Gospel to the Egyptians,"* "When Salome asked (Jesus) how long death would prevail, the Lord said, So long as ye women bear children." . . . When Salome asked when those things about which she questioned should be made known, the Lord said, When ye trample upon the garment of shame; when the two become one, and the male with the female, neither male nor female."—From *"New Sayings of Jesus,"* page 43, Oxford University Press.

will live and reign with Christ (with their knowledge and realization of Truth) on a perfected and glorious earth, in a glorified sense still material, but freed from natural cataclysms, such as famines, floods, and earthquakes, and made fruitful in every way,—an earth on which the kingdom of God, the kingdom of harmony, has come, as it is in heaven, just as far as it is possible to have heavenly harmony and completeness exemplified in connection with matter. At this time will commence a period of mental harmony and unity among the inhabiters of earth, which is spoken of as "the millennium", during which satan (discord) is suppressed as described in 20:1-3.

Resurrection

The period having arrived when people do not die any more, the only thing remaining to demonstrate completely the unreality of death is to prove that those of former generations seeming to have died did not die,—that their estate was not changed,—that their seeming to have died was only a false belief imposed on humanity by the devil. This demonstration can be made by bringing those who seemed to have died, and to have passed to "the other side" (into the next belief) visibly into the presence of those living "here" (in this belief). There is no space in truth, in the true consciousness; and, on careful analysis, it can be seen that there is no space in error, since error is merely false consciousness. The belief of space inheres in the belief in matter; but matter itself is merely a false belief, an objectified state of general mortal belief. Matter being merely an illusory dream, the sense of space is only a part of this dream. At the root both truth and error are states of consciousness; and to consciousness, whether true or false, everything is presence, if in consciousness at all, and there is no absence. Hence, those "here" are separated from those "there", not by space, but merely by a difference of conditions in the two beliefs,—the two beliefs formed by general mortal belief and mesmerically imposed on those "here" and those "there", until general mortal belief shall have been so much overcome by the knowledge and application of the truth, that it can no longer maintain this imposition. As those "here" and those "there" work and demonstrate their way toward the same truth, they will demonstrate their way more and more toward the one Christ-consciousness, and finally they will do this to such an extent that there will be no difference between their states of belief, because they have come into one consciousness. At this point, the difference of belief which has so long separated those "here" from those "there" will be broken down; and they will all seem to be together in one place, on a glorified earth, and perhaps on an enlarged sense of the earth. When those "there" thus come visibly into the presence of those "here", it will appear to those "here" like a "resurrection of the dead."

The First Resurrection

It is entirely reasonable to suppose that those who have been spiritually minded and loyal to Truth "here" will be those who, on passing on, will maintain spiritual leadership among the inhabitants of "there", and that these will be more ready than the less spiritual among those "there" to come into unity of understanding with the spiritually minded "here" in the last days. Hence, it is reasonable to expect that some of the so-called dead will come visibly into the presence of those "here" in the last days before others of the so-called dead; and the 20th chapter of Revelation seems to teach this. *"This is the first resurrection"*, spoken of in Rev. 20:5. John indicates that this "first resurrection" will take place at the beginning of the millennium or thousand-year period already spoken of, so that those reappearing in the first resurrection will dwell on the earth (that is, in "this belief") during the millennial period along with the generation of those who will not experience death; but John foresees that there will have to be a further growth in spirituality before the remainder of the so-called dead can be resurrected, and says that this will not take place until after the thousand-year period is ended.

The Loosing of Satan

At the end of this long period of harmony among men, he tells us that satan (discord) will be loosed again for a season, and will bring mankind under its sway. It is not difficult to see what the occasion for this discord may be. It may arise over the question of going on to overcome the one remaining false belief named matter, with the sense of material bodies, and all attendant material circumstances. Everybody is, and always will be, glad to overcome disease, poverty, accident, and death; and a person need not become very spiritual to be willing to dispense with sin. It is, therefore, easy to see that, after the theory of Divine Science becomes generally understood, all will willingly co-operate to overcome everything except the belief of matter; but it is entirely conceivable, that, after these other beliefs have been overcome, there will be some who will mentally struggle to go still farther and overcome the belief of matter, while there will be many more who will cling to the material sense, and to the sense of material selfhood, because they do not wish to lose their human so-called "individuality", as will happen when all attain the true individuality by putting on Christ and thus becoming one. Such will say that endless life on the earth, where there is no want, no sin, no disease, or death, is good enough for them. They may not see that, good as such a life is from a comparative standpoint, it is yet far short of the completeness and joy of limitless life in God. Thus, there may arise a mental division between those desiring to go on and those clinging to the material order. This will be the period, spoken of in Rev. 20:3, when the devil (discord) "must be loosed a little season." But absolute spirituality will, of course, triumph in the end, and then will come the destruction of the devil, discord.

The General Resurrection

All love for materiality, and desire to cling to corporeal selfhood, having been thus eliminated from the consciousness of humanity, mankind will have become sufficiently spiritual to demonstrate the second or general resurrection as described in 20:11-13, at which time will occur the general judgment; that is, the final separation between good and evil in the minds of men, and the destruction of the evil.

The Final Destruction of Evil

Then will follow the absolute and final destruction of general evil, general mortal belief, and all remnants of error as described in 20:14-15. This event John speaks of as "the second death."

The Destruction of the Matter-Belief

Then will come the demonstration over the belief of matter and the material universe, as forecast in 21:1.*

---

*There are several earnest, intelligent, and highly successful Christian Scientists who hold that matter will be demonstrated over and mortal belief brought to the end of its false appearance within the next few years. The writer earnestly hopes that they are right, but he is unable to interpret prophecy or "read the signs of the times" that way. He will be glad to have anyone write him who feels that he has any important evidence to present, on this subject.

The Scripture as to "The Last Days."

(Chapter xx)

These are the different events which are forecast to happen in "the last days"; and they are all spoken of by St. John in chapters 16-20. We may now comment briefly on the various verses in these chapters with interest and advantage.

1-3 *"And I saw an angel come down from heaven, having the key of the bottomless pit and a great chain in his hand. And he laid hold on the dragon, that old serpent, which is the Devil, and Satan, and bound him a thousand years, and cast him into the bottomless pit, and shut him up, and set a seal upon him, that he should deceive the nations no more, till the thousand years should be fulfilled: and after that he must be loosed a little season."*

As already indicated, chapter 20:1-3 refers to the period of harmony among men and in general human consciousness, lasting something like a thousand years, before the final occasion of discord above spoken of arises.

4-5 *"And I saw thrones, and they sat upon them, and judgment was given unto them: and I saw the souls of them that were beheaded for the witness of Jesus, and for the word of God; and which had not worshipped the beast, neither his image, neither had received his mark upon their foreheads, or in their hands; and they lived and reigned with Christ a thousand years. But the rest of the dead lived not again until the thousand years were finished. This is the first resurrection."*

Chapter 20:4-5 refers to "the first resurrection" and those who have part in it, and to those who must wait for the second resurrection.

6 *"Blessed and holy is he that hath part in the first resurrection: on such the second death hath no power, but they shall be priests of God and of Christ, and shall reign with him a thousand years."*

Verse 6 speaks of "the second death." "The second death" refers to the final and complete destruction of error, even of death and hell themselves, as shown in verse 14. Verse 6 declares that those who have part in the first resurrection are so purified from error that there is nothing in their consciousness to be destroyed at or by the second death, the general destruction of error.

7-9 *"And when the thousand years are expired, Satan shall be loosed out of his prison, and shall go to deceive the nations which are in the four quarters of the earth, Gog and Magog, to gather them together to battle: the number of whom is as the sand of the sea. And they went up on the breadth of the earth, and compassed the camp of the saints about, and the beloved city: and fire came down from God out of Heaven, and devoured them."*

Verses 7-9 refer to the final period of discord above spoken of, when those who desire to cling to materiality mentally camp against those who desire to make the complete spiritual demonstration; but "fire" (purifying truth) comes down from God out of heaven (verse 9) and devours the mortal factor in the mentalities of all these, while leaving the immortal factor in their mentalities untouched.

10 *"And the Devil that deceived them was cast into the lake of fire and brimstone, where the beast and the false prophet are, and shall be tormented day and night for ever and ever."*

Verse 10 refers to the final destruction of mortal mind, the devil. *"The lake of fire and brimstone"* is simply a figurative expression for the consuming of general evil and of all false factors of consciousness, and the phrase *"they shall be tormented day and night forever and ever,"* should be taken to signify, not endless torment, but the absoluteness of the destruction.

11 *"And I saw a great white throne, and him that sat on it, from whose face the earth and Heaven fled away; and there was found no place for them."*

Verse 11 refers to the complete realization or perception of God, so that, as He is fully perceived and realized mentally, the material sense of earth and heaven *"fled away from before his face"*, His realized presence.

12-13 *"And I saw the dead, small and great, stand before God; and the books were opened: and another book was opened, which is the book of life: and the dead were judged out of those things which were written in the books, according to their works. And the sea gave up the dead which were in it; and death and hell delivered up the dead which were in them: and they were judged every man according to their works."*

Verses 12-13 refer to the final destruction and the final judgment. The so-called dead, who do not have part in the first resurrection, will be resurrected at this time, and will be judged according to the standard of God. The records of their past lives will be disclosed, and the laws of life will also be disclosed; and according as the records of their lives shall bear comparison with the laws of life, will the resurrected dead be judged.

14-15 *"And death and hell were cast into the lake of fire. This is the second death. And whosoever was not found written in the book of life was cast into the lake of fire."*

Verses 14 and 15 refer to the complete destruction of evil above spoken of.

In verse 15 we are taught that the mortal or false factor of every man's consciousness *"was not found written in the book of life"* and so *"was cast into the lake of fire"*, along with general evil, to be destroyed. "Mortals" are constituted of the false factors in the mentalities of human beings, while "immortals" are the true factor, the knowledge of truth, in the mentalities of men. All "immortals" are eternally safe, because they have part in the reflection of the one Mind, which is forever. All "mortals", all false mentalities or beliefs of falsehood, are predestined to be destroyed. This is the true doctrine of predestination. In this connection Romans 8:28-30 is interesting.*

With the final destruction of the false claims of evil and matter, which immediately follow the final judgment, the time-consciousness passes away; for all men will then attain the spiritual, eternal consciousness, which is opposite to the time-belief. As Mrs. Eddy says in "Science and Health" (page 468), "Eternity, not time, expresses the thought of Life, and time is no part of eternity. One ceases in proportion as the other is recognized." Accordingly, when the events forecast in chapter 20 have transpired, the consciousness of measured duration will have ceased. Hence, here ends the period or the experience of humanity called "the last days."

---

* Mr. F. L. Rawson writes: "Every single thing that one does, says, and thinks is predestined. Predestination can be spoken of as phenomenal matter existing in the form of thought before it is seen, but that which is predestined is more accurately looked upon as cinematographic pictures, since such pictures present less the appearance of power than 'thoughts' do. The nearer we can get in statement to presenting non-reality, the better. All the cinematographic picures were in position over a million years ago, and all that we can do is to turn in thought to God in such a way as to open our human minds, and then the action of God destroys the evil in the cinematographic pictures, that is, thins the mist of materiality, so that we see heaven a little more like what it really is."

REVISED TRANSLATION AND SUGGESTIVE PARAPHRASE

SECTION VI

THE FINAL CONFLICT

Chapter XV. The Angels of the Vials

A Praise Service

Amended Revised Version

1 And I saw another sign in heaven, great and marvellous, seven angels having seven *scourges* (plagues), which are the last, for in them is *accomplished the eager desire* (finished the 2 wrath) of God. And I saw as it were a glassy sea mingled with fire; and them that come victorious from the beast, and from his image, and from the number of his name, standing by the glassy sea, having harps 3 of God. And they sing the song of Moses the servant of God, and the song of the Lamb, saying, Great and marvellous are thy works, O Lord God, the Almighty; righteous and true are thy ways, thou King of the 4 ages. Who shall not *reverence* (fear), O Lord, and glorify thy name? for thou only art holy; for all the nations shall come and worship before thee; for thy righteous acts have been made manifest.

Suggestive Paraphrase

And there was revealed to me, in the form of seven visions, a marvellous overcoming by Truth, which will later take place, indicating to me the full measure of God's redemptive power. And I saw the truth to be mentally transparent as glass and destructive of evil as fire: and those who have gotten the victory over worldly authority and rule, and over idolatrous worship thereof, and over outward slavery thereto, will be upheld by truth, and will rejoice with the joy of good. And they will proclaim the law of Moses, and the gospel of Christ, and will say, Great and marvellous are thy works, Lord God Almighty; just and true are thy ways, eternal King. Who shall not reverence thee, O Lord, and praise all thy manifestations? for thou only art holy: for all nations shall be converted to thy service; for thy judgments are become manifest.

A Further Revelation from the Spirit of Prophecy

5 And after these things I saw, and the temple of the tabernacle of the testimony in heaven was opened.

And after that the very inmost and deepest hidden of things to happen were revealed to me.

The Angels of the Bowls

Amended Revised Version

6 And there came out from the temple the seven angels that had the seven *scourges* (plagues) arrayed with precious stones, pure and bright, and girt about their breasts with golden girdles. 7 And one of the four living creatures gave unto the seven angels seven golden bowls full of the *ardor* (wrath) of God, who liveth *unto the ages of the ages* 8 (for ever and ever). And the temple was filled with smoke from the glory of God, and from his power; and none was able to enter into the temple, till the seven *scourges* (plagues) of the seven angels should be finished. 1 And I heard a great voice out of the temple, saying to the seven angels, Go ye, and pour out the seven bowls of the *ardor* (wrath) of God into the earth.

Suggestive Paraphrase

And out of the depths of this revelation came now the visions of the seven manifestations of the Christ-mind, which are to uncover and destroy all the phases of evil, these visions of Truth clothed with purity and engirt with holiness. And the Holy Spirit will give unto these seven manifestations of Truth the power to uncover and destroy all of the phases of error,—the power being of God, who liveth for ever and ever. And the deepest things in the realm of consciousness now seemed obscured by the overwhelming brightness of God's glory, and the greatness of His power; and no man will be able to penetrate to these depths, till all the phases of evil have been destroyed.

Chapter XVI

And I seemed to hear a divine Voice saying to the seven manifestations of God, Perform your office; proceed to uncover and remand to self-destruction all phases of evil.

Spiritual Aspiration versus Materiality and Sensuality

2 And the first went, and poured out his bowl into the earth; and there came (it became) a noisome and grievous sore upon the men which had the mark of the beast, and which worship his image.

And the human consciousness will become energized with Spiritual Aspiration and will mentally enforce the law of God against materiality and sensuality, and men who worship worldly government and the man-made sense of God will be sorely afflicted.

Spiritual Reason versus Sensuousness and Psychism

3 And the second poured out his bowl into the sea; and it became blood as a dead man; and every living soul died, even the things that were in the sea.

And the human consciousness will become energized with Spiritual Reason, which will combat sensuousness and psychism, and their activity will cease.

Executive Mind versus Human Emotions

Amended Revised Version

4 And the third poured out his bowl into the rivers and the fountains of the waters; and *they* (it) became blood.
5 And I heard the angel of the waters saying, Righteous art thou, which art and which wast, thou Holy One, because thou didst
6 thus judge: for they poured out the blood of saints and prophets, and blood hast thou given them to drink: they
7 are worthy. And I heard the altar saying, Yea, O Lord God, the Almighty, true and righteous are thy judgments.

Suggestive Paraphrase

And the human consciousness will attain the life of Mind, Spirit, replacing human emotions, whose discordant aspects will be brought to the surface. And I heard the Christ, manifesting Executive Mind, Life, saying, Righteous art thou, holy and eternal God, in excluding human emotions from harmony; for they have caused Christ's people and the proclaimers of thy law to be killed, and now they are reaping like destruction, which they deserve. And the spiritual church affirmed the justice of God's judgments.

Spiritual Intuition versus Worldly Wisdom

8 And the fourth poured out his bowl upon the sun; and it was given unto it to
9 scorch men with fire. And men were scorched with great heat: and they blasphemed the name of the God which hath the power over these *scourges* (plagues); and they repented not to give him glory.

And the human consciousness will attain Spiritual Intuition, which will assert itself against mortal intellect, driving it to display more violently than ever its discordant activity, thus "scorching" the men who are still under its sway; but they will not recognize false intellect as the source of their torment, but will curse God as the supposed source of their trouble, who would destroy their plagues, if they would turn to Him; and they will not turn from their evil way and give God glory.

Divine Love versus Fleshly Desires

10 And the fifth poured out his bowl upon the throne of the beast; and his kingdom was darkened; and they gnawed their tongues
11 for pain, and they blasphemed the God of heaven because of their pains and their sores; and they repented not of their works.

And the human consciousness will attain to a knowledge of divine Love, which will assert itself against the belief that life, intelligence and pleasure are in matter; and the realm of material sense will be full of darkness and discord; and the licentious will be afflicted with grievous diseases and pains and they will blaspheme God because of their diseases, falsely attributing them to Him, and will not repent of their deeds.

Perception of Reality versus Idolatry

Amended Revised Version

12 And the sixth poured out his bowl upon the great river, the river Euphrates; and the water thereof was dried up, that the way might be made ready for the kings that come from the sunrising.

Suggestive Paraphrase

And the human consciousness will attain the Perception of Reality, which will bring to final destruction the great stream of superstition in mortal mind, and mankind will turn from it, so that the way for the advance of Christ's people will be prepared.

Hypnotism, Materia Medica, and Faith Cure

13 And I saw coming out of the mouth of the dragon, and out of the mouth of the beast, and out of the mouth of the false prophet, three unclean spirits, as it were
14 frogs: for they are spirits of devils, working signs; which go forth unto the kings of the whole world, to gather them together unto the war of the great day of
15 God, the Almighty. (Behold I come as a thief. Blessed is he that watcheth, and keepeth his garments, lest he walk naked, and they
16 see his shame.) And they gathered them together into the place which is called in Hebrew Har-Magedon.

And I saw that there will be unclean methods of working what men will call miracles,—methods as loathsome as frogs. From worldly government will issue legalized *materia medica;* from the worldly church will issue healing through blind faith, shrines, relics etc.; from mortal mind, the devil, will issue hypnotism, mental therapeutics, suggestion, etc. These false methods of doing seemingly wonderful things will lay hold upon the allegiance of the men who will rule in worldly thought, and will hold many of them even to the time when Truth will finally destroy all falsehood and evil. And behold! this time will come unexpectedly. Fortunate will be those who shall keep themselves ever ready, clothed with righteousness, lest their evil deeds which they think are hidden shall be unexpectedly uncovered, and they be brought to shame. And through the work of truth these evil methods and influences will be "rounded up" for their final destruction.

Perception of Substance versus Belief of Matter as Life and Substance

17 And the seventh poured out his bowl upon the air; and there came forth a great voice out of the temple, from the throne, saying,
18 It is done: and there were lightnings, and voices, and thunders; and there was a great earthquake, such as

And human consciousness will attain the Perception of Spirit as the only Substance, and will thus uncover for final destruction the hidden, omnipresent parent of all special and particular evils, namely, mortal mind; this will bring the whole contest to an end. The Holy Spirit will be ac-

Amended Revised Version

19 was not since there were men upon the earth, so great an earthquake, so mighty. And the great city was divided into three parts, and the cities of the nations fell: and Babylon the great was remembered in the sight of God, to give unto her the cup of the wine of the *ardor of his zeal* (fierceness of his 20 wrath). And every island fled away, and the moun-21 tains were not found. And great hail, every stone about the weight of a talent, cometh down out of heaven upon men: and men blasphemed God because of the *scourge* (plague) of the hail; for the *scourge* (plague) thereof is exceeding great.

Suggestive Paraphrase

tive; and there will be such a general upheaval among men as was never known before. And Worldly Lust (in which all mortals dwell) will be dismembered, and the special phases of evil which hold men in subservience will be overthrown: and Worldly Lust will be brought into judgment for final destruction by Truth. And every human institution which had seemed established and enduring will vanish away. And during this final contest wicked and unrepentant mortals will be exceedingly tormented and destroyed, as though huge hail stones should fall upon them; and they will curse God and blaspheme Him by falsely attributing this torment to Him; for the punishment will be very severe.*

CHAPTER XVII. BABYLON AND HER RELATION TO THE BEAST

The Judgment of Worldly Lust

1 And there came one of the seven angels that had the seven bowls and spake with me, saying, Come hither. I will shew thee the judgment of the great harlot that sitteth upon 2 many waters; with whom the kings of the earth commit fornication, and they that dwell in the earth were made drunken with the wine of her fornication.

And one of the seven manifestations of Truth, which will finally destroy all error, caused me to see in vision the punishment which will finally overwhelm Worldly Lust, which holds in idolatrous service many nations and peoples (see verse 15): with which, and through which, the great men of the world have been untrue to God, and all the inhabitants of the world have been intoxicated with the sinful pleasures of Lust.

A Vision of the Great Harlot

3 And he carried me away in the spirit into a wilderness: and I saw a woman sitting upon a scarlet-coloured beast, full of names of blasphemy, having seven

So I seemed to be transported into a state of consciousness apart from the ordinary; and I saw Lust upheld by a vast world-organization (including the worldly church and the

---

* Then cometh the end of evil, as predicted at the end of verse 17.

Amended Revised Version

4 heads and ten horns. And the woman was arrayed in purple and scarlet, and decked with gold and precious stones and pearls, having in her hand a golden cup full of abominations, even the unclean things of 5 her fornication, and upon her forehead a name written, MYSTERY, BABYLON THE GREAT, THE MOTHER OF THE HARLOTS AND OF THE ABOMINATIONS 6 OF THE EARTH. And I saw the woman drunken with the blood of the saints, and with the blood of the martyrs of Jesus. And when I saw her, I wondered with 7 a great wonder. And the angel said unto me, Wherefore didst thou wonder? I will tell thee the mystery of the woman, and of the beast that carrieth her, which hath the seven heads and the ten 8 horns. The beast that thou sawest was, and is not; and is about to come up out of the abyss, and to go into perdition. And they that dwell on the earth shall wonder, they whose name hath not been written in the book of life from the foundation of the world, when they behold the beast, how that he was, and is not, and 9 shall come. Here is the mind which hath wisdom. The seven heads are seven mountains, on which the 10 woman sitteth: and they are seven kings; the five are fallen, and one is, the other is not yet come; and when he cometh, he must con-11 tinue a little while. And the beast that was, and is not, is himself also an

Suggestive Paraphrase

worldly state), making blasphemous claims to authority, and manifest in all empires and kingdoms of the world. And Lust seemed arrayed in purple and scarlet color, and decked with gold and precious stones and pearls, the licentious pleasures which it offers appearing fair from their outward appearance and promise. And Worldly Lust may be briefly characterized thus: Its origin and nature are mysterious: it seems wicked and powerful as Babylon; it is the parent of all apostasy from God and of all the wickedness of men. And I saw Lust as fairly intoxicated with the slaughter of holy men, and of witnesses of Christ: and I was amazed beyond measure at what I saw. And then the vision seemed to inquire, Why are you amazed and mystified? I will interpret for you the significance of Lust, and of the worldly organization that upholds it, and is manifest in all worldly empires and kingdoms. Worldly organization seems to be but is not, (appears, but is unreal); and comes from nothingness, and shall go to destruction and nothingness; and all except those who have spiritual understanding are astonished and awestruck at the seeming power of worldly government, though it actually is unreal. Now here is the understanding of these things. All phases of worldly government are the supports of Lust, and they are rulers in human consciousness, where a large portion of them have lost their power, but a portion is very active, and a portion is yet to become active, and will continue active for a time. And worldly government, though unreal, will continue in evidence after its more specific manifestations have passed away, but will

Amended Revised Version

eighth, and is of the seven; and he goeth into perdition.
12 And the ten horns that thou sawest are ten kings, which have received no kingdom as yet; but they receive authority as kings, with the
13 beast, for one hour. These have one mind, and they give their power and author
14 ity unto the beast. These shall war against the Lamb, and the Lamb shall overcome them, for he is Lord of lords, and King of kings; and they also shall overcome that are with him, called and
15 chosen and faithful. And he saith unto me, The waters which thou sawest, where the harlot sitteth, are peoples, and multitudes, and
16 nations, and tongues. And the ten horns which thou sawest, and the beast, these shall hate the harlot, and shall make her desolate and naked, and shall eat her flesh, and shall burn her ut
17 terly with fire. For God did put in their hearts to do his mind, and to come to one mind, and to give their kingdom unto the beast, until the words of God should
18 be accomplished. And the woman whom thou sawest is the great city, which reigneth over the kings of the earth.

Suggestive Paraphrase

ultimately go to destruction. And worldly government will take form as all kingdoms, which have not appeared as yet; and they will represent worldly authority for a short period. These will all agree in this, that they will bolster up worldly organization and government. These will strive against the truth, but Truth will overcome them: for Truth is Lord of lords, and king of kings: and they that side with Truth have heard and chosen Truth, and are faithful thereto. And the vision made known to me, that the support of Lust is found in the service of the multitudes of humanity. But mankind will ultimately turn against Lust, and leave it without support, and Truth apprehended will strip it of its gauds, and will consume its seeming substance, and will reduce it to nothingness. For at last men will open their hearts to God, to fulfil His will, though, before then, they will agree in recognizing the authority of worldly organization, until such time as the purposes of God shall be made evident. And Worldly Lust is the great mental habitation, in which, and in subservience to which, dwell the great men of this world.

CHAPTER XVIII. FALLEN BABYLON

Note.—*If it be remembered that "Babylon" symbolizes Worldly Lust, the vision or prophetic perception presented in this chapter will not need further paraphrasing.*

1 After these things I saw another angel coming down out of heaven, having great authority; and the earth was lightened with his glory.

The Wickedness of Lust

2 And he cried with a mighty voice, saying, Fallen, fallen is Babylon the great, and is become a habitation of devils, and a hold of every
3 unclean spirit, and a hold of every unclean and hateful bird. For by the wine of the *ardor* (wrath) of her fornication all the nations are fallen; and the kings of the earth committed fornication with her, and the merchants of the earth waxed rich by the power of her wantonness.

How Christ's People are to Deal With Lust

4 And I heard another voice from heaven, saying, Come forth, my people, out of her, that ye have no fellowship with her sins, and
5 that ye receive not of her *scourgings* (plagues): for her sins have reached even unto heaven, and God hath remembered her iniquities.
6 Render unto her even as she rendered, and double unto her the double according to her works: in the cup which she mingled,
7 mingle unto her double. How much soever she glorified herself, and waxed wanton, so much give her of torment and mourning: for she saith in her heart, I sit a queen, and am no widow, and shall in no wise see mourning.

The Destruction of Lust Foretold

8 Therefore in one day shall her *scourgings* (plagues) come, death, and mourning, and famine; and she shall be utterly burned with fire; for strong is the Lord God which judged her.

Grief of the Worldly

Sorrow and Terror of the Ruling Class

9 And the kings of the earth, who committed fornication and lived wantonly with her, shall weep and wail over her, when they look
10 upon the smoke of her burning, standing afar off for the fear of her torment, saying, Woe, woe, the great city, Babylon, the strong city! for in one hour is thy judgment come.

Sorrow and Terror of the Business Class

11 And the merchants of the earth weep and mourn over her, for
12 no man buyeth their merchandise any more; merchandise of gold, and silver, and precious stones, and pearls, and fine linen, and purple, and silk, and scarlet; and all thyine wood, and every vessel of ivory, and every vessel made of most precious wood, and of brass, and

13 iron, and marble; and cinnamon, and spice, and incense, and ointment, and frankincense, and wine, and oil, and fine flour, and wheat, and cattle, and sheep; and merchandise of horses and chariots and
14 slaves; and *lives* (souls) of men. And the fruits which thy soul lusted after are gone from thee, and all things that were dainty and sumptuous are perished from thee, and men shall find them no
15 more at all. The merchants of these things, who were made rich by her, shall stand afar off for the fear of her torment, weeping
16 and mourning; saying, Woe, woe, the great city, she that was arrayed in fine linen and purple and scarlet, and decked with gold
17 and precious stones and pearl! for in one hour so great riches is made desolate.

Sorrow and Terror of the Working Class

And every shipmaster, and every one that saileth any whither, and mariners, and as many as gain their living by sea, stood afar off,
18 and cried and cried out as they looked upon the smoke of her burn-
19 ing, saying, What city is like the great city? And they cast dust on their heads, and cried, weeping and mourning, saying, Woe, woe, the great city, wherein were made rich all that had their ships in the sea by reason of her costliness; for in one hour she is made desolate.

Rejoicing of the Saints

20   Rejoice over her, thou heaven, and ye saints, and ye apostles, and ye prophets; for God hath judged your judgment on her.

The Destruction of Lust Complete

21   And a strong angel took up a stone as it were a great millstone, and cast it into the sea, saying, Thus with a mighty fall shall Babylon, the great city, be cast down, and shall be found no more
22 at all. And the voice of harpers and minstrels and flute players and trumpeters shall be heard no more at all in thee; and no craftsman, of whatsoever craft, shall be found any more at all in thee; and
23 the voice of a millstone shall be heard no more at all in thee; and the light of a lamp shall shine no more at all in thee; and the voice of the bridegroom and of the bride shall be heard no more at all in thee; for thy merchants were the princes of the earth; for with
24 thy sorcery were all the nations deceived. And in her was found the blood of prophets and of saints, and of all that have been slain upon the earth.

Chapter XIX. Triumph of the Lamb
Rejoicing of the Spiritually-minded

Amended Revised Version

1 After these things I heard as it were a great voice of a great multitude in heaven, saying, Hallelujah; Salvation, and glory, and power,
2 belong to our God: for true and righteous are his judgments; for he hath judged the great harlot, which did corrupt the earth with her fornication, and he hath avenged the blood of his servants at her hand.
3 And a second time they say, Hallelujah. And her smoke goeth up *unto the ages of the ages* (for ever and
4 ever). And the four and twenty elders and the four living creatures fell down and worshipped God that sitteth on the throne, say-
5 ing, Amen; Hallelujah. And a voice came forth from the throne, saying, Give praise to our God, all ye his servants, ye that fear him, the
6 small and the great. And I heard as it were the voice of a great multitude, and as the voice of many waters, and as the voice of mighty thunders, saying, Hallelujah: for the Lord our God,
7 the Almighty reigneth. Let us rejoice and be exceeding glad, and let us give the glory unto him: for the marriage of the Lamb is come, and his wife hath
8 made herself ready. And it was given unto her that she should array herself in fine linen, bright and pure: for the fine linen is the righteous acts of the saints.

Suggestive Paraphrase

And after this I seemed to hear the collective testimony of a great multitude of men who had attained spiritual consciousness, saying Alleluia: Let the salvation of the world, and glory, and honor, and power, be ascribed unto the Lord our God: for true and right are His standards; by which have been judged and found wanting Worldly Lust, which corrupted mankind with its apostasy from God, but which has been punished for all its persecution of His servants. And again I seemed to hear them cry, Alleluia; for the destruction of Lust is complete. And the whole spiritual church humbled itself before creative Mind enthroned with power, saying Amen; Alleluia. And I seemed to hear the Holy Spirit saying, Praise our God, all ye who serve and reverence Him, both great and small. And I heard the testimony of a great multitude, in many languages, and with great volume, saying, Alleluia: for the all-powerful God has triumphed. Let us be glad and rejoice, and give honor to Him; for the time has come for the human consciousness as the church to be wholly united, having put on Christ. For it has been granted to human consciousness to become purified with the righteousness which belongs to God's people.

Doing Honor to God's Messenger Forbidden

Amended Revised Version

9 And he saith unto me, Write, Blessed are they which are bidden to the marriage supper of the Lamb. And he saith unto me, These are true words of
10 God, And I fell down before his feet to *do honor to* (worship) him. And he saith unto me, See thou do it not: I am a fellow-servant with thee and with thy brethren that hold the testimony of Jesus: *do honor to* (worship) God: for the testimony of Jesus is the spirit of prophecy.

Suggestive Paraphrase

And the voice said to me, Write, Fortunate are they who are prepared to put on Christ. This is truly a message from God. And I humbled myself before the divine, incorporeal messenger. But it was revealed unto me, that I ought not to do this: for this messenger, or truth-revealing message, was but serving God, even as was I myself, and those of my brethren who have the spirit of prophecy. I saw that I ought to worship the Creator only: for to bear testimony to the Christ requires the spirit of prophecy.

A Vision of the Impersonal Mediatorial Christ

11 And I saw the heaven opened; and behold, a white horse, and he that sat thereon, called Faithful and True; and in righteousness he doth judge and make
12 war. And his eyes are a flame of fire, and upon his head are many diadems; and he hath a name written, which no one knoweth but
13 he himself. And he is arrayed in a garment sprinkled with blood: and his name is called the Word
14 of God. And the armies which are in heaven followed him upon white horses, clothed in fine lin-
15 en, white and pure. And out of his mouth proceedeth a sharp sword, that with it he should smite the nations: and he shall rule them with a rod of iron: and he treadeth the winepress of the *ardor* (fierceness) of the *zeal* (wrath)

And there was disclosed to me the eternal mental realm, in which all pure ideas are active (See chap. 6:2); and the Christ, up-borne by all pure ideas, was declared faithful and true. His standards are right, and with right does he make war against evil. The vision of the Christ-consciousness is very clear, quick and penetrating; and is endowed with all authority; and nobody understands his character or manifestation but he himself.* And his appearance is the manifestation of Life: and he is properly described as the complete utterance† of God. And the multitudes of men which have attained spiritual consciousness follow the Christ, up-borne by pure thoughts, and mentally clothed with righteousness (See v. 8). And the message proceeding from the Christ is very "quick and powerful," and smites the evil which has attached itself to the nations of men: and the Christ shall rule the nations according to the inflexible Principle: and he relentlessly excludes evil from harmony, and re-

---

* Men do not understand the Christ until they "put on Christ."
† Outer-ance.

Amended Revised Version

16 of Almighty God. And he hath on his garment and on his thigh a name written, KING OF KINGS, AND LORD OF LORDS.

Suggestive Paraphrase

mands it to its own realm of discord and destruction. Both in his appearance and in his substance, Christ is manifest as, KING OF KINGS, AND LORD OF LORDS.

The Christ Summons All Spiritual Ideas to Destroy the Seeming Substance of the Ungodly

17 And I saw *a lone* (an) angel standing in the sun; and he cried with a loud voice, saying to all the birds that fly in mid heaven, Come and be gathered together unto the great supper of God; 18 that ye may eat the flesh of kings, and the flesh of captains, and the flesh of mighty men, and the flesh of horses and of them that sit thereon, and the flesh of all men, both free and bond, and small and great.

And I seemed to see the Christ established in Mind and powerfully proclaiming to all the right ideas which are in the mental realm, Prepare yourselves to do the work set for you in accord with your nature as manifestations of God: that you may utterly destroy the seeming substance of all mortals, whether as bodies or as false mentalities, irrespective of their rank according to worldly sense.

Worldly Government and the Worldly Church and Their Adherents Destroyed

19 And I saw the beast, and the kings of the earth, and their armies, gathered together to make war against him that sat upon the horse 20 and against his army. And the beast was taken, and with him the false prophet that wrought the signs in his sight, wherewith he deceived them that had received the mark of the beast, and them that worshipped his image: they twain were cast alive into the lake of fire that burneth 21 with brimstone: and the rest were killed with the sword of him that sat upon the horse, even the sword which came forth out of his mouth; and all the birds were filled with their flesh.

And I saw worldly organization, and the rulers of all worldly kingdoms, and their armies, mustered to make both mental and physical war against the Christ, and those who follow him. And I saw that worldly government will be overthrown, and along with it the worldly church (see chap. 13:11-14) that wrought seeming wonders in the presence of worldly government, and thus deceived those who were loyal to worldly authority, and who worshipped the man-made sense of God. Both worldly government and the worldly church will be utterly destroyed. And the remnant of mortal beliefs serving them will be destroyed by the manifestation of the Christ: and all right ideas will accomplish the destruction of the seeming substance or appearance of evil.

CHAPTER XX. THE MILLENNIUM AND THE FINAL JUDGMENT
Discord Suppressed for a Long Season

Amended Revised Version

1 And I saw an angel coming down out of heaven, having the key of the abyss and a great chain in his
2 hand. And he laid hold on the dragon, the old serpent, which is the Devil and Satan, and bound him for
3 a thousand years, and cast him into the abyss, and shut it, and sealed it over him, that he should deceive the nations no more, until the thousand years should be finished: after this he must be loosed for a little time.

Suggestive Paraphrase

And I saw that the Christ-mind is able to uncover the most hidden depths of error (nothingness), and, clothed with power, will reduce to subjection primeval error, which is spoken of as a dragon, an old serpent, the devil and satan, and will hold it in subjection for a long but indefinite period, and will keep it in inactivity till the end of this period: and after that, error will become active again for a short time.

The First Resurrection

All men on earth, having become highly spiritual, now demonstrate the resurrection of the saintly among the so-called "dead," and they join in living harmoniously on earth with the truth in consciousness.

4 And I saw thrones, and they sat upon them, and judgment was given unto them: and I saw the souls of them that had been beheaded for the testimony of Jesus, and for the word of God, and such as worshipped not the beast, neither his image, and received not the mark upon their forehead and upon their hand; and they lived, and reigned with Christ a
5 thousand years. The rest of the dead lived not until the thousand years should be finished. This is the first resurrection.
6 Blessed and holy is he that hath part in the first resurrection: over these the second death hath no power; but they shall be priests of God and of Christ, and shall reign with him a thousand years.

And I saw that authority and power will be given those who were beheaded for exercising the spirit of prophecy and for loyalty to the word of God, who had not given either inward or outward allegiance to worldly government, when it conflicted with God's government, and who had not worshipped the false sense of God; and I saw that these will live and reign on earth with the Christ or truth in consciousness during the millennial period; for these will be the first to be raised from the dead. But the remainder of the dead will not be raised until after the millennial period is finished. Blessed and holy are those who will be raised up first: they are so pure that the final destruction of evil (See v. 14) will not affect them at all, but they will reign as priests of God and His Christ during the thousand years.

The Return of Discord

Amended Revised Version

7 And when the thousand years are finished, Satan shall be loosed out of his
8 prison, and shall come forth to deceive the nations which are in the four corners of the earth, Gog and Magog, to gather them together to the war: the number of them is as the sand of the
9 sea. And they went up over the breadth of the earth, and compassed the camp of the saints about, and the beloved city: and fire came down out of heaven, and devoured them.

Suggestive Paraphrase

Then discord will become active again.* And satan will deceive the nations all over the earth, Gog and Magog, and will muster them for battle, in numbers like the sands of the sea. And the followers of error will surround the followers of Christ, and will mentally camp against the spiritual consciousness: but the truth of God will be mentally enforced against the minions of error and will destroy them.

* The probable occasion of this will be that many will resist the demonstration over the last phase of error, namely, the belief in matter and separate, corporeal selfhood.

Discord Finally Destroyed

10 And the devil that deceived them was cast into the lake of fire and brimstone, where are also the beast and the false prophet; and they shall be tormented day and night *unto the ages of the ages* (for ever and ever).

And the fundamental error that deceived them will be cast to destruction, as worldly government and the worldly church had been before it.

The Destruction of Matter

11 And I saw a great white throne, and him that sat upon it, from whose face the earth and the heaven fled away; and there was found no place for them.

And I saw enthroned in pure spiritual power the creative Mind, before whose militant manifestation the material sense of earth and heaven will be dissolved, so that they will no longer appear.

The Final Resurrection and the Final Separating Out and Destruction of All Accumulated Evil from the Mentalites of Men

12 And I saw the dead, the great and the small, standing before the throne; and books were opened; and another book was opened; which is the book of life: and the dead were judged out of the things which were written

And I saw that the remainder of the so-called dead, whether small or great according to human estimate, will be judged according to the standard of God; the records of their past lives* will be disclosed: and the laws of life will also be disclosed: and

* The accumulations stored in their sub-conscious mentalities.

Amended Revised Version

13 in the books according to their works. And the sea gave up the dead which were in it; and death and Hades gave up the dead which were in them: and they were judged every man according to their works.
14 And death and Hades were cast into the lake of fire. This is the second death,
15 even the lake of fire. And if any was not found written in the book of life *it* (he) was cast into the lake of fire.

Suggestive Paraphrase

according as the records of their lives shall bear comparison with the laws of life, will the resurrected be judged; for latent (subconscious) error will give up the dead which are in it; yea, the very Prince of Death will lose his hold upon the dead: and they will be judged according to the records of their past lives.

Then the fundamental beliefs of death and discord will be destroyed. This destruction is spoken of as "the second death." (See chapter 2:11; chap. 20:6.) And whatsoever mental manifestation or activity is not found among the manifestations of Life (God) will be cast to destruction.

(Continued on Page 371.)

NOTES BY THE READER

SECTION VII

THE VISION OF THE SPIRITUAL, ETERNAL CONSCIOUSNESS, SYMBOLIZED AS THE HOLY CITY, THE NEW JERUSALEM

(Chap. 21:1-22:5)

The text from the Bible is not printed here, because the comment upon it is comparatively brief, and because it is printed in connection with the paraphrase which immediately follows. In this paraphrase, the interpretation of the text is indicated clearly without explanation, except in a few points which call for previous comment.

In this act of the drama, no evil characters appear as alive or active, and no conflict is represented. There is merely the description in symbolical language of the consciousness of the spiritual man. There is occasional mention of evil and evil-doers, but such mention is made only to bring out the facts and the blessedness of spiritual consciousness by way of contrast with the material factor in the human order of consciousness.

Chapter 21:1-4 describes the eternal, spiritual heaven and earth and the conditions of the eternal spiritual consciousness. The eternal heaven and earth are spoken of as *"new"* merely because they are new to humanity's advancing understanding, —just as the western hemisphere is spoken of to this day as "the new world"; because it was discovered later, although it is as old in point of existence as any part of the earth.*

---

* Mr. Rawson has written: "The word 'new' is a doublet for 'now,' and it is much more accurate to speak of the 'now earth' and the 'now heaven.' There is no material earth and no material heaven. At best there is only the belief of matter which hides the real earth (spiritual ideas) and the real heaven (the perfect state of consciousness) from us."

"The first heaven and the first earth", spoken of as passing away, are the false material concept of heaven and earth. This false material concept is merely a factor of mortal belief, as is also the *"sea",* which is the symbol of turbulence and division, and which is also spoken of as passing away.

"The holy city, new Jerusalem", is the spiritualized consciousness, coming down to human beings from God out of the realm of harmony. This is, of course, not a coming down from a higher level of space to a lower, but an impartation of higher, heavenly consciousness to the lower order of human thought, destroying that lower order.

Verse 3. *"The tabernacle of God is with men."* This means that man now realizes himself as dwelling in God, infinite Mind.

Verse 4. *"And God (the realized presence and power of eternal good) shall wipe away all tears from their eyes";* and the verse goes on to again prophesy the final destruction of evil.

Verses 5-7. *"And he that sat upon the throne."* The term *"throne"* signifies an exalted state of spiritual consciousness. In this case, God is represented as sitting upon the throne. *"The fountain of the water of life"* is everlasting truth, which washes away error, and, as *"the bread from heaven"* feeds the consciousness of man.

8 *"But the fearful and unbelieving, and the abominable, and murderers, and whoremongers, and sorcerers, and idolaters, and all liars, shall have their part in the lake which burneth with fire and brimstone: which is the second death."*

Verse 8. Here, again, out of chronological sequence, is prophesied the destruction of mortals; that is, of the mortal factors in the minds of human beings. *"The lake which burneth with fire and brimstone"* is the symbol of absolute destruction, and so is again spoken of as *"the second death."*

9 *"And there came unto me one of the seven angels which had the seven vials full of the seven last plagues, and talked with me, saying, Come hither, I will shew thee the bride, the Lamb's wife."*

Verse 9. The angels here spoken of refer back to chapters 15 and 16. *"The bride, the Lamb's wife"*, spoken of in this verse, is the spiritual consciousness.

10 *"And he carried me away in the spirit to a great and high mountain, and shewed me that great city, the holy Jerusalem, descending out of heaven from God."*

Verse 10. *"The great and high mountain"*, spoken of in this verse, is a spiritual state of consciousness, sufficiently exalted so that, from its height, the beholder could understand all spiritual things. *"That great city, the holy Jerusalem"*, is again the spiritual consciousness, the consciousness of God. The glories of this consciousness are spoken of under what seems to our western thought rather extravagant images in verses 11 to 21. In the chapter on "The Apocalypse", in "Science and Health," Mrs. Eddy has given a very beautiful and enlightening interpretation of some of these verses.

16-17 *"And the city lieth four square, and the length is as large as the breadth: and he measured the city with the reed, twelve thousand furlongs. The length and the breadth and the height of it are equal. And he measured the wall thereof, an hundred and forty and four cubits, according to the measure of a man, that is, of the angel."*

Verses 16-17. The significance of the distances mentioned in these two verses has been fully discussed in the comment on verse 20 of chapter 14 (which see on page 323).

Verses 19, 20. "The twelve precious stones are not all identified with certainty, as some of the Greek names are dubious; but, given in the modern terms generally applied to them they are probably as follows: 1, opal; 2, lapis-lazuli; 3, chalcedony; 4, aqua-marine; 5, sardonyx; 6, carnelian; 7, topaz; 8, beryl; 9, chrysolith; 10, chrysoprase; 11, hyacinth; 12, amethyst. Placed in a circle these colored stones form approximately the prismatic scale, and are thus identical with the rainbow (iv: 3) which encircles the throne of God."*

---

* "The Apocalypse Unsealed," page 214.

Verses 22-27. In these verses we are informed that the city of God, the spiritual consciousness, has and needs in it no material structure, nor any material source of light, and that that state of consciousness is constantly lighted spiritually by God Himself.

Chapter 22:1-5. These verses are a continuation of the description of the spiritual consciousness. *"The leaves of the tree"*, the ideas of truth, are for the overcoming of error, *"for the healing of the nations."*

REVISED TRANSLATION AND SUGGESTIVE PARAPHRASE

SECTION VII

THE ETERNAL UNIVERSE

CHAPTER XXI

Humanity Attains Realization of God and Heaven

Amended Revised Version

1 And I saw a new heaven and a new earth: for the first heaven and the first earth are passed away; and the sea is no more.
2 And I saw the holy city, new Jerusalem, coming down out of heaven from God, made ready as a bride adorned for her husband.
3 And I heard a great voice out of the throne saying, Behold, the tabernacle of God is with men, and he shall dwell with them, and they shall be his peoples, and God himself shall be with them, and be their
4 God: and he shall wipe away every tear from their eyes; and death shall be no more; neither shall there be mourning, nor crying, nor pain, any more: the first things are passed away.

Suggestive Paraphrase

And I perceived the kingdom of heaven that is wholly spiritual, the universe of divine ideas, the material sense of heaven, earth and sea having passed away. And I, John, beheld the celestial city, the redeemed and purified consciousness of mankind, approaching union with divine Mind in harmony, a consciousness having the beauty of good. And there came to me a great revelation in consciousness that men will dwell with God, good, and they will be His people: and good realized and demonstrated will wipe away and destroy all that is un-ideal: for the reign of evil will pass away.

A New Sense of the Universe

5 And he that sitteth on the throne said, Behold, I make all things new. And he saith, Write: for these words are faithful and true.
6 And he said unto me, They are come to pass. I am the Alpha and the Omega, the beginning and the end. I will give unto him that is athirst of the fountain of the water

And mind enthroned in power said, Behold, I give mankind a new and eternal sense of being, a spiritual sense to displace their old, false, material sense. And Mind said unto me, Write: for these words are true and faithful. My works are eternal, changeless, and therefore finished. I am the everlasting. I will give unto him who really desires them the ideas

371

Amended Revised Version

7 of life freely. He that overcometh shall inherit these things; and I will be his God, and he shall be my son.
8 But for the fearful, and unbelieving, and abominable, and murderers, and fornicators, and sorcerers, and idolaters, and all liars, their part shall be in the lake that burneth with fire and brimstone; which is the second death.

Suggestive Paraphrase

of Truth and Love freely; and these shall support his consciousness or life. He that overcometh his false sense of matter and evil shall gain the realization of all that is true and good; and he shall know that I am his God, and that he is my son. But all discordant and sinful dispositions and habits shall be removed from the mentalities of men, and shall go to destruction: this will be the final destruction of evil.

A Symbolical Description of the Spiritual Consciousness

9 And there came one of the seven angels who had the seven bowls, who were laden with the seven last *scourges* (plagues); and he spake with me, saying, Come hither, I will shew thee the bride, the wife of the Lamb.
10 And he carried me away in the Spirit to a mountain great and high, and showed me the holy city of Jerusalem, coming down out of
11 heaven from God, having the glory of God: her light was like unto a stone most precious, as it were a jasper stone, clear as crystal:
12 having a wall great and high; having twelve gates, and at the gates twelve angels; and names written thereon, which are the names of the twelve tribes of the children of Israel:
13 on the east were three gates; and on the north three gates; and on the south three gates; and on
14 the west three gates. And the wall of the city had twelve fountains, and on them twelve names of the twelve apostles of the Lamb.

And there came unto me one of the visions which had formerly revealed to me* the full measure of God's redemptive power, saying, Elevate your thought, and I will show you the spiritualized consciousness of mankind which is wedded to Christ, Truth. And this vision raised me into a very exalted state of thought, and showed me the celestial city, the immaterial realm, to which human consciousness will attain, having the glory of God: and this manifestation of Truth is of supreme value and exceedingly clear, devoid of ignorance, mystery, or evil; and this spiritual consciousness excludes all evil thoughts and dispositions, but is open on every side, so that all men can enter, as soon as they have separated evil from themselves, and the entrance is guarded by twelve (all) right ideas, so that no evil can enter. There is entrance for men upon every side, from every condition of need. And the consciousness excluding evil is founded on the teachings of the twelve apostles of Christ Jesus.

---

* See chapters 15 and 16.

A Symbolical Measuring of the Spiritual Consciousness

Amended Revised Version

15 And he that spake with me had for a measure a golden reed to measure the city, and the gates thereof,
16 and the wall thereof. And the city lieth foursquare, and the length thereof is as great as the breadth: and he measured the city with the reed, twelve thousand furlongs: the length and the breadth and the heighth
17 thereof are equal. And he measured the wall thereof, a hundred and forty and four cubits, according to the measure of a man, that is, of an angel.

Suggestive Paraphrase

And I was shown the Principle by which to test and understand the true consciousness, and the mental avenues of entrance thereto, and the action thereof in excluding falsehood and evil. And the spiritual consciousness is genuine, flawless, the same from all points of view, with nothing concealed or hidden, infinite. And the consciousness which excludes evil is spiritual in extent, that is, infinite, according to the measure of spiritual man, in God's image and likeness.

The Protection, the Entrances and the Mental Pathways of the Spiritual Consciousness

18 And the building of the wall thereof was of jasper: and the city was pure gold,
19 like unto pure glass. The foundations of the wall of the city were adorned with all manner of precious stones. The first foundation was jasper; the second, sapphire; the third, chalcedony; the fourth, emerald;
20 the fifth, sardonyx; the sixth, sardius; the seventh, chrysolite; the eighth, beryl; the ninth, topaz; the tenth, chrysoprase; the eleventh, jacinth; the twelfth, ame-
21 thyst. And the twelve gates were twelve pearls; each one of the several gates was of one pearl: and the street of the city was pure gold, as it were transparent glass.

And the substance of the spiritual consciousness which excludes evil is exceeding precious, mentally brilliant and transparent. And the spiritual consciousness excluding evil rests upon or includes every idea of Truth and good, each having its own individuality, and being of exceeding value and beauty, and a necessary part of the complete structure of Mind. And all avenues of approach to the spiritual consciousness are pure and clean. These avenues are all right ideas, each having its own individuality, and being one. The paths in Mind are beautiful and clear.

The Structure and Illumination of the Spiritual Consciousness

Amended Revised Version

22 And I saw no temple therein: for the Lord God the Almighty, and the Lamb, are the temple thereof.
23 And the city hath no need of the sun, neither of the moon, to shine upon it: for the glory of God did lighten it, and the lamp thereof is the Lamb.

Suggestive Paraphrase

There is no material structure in the celestial city, but the spiritual consciousness dwells and worships in God (Mind) and His Christ. And the spiritual realm has no need or place for material light; but is mentally illumined by divine Mind and its reflection, the Christ.

Inhabitants of the Spiritual Consciousness

24 And the nations shall walk amidst the light thereof; and the kings of the earth do bring their glory
25 into it. And the gates thereof shall in no wise be shut by day (for there shall be
26 no night there): and they shall bring the glory and the honour of the nations
27 into it: and there shall in no wise enter into it anything unclean, or he that maketh an abomination and a lie: but only they which are written in the Lamb's book of life.

And man redeemed shall dwell in the light of spiritual understanding: and the kings of the earth will surrender their personal sense of glory, in order that glory may be given to God alone. There is never a time when the avenues of approach to God are either closed or darkened to those who earnestly desire to enter. All worldly glory shall be laid down and surrendered before the glory of Mind. Neither evil nor falsehood can have part or place in the celestial city, but only the ideas of Truth and good, and those who have identified themselves with them.

Chapter XXII

Food and Drink in Spiritual Consciousness

1 And he shewed me a river of water of life, bright as crystal, proceeding out of the throne of God, and of
2 the Lamb. In the midst of the street thereof, and on either side of the river, was the tree of life, bearing twelve (manner of) fruits, yielding its fruit every month: and the leaves of the tree were for the healing of the nations.

And I perceived the stream of divine ideas flowing from God to man, giving to man that knowledge of God which is life eternal. Omnipresent in the immaterial city is Mind, which always gives forth every kind of good and true ideas: and these ideas cleanse and heal the nations of men.

Bliss of the Spiritual Consciousness

Amended Revised Version

3 And there shall be no curse any more: and the throne of God and of the Lamb shall be therein: and his servants shall do him
4 service; and they shall see his face; and his name shall
5 be on their foreheads. And there shall be night no more; and they need no light of lamp, neither light of sun; for the Lord God shall give them light: and they shall reign for ever and ever.

Suggestive Paraphrase

And there shall be no more curse: but God and His Christ shall be enthroned; and men shall serve God. And men shall not be separated from the realization of truth and good; but shall acknowledge only God in their understanding. And there shall be no ignorance of evil in the spiritual consciousness; and no need of material light; for the light of Mind is sufficient; and man shall have everlasting dominion over all that is good and true.

(Continued on Page 381.)

EPILOGUE

(Chapter 22:6-21)

The interpretation of the most of the verses in this passage will be sufficiently evident as given in the paraphrase which follows, without additional explanation. However, it seems well to take special note of certain verses or groups of verses.

The translation as given in the Authorized Version needs amending at several points, which the student can readily discover for himself by comparing the Authorized Version with the revised translation which is given in connection with the paraphrase, and as the basis thereof.

Verses 6 and 7 are so similar in phraseology to the first three verses of the Prologue, that the interpretation of the Prologue is a sufficient interpretation of these first two verses of the Epilogue. The interpretation of verses 8 and 9 is practically the same as that of 19:10, which see.

Verse 10 *"And he saith unto me, Seal not the sayings of the prophecy of this book: for the time is at hand."*

"The injunction not to seal up the teachings has been followed by the Apocalyptist; for although his scroll is written in veiled language, it is not 'sealed'. The Apocalypse surely contains its own key, and is complete in itself, coherent, and scrupulously accurate in every detail. . . . Though the growth of the inner nature is a slow process, the recognition of . . . the imminent higher mind comes upon the man suddenly; as Ioannes reiterates, the Logos [Greek for Christ-mind] comes speedily, unexpectedly, as a thief in the night; and when it does come there is a balancing of merits and demerits. If his nature is sufficiently purified, the mystic tree of life is his, and by means of it he enters the holy city; otherwise he remains with 'those without', until he shall have 'washed his robes.' "*

---

* "The Apocalypse Unsealed," pages 219, 220.

Verse 11 *"He that is unjust, let him be unjust still: and he which is filthy, let him be filthy still: and he that is righteous, let him be righteous still: and he that is holy, let him be holy still."*

This verse indicates that error cannot become truth, and that evil cannot become good. Each must continue in its own state until evil and error are finally destroyed.

Verses 12-17. These verses speak of conditions prevailing from the time of the writer, John, until the final destruction of error. They are conditions that prevail today. Today, *"they that do his commandments have a right to the tree of life, and may enter in through the gates into the city"*,—into the spiritual consciousness,—while outside of that city are the factors of mortal mind, "the dogs, the sorcerers, the fornicators, the murderers, the phantom-servers, and every one who keeps sanctioning and acting a lie"; but, at last, these are all to be destroyed, as indicated in 21:8.

Verse 16 *"I, Jesus, have sent mine Angel, to testify unto you these things in the Churches. I am the root and the offspring of David, and the bright and morning star."*

"Jesus" without doubt connotes the mediatorial consciousness, the impersonal Christ, which is God's angel or messenger, and which, in turn, employs John as its angel or messenger.

This eternal Christ, "the same yesterday, to-day and forever", is "the root", the eternal fact back of every man that cometh into the world, and so is properly spoken of as "the root of David." Any man who attains, as David did, to a high degree of the mediatorial consciousness, the spirit of prophecy, in a sense passes on that impersonal spiritual consciousness to his fellow men of future generations: hence, from the human standpoint, this mediatorial consciousness might speak of itself as "the offspring of David." This impersonal Christ-mind is the anointed Saviour, the way-shower, and so is the harbinger of the coming spiritual day: hence it is, to humanity, *"the bright and morning star."*

Verse 17 *"And the Spirit and the Bride say, Come."*

XXII : 18-21   EPILOGUE   379

"The Spirit" is the Holy Spirit in human consciousness, militant against evil, and "the Bride" is the spiritual factor in human consciousness in its attitude of aspiring after and worshiping God,—it is the true, spiritual church.

Verses 18, 19 *"For I testify unto every man that heareth the words of the prophecy of this book, If any man shall add unto these things, God shall add unto him the plagues that are written in this book. And if any man shall take away the words of the book of this prophecy, God shall take away his part out of the book of life, and out of the holy city, and from the things which are written in this book."*

The "book" referred to in these verses is not the whole Bible, the various books of which had never been selected as especially authoritative, and had never been bound between two covers, at the time that John wrote; but the "book" referred to is this book of Revelation itself. Being the word of truth, it could not be altered in any way by an individual without that individual's straying into error. Should he do so, he would experience the effects of error, and would automatically exclude himself from the realm of truth and good, from the realm of God. However, it must not be understood that God would consciously punish any man, or withhold any good from any man.

Verse 21 *"The grace of our Lord Jesus Christ be with you all. Amen."*

EPILOGUE

Chapter XXII

Amended Revised Version

6 And he said unto me, These words are faithful and true: and the Lord, the God of the spirits of the prophets, sent his angel to shew unto his servants the things which must shortly *be revealed* (come to pass).
7 And behold, I come quickly. Blessed is he that keepeth the words of the prophecy of this book.
8 And I, John, am he that heard and saw these things. And when I heard and saw, I fell down to worship before the feet of the angel which shewed me these
9 things. And he said unto me, See thou do it not: I am a fellow-servant with thee and with thy brethren the prophets, and with them which keep the words of this book: worship God.
10 And he saith unto me, Seal not up the words of the prophecy of this book; for
11 the time is at hand. He that is unrighteous, let him do unrighteousness still: and he that is filthy, let him be made filthy still: and he that is righteous, let him do righteousness still: and he that is holy, let him be holy
12 still. Behold, I come quickly; and my reward is with me, to render to each man
13 according as his work is. I am the Alpha and the Omega, the first and the last, *the origin and the completion* (beginning and the
14 end). Blessed are they that wash their robes, that they may have the right (to come) to the tree of life,

Suggestive Paraphrase

And a voice said unto me, These sayings are faithful and true: and the Lord God of the holy prophets hath sent me unto men who are striving to serve Him to show to them what things they will soon realize. Behold, the Christ-mind will soon be known among men: blessed are they that order their lives in accordance with the truth which is revealed in this book. And I, John, saw these things, and heard them. And when I had heard and seen, I was impelled to pride myself on the exaltation of my consciousness. Then it was said unto me, See that thou do not worship the creature, but worship the Creator only. Do not keep to yourself what has been revealed to you: the time is ripe for it to be given to the world. That which is unjust, let it be called unjust still: and that which is filthy, let it be called filthy still: and that which is righteous, let it be righteous still: and that which is holy, let it be holy still. Mankind will soon approach so near to the Christ-mind, that the separation between good and evil in human experience will be made much more quickly than formerly; and those who do right will receive their reward more quickly, and those who do wrong their punishment more quickly. I am the eternal and changeless. Blessed are the men who keep God's commandments, for they have a right to the knowledge of God which is everlasting life, and they enter into the spiritual consciousness.

Amended Revised Version

15 and may enter in by the gates into the city. Without are the dogs, and the sorcerers, and the fornicators, and the murderers, and the idolaters, and every one that loveth and maketh a lie.
16 And I, Jesus, have sent mine angel to testify unto you these things for the churches. I am the root and the offspring of David, the bright and morning star.
17 And the Spirit and the bride say, Come. And he that heareth, let him say, Come. And he that is athirst, let him come: he that will, let him take the water of life freely.
18 I testify unto every man that heareth the words of the prophecy of this book, If any man shall add unto them, God shall add unto him the plagues which are
19 written in this book: and if any man shall take away from the words of the book of this prophecy, God shall take away his part from the tree of life, and out of the holy city, which are written in this book.
20 He which testifieth these things saith, Yea: I come quickly. Amen: come, Lord Jesus.
21 The grace of the Lord Jesus be with the saints. Amen.

Suggestive Paraphrase

But all evil dispositions and influences are excluded from that consciousness. I, Christ, have appeared to you, to make known these things to the human consciousness. I am the truth which was taught by David, and I am the star of hope to humanity. The divine Mind and the spiritual consciousness say to men, Come. And let him that heareth this message say to others, Come. And let him that desires good come. And whosoever will, let him drink freely of good and truth. If any man shall adulterate the truth, he shall suffer the plagues which are imposed on a wicked and adulterous mentality from the fact that by its own nature it is excluded from the realm of God: and if any man shall omit to heed and obey any portion of the truth, he shall exclude himself from the perfect and indivisible law of good, and as long as he does so, he cannot enter into the spiritual consciousness, and the joys thereof.

The Christ, which maketh known these things, declares, that he will soon be known among men. Amen. So may it be, Oh Christ.

The grace of the mediating Christ be with the spiritually minded.

Amen.

A PERSONAL APPLICATION OF THE LESSONS OF THE APOCALYPSE

A revelation of the things made known in the prophetic consciousness, which emanates from God, to show unto His servants the things which must quickly unfold to them.

Before a person can make any beginning of either understanding or applying the lessons of the Apocalypse, he must have distinctly and purposely entered upon the spiritual life through the service of God as Spirit and substance. He must have learned that Mind and its ideas or manifestations are the only realities.

Then he may understand the Letters to the Seven Churches, and that it is required of him that he should undertake to consecrate to God and to the service of the spiritual order his attention, reason, will, intuition, love, sense of reality, and sense of substance.

While engaged in such effort, there may come to him wonderful visions of the spiritual life, which is the end of attainment,—such as are given in the 4th chapter, and in various other places, in the Apocalypse.

He will recognize the spiritual factor in his consciousness as the indwelling Christ, as the white horse and rider within, and he will know that this higher activity in his consciousness must war with and first control and finally overcome his human will and ambition, his human greed and selfishness, his sense of materiality and sensuality, also any sense of resentment or discouragement on his part, and all phases of superstition and false belief.

He will recognize the stage of his development when the impersonal Christ, as seven Angels of God, is beginning to overcome, and is suppressing in his consciousness, something like a third part, materiality and sensuality, sensuousness and sub-normal psychic tendencies, mortal love and hatred, worldly wisdom, fleshly desires and resultant diseases, superstition and false doctrine, and every other form of evil.

At this stage of attainment, there may come to him fuller revelations of truth and a more distinct and thorough-going uncovering of error.

Then he may be called upon to conquer that tendency in human nature which, through desire or fear, renders allegiance to human or outward authority, rather than to listen to and obey the voice of God within,—that tendency of human nature which, for instance, led Israel of old to demand a king, a human ruler, despite the warnings of the prophet Samuel of the oppression and corruption which would follow. He who would heed the lessons of the Apocalypse must work his way free from human domination, whether personal, political or ecclesiastical, obeying God's law only, both in his thought and in his conduct, at no matter what sacrifice, else he will be numbered among those who "wear the mark of the beast, and his name, and the number of his name, whose names are not written in the Lamb's book of life."

The whole realm of his consciousness will come under the judgment of Christ, and the lower elements will be trodden down,—with great suffering, if his lower nature resists the Christ.

Then the seven Angels whom he recognized as having subdued his mortal nature to something like a third part, he now finds completing their conquest. Then he is shown wonderful visions of the fall of Worldly Lust within and without, and of the universal triumph of the Christ.

Next, he is shown a vision of the millennium on the earth, which can only be *fully* realized after all men shall have entered upon and completed the same spiritual journey which he is taking.

Last of all, there is unfolded to him in vision something of the glories of the spiritual, incorporeal man, dwelling in full, conscious union with God, unto whom he is finally to attain.

To the true and earnest servant of God, this whole vision of the stages of development, here sketched in brief, is *revealed* "quickly" (comparatively so) after he definitely seeks to gain the vision; and much of it *comes to pass* quickly, comparatively so, in actual experience; but the *full measure* of attainment would seem to depend upon the progress of the human race as a whole. It does not appear that any person will fully demonstrate the millennial freedom from *all* sense of discord within and without until all men demonstrate it, both in this world and that to come.

The supreme inquiry prompted and expressed by the Apocalypse has been well put by Mr. J. S. Hughes. It is this:

"Shall Men Rule in Lust by the Power of Brutes, or Shall God Reign in the Power of Love?"

REVELATION

GLOSSARY

Stage Settings for the Drama

A definition of some of those symbols employed in the Apocalypse, which are not defined under the "Cast of Characters" on the chart at the end of the book.

"**Clouds**", "**Smoke**". The Holy Spirit, obscure and blinding to material sense. They often symbolize the majesty and glory of God and of the Christ.

"**Earth**". In the spiritual sense, "the new earth" stands for spiritual consciousness. In the lower sense, the phrase "the earth" symbolizes the lowest phase of the carnal mind,—sensuality, materiality, including belief in matter.

"**Earthquake**". The upheaval produced, mentally or outwardly, when truth meets error in violent conflict.

"**Fire**". The purifying influence of the Holy Spirit.

"**Grass**". In the higher sense, details of spiritual activity in human consciousness, humility. However, in the two places where the term appears in the Apocalypse, it is evidently used in a lower sense, symbolizing the details of ordinary human mental activities.

"**Hail**". The dense, solidified condition of the carnal mind which resists "fire" and "lightning" in their purifying and enlightening work. Because the carnal mind seems to present an active rather than a passive resistance to the work of the Holy Spirit and of the Christ, it is symbolized by "hail", which can fall and strike and hurt, rather than by ice, which would be merely a symbol of passive resistance.

"**Heaven**". In the higher sense, the spiritual consciousness. In the lower sense, the mental realm, where the forces of good and evil are contending. The word is used in connection with situations which represent varying degrees of approach toward harmony and Spirit.

"**Jews**". Chosen people. Spiritual initiates. False Jews are those who claim to be spiritual initiates and teachers, but are not.

"**Lightning**". The Holy Spirit. The utterance and enforcement of Truth, the militant activity of the Christ.

"**Mountains**" and "**islands**". Established customs and institutions of human society. "Law and order", though often not the divine law and order.

"**Rivers and fountains of waters**", "**rivers of waters**", "**fountains**", or "**waters**". Sources and channels of thought and feeling. In the higher sense, these expressions symbolize divine love and the divine ideas, regarded as the support of true consciousness or life. In the lower sense, they represent the human emotional nature, and such intellectual ideas as are naturally associated therewith. Human love, though it is in a sense higher than anything connoted by the word "sensual", is, nevertheless, a manifestation of the "natural man", "who receiveth not the things of the Spirit of God". These expressions also stand for the human emotions which are the obverse of human love, such as hatred, malice, envy, jealousy, and for such intellectual activity as naturally accompanies them.

"**Sea**". In the higher sense, "the sea of glass" stands for spiritual consciousness, the redeemed human consciousness, the Holy Spirit. In the lower sense, "the sea" symbolizes the sensuous and so-called psychic element in human nature, the "psuchê" into which St. Paul says "the first Adam" is born (1 Cor. 15:45).

"**Ships**". Human beings regarded as carriers, or messengers, of either good or evil.

"**Thunder**" or "**thunders**". The utterance or proclamation of God and of the Holy Spirit. The term does not seem to be used in the Apocalypse in a reversed sense.

"**Sun, moon and stars**". In the higher sense, the light of spiritual intelligence. Specifically, "the sun" symbolizes divine Mind; "the moon", the Christ; and "stars", right ideas, or even human teachers or messengers of Truth. In the lower sense, these symbols stand for "the wisdom of this world", or for "the carnal mind", which "is enmity against God". Specifically, in this lower sense, "the sun" stands for "satan"; "the moon" for "man-wisdom" or "man-rule"; and "stars" for "fallen stars", evil influences, or even human teachers who have fallen away from good. As to whether, in any given instance, these expressions are employed in the higher or in the lower sense must be determined by the context.

"**Tree**", or "**trees**". In the higher sense, "the tree of life", "the two olive trees", the Holy Spirit, or any particular line of spiritual activity among men. In the lower sense, any well-established human doctrines, customs and habits of thought. These, though highly respected among men, are often strongholds of error.

APPENDIX

ST. JOHN THE EVANGELIST

Abstract of an Address Delivered by the Rev. A. B. Beresford, D. D., Pastor of the Universalist Church of Walnut Hills, Cincinnati, Ohio.

(By permission of the Author)

The blackness of oblivion buries in its robe of obscurity that vast throng that has walked the earth—only one, here and there, is remembered. Since John the Evangelist lived nearly one hundred billions of humans have trod this globe. How few have left any trace, any memorial of themselves! One of the sons of light, one of the choicest of the children of the spirit—one of the torch-bearers in this human procession—who was reserved for a high destiny and whose memory is fadeless, is John the Evangelist. The all-encompassing darkness of forgetfulness has not engulfed him—it is but background for his luminous personality to radiate forth its deathless influence. He was not born to die—he is one of the immortal ones. His life and its lessons will claim our attention for the hour.

He was born in Bethsaida on the shores of the Sea of Galilee in the Holy Land. His birth year was about the first of the Christian era—and thus he was about four or five years younger than Jesus, with whom his name is imperishably associated. (It will be remembered that a miscalculation was made in fixing the Christian era, and Jesus was born "4 B. C."—and really we live in the year 1918.)

Behind him—as behind so many notable men of history—stands the unusual mother. His mother was Salome, the sister of Mary the mother of Jesus. Thus he and the foremost man of all this world—Jesus of Nazareth—were first cousins. They had no small share of the same massive moral strength and the same far-seeing spiritual faculty. His father was Zebedee, a man of business importance in the fisheries. He was prosperous, was an employer of labor, had extensive business connections with distant cities—his son, John, making many business trips to Jerusalem in the interests of the business. One of the business partners of Zebedee was Jonas, the father of Peter and Andrew. Thus by inheritance, surroundings, associations, social and business prominence, the Evangelist was far above the level of the average of his day and country. His education doubtless was identical with that of all Jewish boys of his time, the history, tradition, hopes, and the spiritual life of his people, and a trade—for every Jewish boy was taught a trade or handicraft. Jesus and Paul were no exceptions. He was in business with his father—fishing, buying, preserving, selling fish. "The grasp of every situation," which is the characteristic of well trained business men, zeal in the cause at hand, energetic pursuit of worthy ends, vigor and even vehemence—which gave him the sobriquet of "Boanerges," or son of thunder—all bespoke a pronounced and persuasive personality. By inheritance and circumstance he was being fitted for a high destiny.

However, had he been contented to remain a member of the prosperous firm of "Zebedee, Jonas & Co.," he would now have no claim upon us. Man's nature is larger than business; it has capacities higher than even the largest business can fully employ. Doubtless he often conversed—in the glowing fervor of early youth—with his great kinsman, Jesus of Nazareth. With largeness and fineness of nature he readily comprehended the noble passions, ambitions, visions of the Man of Galilee. Sons of two sisters, they shared the blood bond of family—and what is more, they had many capacities and character-traits that were similar. Out of this boyish friendship came their spiritual partnership—which lasted during all their mortal lives. John became the first disciple of Jesus—and of all living men was nearest to the soul of his Master, toiled like a brother in his affairs, was his "bosom comrade," and is best remembered as the "beloved disciple." In him we find the coronation of friendship—the apotheosis of man's love for man. "His love to me was wonderful"—"More than brothers are to me"—this Jesus might have said. He was truly human —had a heart in his breast and red blood in his veins!

He was the inseparable companion of Jesus during the four stormy and stressful years of the Master's public life. He was helper in plan-making, heard His most confidential teachings, and was present at the great public discourses. He was with Jesus upon the Mount of Transfiguration, and was thus by an object demonstration made to see that "in man there is an ethereal essence" that can never die. When the stars are old and the sun grows cold—even then shall the soul of man live on!

He was at the gate of Gethsemane—saw the supreme agony of a great soul, fated to tread the wine-press of pain, peril, and premature death. He was at the side of Jesus at the Last Supper, at the betrayal, the arrest, and, because of some friendly relations with Caiaphas, the high priest—acquaintance made during the earlier business days—he was in the council chamber where Jesus was first arraigned; was beside Jesus in the Pretorium when Pilate sat in judgment upon a cause he understood not; followed Jesus to Calvary! and received His last request from the cross, "Care for my mother."

He saw the death-agony; and he more than any other man created the Christian crusade; he took the wooden cross—a symbol of shame—made it the sign of a new power liberated upon earth, and with a little band went forth to conquer the world! Well might the soldier and civilian who saw "the head fall upon his breast when he gave up the ghost" on the cross, say, "Another delusion is gone; another delusionist is dead; here is an end that has no new beginning." But alas—the end was not yet—from Golgotha went forth the power, conquering and to conquer! Doubtless it is to John, more than to another man under God, that we owe this world-victory of the Cross.

A stone was once hurled at Wendell Phillips—to silence his speech for human freedom. He picked it up, calmly showed it to the excited audience, and said, "He who threw this was not wise; you cannot kill an idea with a stone." The cross is not the end of the human story.

John was the first to recognize Jesus as "he rose." The resurrection body—the kind of body souls shall wear through eternity—is a "border land question;" John was the first to see the identity of the risen spirit with his former Master. "He was the same yet different," but identity was completely established. "The grave is not the goal"—any more than the cross was the end of his career. With this conviction born in his heart of heart, John rallied the other disciples—and began the new era.

He was present at the Ascension and the Day of Pentecost. The power of a new conviction and the force of a new faith were born in the soul! This "faith," this "power," enabled John and the little band to stand up against the persecutions—for opinion's sake—that were to burst out in hot flame, stopping at nothing—imprisonment and death came to many. He is humanity's everlasting leader of those elect ones who can side with unpopularity and be strong in present failure!

Next we see him in the "Council of Jerusalem," in the year 51 of our era. He is accounted "one of the three pillars" of the church. The issue before the council was a simple one; should all disciples of Jesus first conform to the Levitical Law—in all its demands and its ceremonies? Can only Jews be Christians? Or, is Christianity a world-religion—and has it a spiritual message and a social gospel for all men, irrespective of race, blood, land, age?

It was the hour of fate. Upon the council's reply to these questions hung the future of the world—because that hung upon the nature of Christianity. Should it be a religion for all men, or only for Jews? Should it be national or universal?

John stood for the universal—the cosmopolitan, the world-religion—and so launched Christianity upon its happy way. "Fear not, for I bring you good tidings of great joy which shall be unto all peoples." Had the other decision been made, then Palestine would indeed have remained the cradle of Christianity, and its grave.

Through nearly two millenniums the influence of that act of the Evangelist is a controlling force. If it had not been for the stand taken on that day and hour for a universal gospel we would not now be in his church; this present holds all the good the past has had!

Tradition now takes up the tale of this fruitful life; and herein tradition is, probably, as trustworthy as history. He continued to preside over the fate of the church; was persecuted under Domitian; sent to Rome—in his appeal to Caesar; was subjected to "the third degree" of torture to extort evidence (the story runs that he was cast into boiling oil—but sustained no hurt); was then exiled to work as a slave in the mines of Patmos—a rocky isle in the Mediterranean; was released under Nerva; went to Ephesus—where there was a strong Christian Church; there lived and wrote—being gathered to his fathers at a ripe age. Tradition fixes it variously at from ninety to 120. Like all the other disciples, the place, date, and manner of his death are unknown. "No man knoweth his sepulchre."

The best in the New Testament is a family legacy to mankind. The four gospels carry the message of Jesus. The Epistle of St. James is "from the brother of the Lord"—the Fourth Gospel, the three Epistles of John, the Book of Revelation, are from the blood-cousin of Jesus—the beloved disciple whose day we are commemorating.

The marvel is, not that we have so little in writing from this gifted family, but that we have so much. A great man uttered his soul—a few heard his words, felt their sweetness and light, were moved by their power, and spoke them to others! Thus came our Gospels. John wrote his thoughts, emotions, dreams, upon parchment—gave it to the breeze to float or fall—others caught it up—read the mystic and mighty words—preserved and re-wrote them—and so through the ages have come the epistles and the apocalypse. Words—freighted with a message from on High—are more enduring than the pyramids.

To but few men has it been given to so controllingly influence the history of man as it was to John the Evangelist. Millions of men have borne his name. To him was given the insight—than which nothing has reached loftier levels—to disclose to men the inmost nature of the Supreme Unseen Spiritual Power—"God is Love" is his master gift to man. Churches and cathedrals—the world over—are dedicated to St. John the Divine."

In retrospect John—with his mind's eye—saw Jerusalem and the three Temples, Solomon's, Zerubbabel's, Herod's, all to suffer destruction from the ravages of time and barbarous force. The last temple had fallen when he was seventy years of age; but he had his cheering visions of the future—he saw another and a better Jerusalem, the New and the Holy City. Of its many wonders one was of startling surprise, "I saw no Temple therein." What is the meaning of this portent? The future would have many temples: men, with flawless lives, wills set in righteousness, purified and perfected souls—these are the living temples dedicated to the Living God. "Nothing shall enter in that defileth." "I John, saw the Holy City the New Jerusalem coming down from God out of Heaven; and the glory of God did lighten it, and Christ is the Light of it." "This temple is holy, which temple ye are."

CAST OF CHARACTERS

GOD

SATAN
The Father of Lies

CHRIST
The Lamb
The Son

THE BEAST
Worldly Government

THE HOLY SPIRIT
"The Faithful and True Witness," the True Prophet

THE SECOND BEAST
The False Prophet
The Worldly Church

APOSTLES OF CHRIST
Collection: the same as the

This chart is not presented as a complete classification of all of the symbols in the Book of Revelation, but of most of them,—sufficient to give an intelligible view of the general structure and character of the Book.

A chart prepared by Rev. G. A. Kratzer.
January 23, 1912.

THE BOOK OF REVELATION.

THE DRAMA OF THE CONFLICT BETWEEN GOOD AND EVIL ON THE FIELD OF HUMAN CONSCIOUSNESS, AND OF THE FINAL TRIUMPH OF GOOD.

DISTRIBUTION OF CHARACTERS BY ACTS.

PROLOGUE (Chap. 1:1-3)

EPILOGUE (Chap. 22:6-21)

CAST OF CHARACTERS	Act I (1:4-3:22) THE SEVEN LETTERS	Act II (4:1-8:1) THE SEVEN SEALS	Act III (8:2-11:18) THE SEVEN TRUMPETS	Act IV (11:19-13:18) WOMAN, DRAGON AND BEASTS	Act V (14:1-14:20) SEVEN HARVEST ANGELS	Act VI (15:1-20:15) THE FINAL CONFLICT	Act VII (21:1-22:5) THE NEW CREATION
GOD Divine Mind The Father	"Him which is, and which was, and which is to come" (Chapter 1:4)	"One sat on the throne" (4:2)	"A great voice from heaven" (11:12)	God (12:5)	God (14:10)	"The lord our God" (19:1) "He that sat on the throne" (20:11)	God Lord God Almighty. NOTE.—None of the evil characters appear in Act VII.
SATAN Mortal Mind The Father of Lies	The devil (2:10)	Four winds of earth (7:1) Red horse with rider (6:4)	"Hail" (8:7). "Earthquake" (8:5) Abaddon and Apollyon (9:11) Court without temple (11:2)	"Hail" (11:19) "Great red dragon" (12:3) "The serpent" (12:14)		"A great hail" (16:21) "The "Devil and satan" (chap. 20)	
CHRIST The Lamb. The Son	"Jesus Christ" (1:5) "One like unto the Son of man" (1:13). "The morning star" 2:28)	"The lion of the tribe of Juda, the root of David" (5:15). "Lamb" (5:6). White horse and rider (6:2). "Angel from East" (7:2)	"His Christ" (11:15)	"Christ Jesus" (12:5) "Michael" (12:7) "The Lamb" (12:11)	"Lamb on mount Sion" (14:1) "Son of man on cloud" (14:14)	The Lamb (17:14; 19:7) Whitehorse and rider (19:11) Angel in sun (20:1)	The Lamb
THE BEAST Worldly Government	"Where satan's seat is" (2:13)	Black horse and rider (6:5)		"The beast" (11:7; 13:1-10)		The beast (17:3, 8, 11; 19:19)	
THE HOLY SPIRIT "The Faithful and True Witness," the True Prophet	"The seven Spirits" (1:4), identical with "the seven stars" (1:16), and "the angels of the seven churches" (1:20). "Voice as a Trumpet" (1:10). "The isle that is called Patmos" (1:9), which symbolizes withdrawal from material sense into spiritual consciousness. "In the Spirit on the Lord's day" (1:10). "Antipas, my faithful witness" (2:13) NOTE.—The spiritualized human consciousness in a militant attitude, spreading the truth and destroying evil, is the Holy Spirit, which is the activity in the human realm of the Father and the Son; in its attitude of worship, the spiritualized human consciousness is the true church, "the Bride, the Lamb's wife", the Spiritual Woman.	"Throne" (wherever it appears) "The voice of a trumpet" (4:1) "Lightnings and thunderings and voices" (4:5) "The seven lamps of fire" (4:5) "The face of Him that sitteth on the throne, and the wrath [zeal] of the Lamb" (6:16) "The sea of glass" (4:6) "The four beasts" (4:6) NOTE.—The last two also belong under "The True Church", the "Spiritual Woman", in the Cast of Characters.	"Voices, lightnings and thunders" (8:5). "The reed like a rod" (11:1). (The Holy Spirit, the Spirit of Truth, is the only proper measure of human consciousness, separating truth from error). "Angel flying in heaven" (8:13). "Voice from the altar" (9:13). "Seven thunders" (10:2). "Two witnesses" (truth and love), "two olive trees," and "two candlesticks" (11:3, 4)	"Lightnings, voices and thunderings" (11:19) "In His temple the ark of His testament" (11:19) "A loud voice in heaven" (12:10). "The wilderness" (withdrawal from material into spiritual sense) (12:6, 14). "The two wings [truth and love] of an eagle" (12:14) NOTE.—The Authorized Version and nearly all others translate the Greek orge and thumos "wrath" or "indignation". Orge means literally orgy; but it is an orgy of love, not of anger. It is the divine passion or zeal to overcome evil with good. In the same sense is thumos, the divine ardor to save. Divine Love is not "wrath", yet it is a consuming fire to evil.	"A voice from heaven" (14:2, 12). "Wine of the wrath [ardor] of God poured out into the cup of His indignation" [zeal or passion]. (14:10) "Angel of fire" (14:18) "Fire and brimstone" (14:10) "A white cloud" (14:14) "Wine press of the wrath [zeal] of God" (14:19) "Horse bridles" (14:20)	"Vials of the wrath [zeal] of God" (chaps 15 & 16). "The temple of the tabernacle of the testimony in heaven (15:5). "Smoke from the glory of God" (15:18). "A great voice out of the temple" (16:17) "Voices and thunders and lightnings" (16:18). "The cup of the wine of the fierceness of His wrath [zeal]" (16:19). "Angel from heaven (18:1). "A great voice of much people in heaven" (19:1). The milennial consciousness (20:4-6). The camp of the saints" and "the beloved city" (20:9). "Fire from God out of heaven" (20:9). "The book of life" (20:12)	"The new heaven and the new earth" (21:1). "The holy city, new Jerusalem" (21:2). "A great voice out of heaven" (21:3). "The fountain of the water of life" (21:6). "Seven vials full of the seven last plagues" [to evil] (21:9). "A great and high mountain" (21:10). "That great city" (21:10). "The glory of God" (21:10). "Her light" (21:11). "A wall great and high" (21:12). "The golden reed" (21:15). "The measure of. . the angel" (21:17). "The street of the city" (21:21). "The nations of them which are saved" (21:24). "The light of it" (21:24). "The glory and the honor of the kings and of the nations" (21:24, 26). "They which are written in the Lamb's book of life" (21:27). "A pure river of water of life" (22:1). "The tree of life" (21:22)
THE SECOND BEAST The False Prophet The Worldly Church	Balaam; also the wicked influence deceiving the Nicolaitanes (2:14, 15)	The darkening of the sun and moon (6:12), due to false doctrine.		"The two-horned beast" (13:11) "The image of the beast" (13:14); i. e., the anthropomorphic sense of God, set up by the false prophet.		The false prophet (19:20)	
APOSTLES OF CHRIST Angels, Messengers Collectively, the same as the Holy Spirit	Angels of the Seven Churches	"Elders about the throne" (Chapter 4 and elsewhere) "Four angels on four corners of the earth" (7:1)	"Ships" (8:9) Angels of the Trumpets (9:14) "Four angels at Euphrates" (9:14)	Angels of Michael (12:7)	Harvest Angels	Angels of the Vials.	"Twelve apostles of the Lamb" (21:14)
APOSTLES OF SATAN	False Apostles (2:2) False Jews (3:9)	"Trees" (7:3), established and respected human institutions which are strongholds of error.	Locusts of the Pit (8:3) "Trees" (8:7; 9:4)			"Three unclean spirits" (16:13)	
THE SPIRITUAL WOMAN "The Bride" The True Church	"The seven golden candlesticks" (1:20) NOTE.—Nearly the whole of chap. 1:13-16 is a figurative description of the Christ, or the Holy Spirit.	"The sea of glass " (4:6) "The four beasts" (4:6) (See also, Holy Spirit)	"The temple of God, and the altar, and worshipers" (11:1) Chap. 8:3 also describes the church.	"The woman clothed with the sun" (12:1); also "the wilderness" (12:6, 14)	"The redeemed", described in 14:2-5. This company of the redeemed appears in nearly every Act	The Lamb's wife (18:7). The redeemed (15:2-3). "The voice of a great multitude" (19:6). "Great white throne" (20:11).	"The bride" (21:9; 22:17). "The Holy City, New Jerusalem," which is also the Holy Spirit. "Twelve gates to the city" (21:21). "Honor and glory of the kings and of the nations" (21:24, 26)
THE CARNAL WOMAN "Babylon" Worldly Lust	Jezebel (2:20) NOTE.—As the spiritual woman is closely allied with the Holy Spirit, the true prophet, so the carnal woman is closely identified with the two-horned beast, the false prophet, the worldly church.	"The pale horse and his rider" (6:8)	"The star Wormwood" (8:11) "The fallen star" (9:1). "The city (12:1); Sodom and Egypt (11:8)		Fallen Babylon (14:8)	"Babylon" (16:19 and chap. 18) "The great whore" (17:1; 19:2) Woman on a scarlet beast (17:3, 18).	
FOLLOWERS OF CHRIST	The Seven Churches, (Chapters 2-3)	"One hundred and forty-four thousand" (7:4)	"The horsemen" (9:16)	"Our brethren" (12:10) "Remnants of her seed" (12:17)	"144 thousand" (14:1) "The dead who die in the Lord" (14:13)	Armies in heaven (19:18). Fowls that fly in heaven (19:17). Those describid in 20:4	"The nations of them which are saved" (21:24)
FOLLOWERS OF SATAN	Followers of Balaam, and the Nicolaitanes (2:14, 15)	"Souls under the altar" (6:9) These manifest discouragement and revenge, attributes of satan.	"Green grass" (8:7). "Grass of the earth" (9:4). "Creatures in the sea" (8:9). "Men dying of the waters" (8:11). "Those not having the seal of God" (9:4). The idolaters (9:20). Gentiles (11:12)	Angels of the dragon (12:7) "The earth" (12:16)	Worshipers of the beast (14:9)	Practically the same as in Act III, and those described in 19:18	

of the symbols in the Book
view of the general struc-

THE BOOK
THE CONFLICT BETWEEN GOOD AND EVIL ON THE
DISTRIBUTION

	Act II (4:1-8:1) THE SEVEN SEALS	Act III (8:2-11:18) THE SEVEN TRUMPET
was	"One sat on the throne" (4:2)	"A great voice from heav (11:15)
	Four winds of earth (7:1) Red horse with rider (6:4)	"Hail" (8:7). "Earthquake" Abaddon and Apollyon (9:11) Court without temple (11:2)
	"The lion of the tribe of Juda, the root of David" (5:15). "Lamb" (5:6). White horse and rider (6:2). "Angel from East" (7:2)	"His Christ" (11:15)
	Black horse and rider (6:5)	
anti- 16), even 3, a it is ym- rial ess, ay, wit-	"Throne" (wherever it appears) The voice of a trumpet" (4:1) "Lightnings and thunderings and voices" (4:5) "The seven lamps of fire" (4:5) "The face of Him that sitteth on the throne, and the wrath [zeal] of the Lamb" (6:16) "The sea of glass" (4:6) "The four beasts" (4:6) NOTE.—The last two also belong un- der "The True Church", the "Spiritual Woman", in the Cast of Characters. man consciousness is a militant attitude. evil, is the Holy Spirit, which is the activity and the Son; in its attitude of worship, the is the true church, "the Bride, the Lamb's	"Voices, lightnings and thund (8:5). "The reed like a rod" 1). (The Holy Spirit, the S of Truth, is the only proper m ure of human consciousness, s rating truth from error). "A flying in heaven" (8:13). " from the altar" (9:13). "Se thunders" (10:2). "Two with es" (truth and love), "two o trees", and "two candlestic (11:3, 4).

WORKS PUBLISHED
by
The Central Christian Science Institute
5521 CORNELL AVE., CHICAGO, ILLINOIS

From which, and from dealers, they may be purchased at prices announced below.

"DOMINION WITHIN"
By
Rev. G. A. Kratzer

A book of 224 pages, printed in large type on heavy paper, bound in dark green cloth. Price, $1.25, postpaid.

This book consists of twenty-five articles, mostly dealing with the practical application of Christian Science to the overcoming, in human experience, of sin, disease, accident and poverty. In the two years since it was published, over six thousand copies have been purchased by readers from nearly every civilized country in the world, attesting its usefulness.

"SPIRITUAL MAN"
By
Rev. G. A. Kratzer

This book is uniform in size, style and price with "Dominion Within." It consists of articles dealing with the theory and practice of Christian Science. It is of especial use to those who wish to go into the deeper things of Christian Science metaphysics, and who wish to understand what are ordinarily considered the "hard problems" of this Science. It already has a world-wide circulation.

"REVELATION INTERPRETED"
By
Rev. G. A. Kratzer

The book now in the reader's hand. Price, $3.00, postpaid. Full morocco, flexible covers, $5.00.

This book is much more expensive to print and publish than its mere size indicates. Hence, the larger price.

"COMPLETE IN HIM"
By
Elizabeth Cary Kratzer

A book of 236 pages, excellent type and paper, bound in blue cloth. Price, $1.25, postpaid.

This work is in story form and deals especially with the application of Christian Science to the solution of the sex problem. Also, a reader will get from perusing the book an excellent idea of the method of applying Christian Science to the healing of sin and disease and is sure to gain much of inspiration and spiritual uplift. The book has been widely circulated and highly commended by some of the best Science teachers and workers in the world.

"WHAT IS TRUTH?"
By
Rev. G. A. Kratzer

A pamphlet of 50 pages, with heavy paper covers, large type, excellent paper, pocket size. Second edition. Price, 20 cts. per copy, $2.00 per dozen, postpaid.

This pamphlet was published at the request of several active workers in Christian Science, who urged the author to prepare a simple, brief and comprehensive statement of this Science, with plentiful quotations from the Bible in support of its leading doctrines, being designed especially to hand to that numerous class of people who are now just at the point of inquiring what Christian Science is, and what it teaches. Older students of Science will find in the pamphlet much that will be helpful. An instructive case of healing is described, and useful inferences are drawn.

"THE CAUSE AND CURE OF WAR"
By
Rev. G. A. Kratzer

A pamphlet of 44 pages, uniform in type and paper, with "What Is Truth?" and sold at the same price.

This pamphlet is an interpretation and application of the thirteenth chapter of Revelation. It clearly makes known, in the light of St. John's prophecy, the cause and cure of all human strife. Incidentally, other matters of interest are discussed. The pamphlet also exhibits what can be done, in the light of Christian Science, in disclosing the hidden meaning of that book of the Bible which has long been regarded, to a large extent, as the hopeless riddle of the ages. The reader will see the meaning of one of its most difficult chapters as clearly as he sees the meaning of the Ten Commandments or the Beatitudes.

CPSIA information can be obtained
at www.ICGtesting.com
Printed in the USA
LVHW082140170219
607838LV00023B/708/P